Generals

Generals

The Best and Worst Military Commanders

Gerald Suster

Robson Books

To Nick Austin

First published in Great Britain in 1997 by Robson Books Ltd, Bolsover House, 5–6 Clipstone Street, London W1P 8LE

Copyright © 1997 Gerald Suster

The right of Gerald Suster to be identified as author of this work has been asserted by him in accordance with the Copyright, Designs and Patents Act 1988

British Library Cataloguing in Publication Data
A catalogue record for this title is available from the British Library

ISBN 1 86105 018 6

Photoset in North Wales by Derek Doyle & Associates, Mold, Flintshire. Printed in Great Britain by St Edmundsbury Press, Bury St Edmunds, Suffolk

Contents

Preface

Generals: The Best and Worst of Military Commanders is a work intended to make scholarship in military history and biography accessible to the layperson. It demonstrates both the nobility and the folly of war, in addition to its influence on human evolution and civilization. War shows both the astonishing bravery of men and the equally astonishing fatuity of some of their commanders.

As Winston Churchill remarked about the British people during the 1930s: 'These are the bravest of the brave, presently led by the vilest of the vile.' However, the purpose of this work is also to examine the sheer brilliance of the finest commanders in moving men around a space at a particular time, analysed within its context. It is necessary to remark upon the psychology of these remarkable men and women. It is essential for particular battles to be described, since these demonstrate not only high intelligence, on the one hand, and appalling stupidity, on the other, but also the ways in which a battle can change the course of history.

This matter is approached by studying a series of battlefield commanders, placing them in the context of their era and describing the effects of their actions upon their own time. It is written for the lay reader of military history, though it is hoped that specialists and scholars will find the work satisfying. Obviously, one will be criticized for including some commanders and excluding others, for on these matters one can never satisfy everybody. I have simply selected those I regard as being the best and the worst, and hope that this approach will strike sparks for future fruitful debate.

I make no apology for structuring this work in terms of individuals. Marxist historians declare the individual to be of no importance, and merely a product of the environmental conditions of his or her time. Obviously every individual is a product of a genetic code and of environmental conditioning, but to dismiss a particular individual as being of no more than robotic importance is surely among the crassest of intellectual follies, especially when it is evident that a military decision by an individual general at a crucial moment has affected the subsequent course of civilization.

This work will therefore proceed to examine the influence of individuals upon the evolution of human history.

Introduction

'War! What is it good for? Absolutely nothing!'

These were the words of an excellent popular song of the 1960s: yet it cannot be denied that war has been a principal, dominant factor in the evolution of humankind. Anyone who wants worldwide peace needs therefore to study the evolution of war.

Organized warfare was actually unknown before the advent of civilization, paradoxically enough. In his treatise, *On Perpetual Peace*, the great philosopher Immanuel Kant suggests that, in the long run, wars unite the human race, for they bring about groupings which lessen their incidence.

This is a doubtful proposition, since in an era in which the world is habitually referred to as being a 'Global Village', there are more wars being fought on our planet than ever before. Consequentially, it is hard to agree with Major-General J.F.C. Fuller in his otherwise outstanding three-volume work. *The Decisive Battles of the Western World, and Their Influence upon History*:

> It would appear that though Nature's goal is concord, her driving force is discord. Thus, the tribe, by striving to remain a tribe, through inter-tribal warfare becomes a multi-tribal community or people. Similarly, a people, striving to remain a closed community, through inter-community wars becomes a nation, and a nation, striving to remain a nation, through international wars grows into an empire. So it comes about

that the unit, at any particular time, though striving to remain single, inevitably is duplicated through absorbation until ultimately, then the biological and economic frontiers of the globe are reached.

Fuller was a brilliant military strategist and the principal pioneer of tank warfare and *Blitzkrieg* (lightning war), as this work will demonstrate. He was also an excellent military historian; but the break-up of the former USSR and of Yugoslavia demonstrates the flaws in his thesis.

It is obvious, of course, that war has dictated the evolution of humankind, for better or for worse. The matter began with the advent of two sorts of civilization: the agriculturalists and the hunter-gathers. The former settled in the Nile Valley, connected by trade and travel to the Upper Euphrates and the Persian Gulf. These were human beings who had discerned that certain grass seeds could be cultivated so as to grow plants which could sustain life. Settling down in various areas which gave easy access to water, they grew crops, farmed the land, eventually built walled cities and endeavoured to protect themselves from predatory marauders.

The civilization of the hunter-gatherers appears to have arisen on the steppes by the northern shores of the Caspian Sea. These people made use of the domestication of the horse and the invention of the wheel and the wagon, which increased their powers of mobility. For centuries, these tribes of Indo-Europeans moved in great migrations, taking all they could from the lands over which they travelled. Meanwhile, the agriculturalists, who appear to have been Semitic in origin, did all they could to resist them. It is perhaps ironic that at this time, the Semites represented Europe with their sacred symbol of the ankh; and the Aryans – the tribes of Indo-European origin – represented Asia with their sacred symbol of the swastika. Both symbols mean *Light*.

Many battles took place, such as that at Megiddo, in what is now northern Israel, in 1469 BC, which was won by Pharaoh Thutmose III of Upper Egypt against the Canaanites. He armed his soldiers with bows and spears and shields and made use of the chariot. As we shall see, throughout history, superior technology usually wins wars. On this occasion, when the besieged city of

Kadesh surrendered, Thutmose took 924 chariots, 2,238 horses, 200 suits of armour and a vast quantity of gold and silver. Rather than raze the rebellious city to the ground, in the manner of his predecessors, Thutmose III preferred to make a peace based upon reason, enabling him further to chase the invaders from the land he regarded as being his own.

Obviously, Thutmose III was a fine commander in the context of his own time. One of the many purposes of this book is to investigate the question of what makes a man or woman a good military commander. How does one move sets of warriors intelligently in order to win a battle, the outcome of which may affect the development of a country or even, on occasion, the course of future civilization? It is initially difficult to discern just what constitutes the principles of excellent generalship but studies have made clear the factors which unite gross inefficiency, utter incompetence, blundering stupidity and useless bungling.

One finds a belief in spurious mystical forces such as fate and luck; and news from the front is suppressed or distorted on the grounds of 'morale' or 'security'. Scapegoats are blamed for military setbacks. There is a failure to make use of surprise and deception, replaced by a belief in sheer toughness rather than intelligence. This leads to orders for frontal assault against the strongest defence of the enemy, owing to failure in undertaking adequate reconnaissance. Even if the ground is gained, the advantage is not exploited.

There is an obstinate persistence in a given task despite clear evidence that this contradicts its purpose or effectiveness, hardly helped by a commander's lack of decision, underestimation of the enemy and over estimation of the abilities of his forces. This blinkered mind is reinforced by its tendency to reject or ignore information which throws preconceptions into doubt. The cause lies in a clinging to outmoded tradition, a refusal to admit past mistakes and an inability to employ new and relevant technology without even learning from the past. The consequence is a serious wastage of human resources since in the worst commanders, there is no notion of economy of force.

These simple points were most cruelly demonstrated in the First World War and in the United States of America's war upon North Vietnam. In the latter case, a nation of vastly superior wealth, technology and military might lost – to its amazement – because it had committed every blunder cited above. Inciting American schoolchildren to 'kill a gook for God' is hardly the way to win a war allegedly fought for freedom and democracy.

What *is* the way to win a war? As we shall see, it is through a combination of strategy and tactics. Strategy involves the use of political and economic alliances, and of propaganda for the motivation of public support in a context much larger than that of a mere battlefield. Tactics is the science and art of movement or manoeuvre, such as deploying a division from one part of the battlefield to another, in the knowledge that, as on a chessboard, a pawn can be as powerful as a rook if positioned rightly; and that the tactics of a battle will affect the entire course of overall strategy.

Why is it, therefore, that when crucial issues are at stake, some generals nevertheless order actions which any person of common sense, though without detailed military knowledge, would judge to be stupid? There seems to be a rigid automatism in so much military thinking. The conclusions of both American and British psychologists have been in accord and can be summarised.

A bad commander has a rigid adherence to conventional, middle-class values and a submissive, uncritical attitude towards the authorities of the group with which he identifies. This leads him to condemn, reject and punish people who violate conventional values with an especial dislike of anyone who questions or doubts. Individuals of this nature sometimes win battles but do not, on the whole, win wars, mainly on account of their tendency to think only within rigid categories.

Although this work will analyse the failures, its principal enquiry is into the nature of military commanders who were not guilty of stupidity and who consequently won their battles and their wars to the lasting benefit of human evolution. There are also cases of paradox. Major-General J.F.C. Fuller, for instance, was the architect of tank warfare and his appreciation of flexibility contributed to his superb works of military history. The insights which inspired his works, both in words and in practical action, was hardly done credit by his embrace of fascism, a political system devoid of mentation, characterized by stupidity, rigidity, barbarism and all other hallmarks of failure which Fuller, in

military terms, abhorred. Even more paradoxically, his ideas of
Blitzkrieg were rejected by British High Command and embraced
by the Germans with stunning success for a time: had the British
accepted Fuller's ideas, fascism could probably have been crushed
by 1941, leaving the British Empire more powerful than before, in
terms of having democratic influence upon Europe.

From intelligent commanders, we can learn so much about
human ingenuity in the movement of men and supplies, so much
about the evolution of civilization, so much about the application
of human intelligence as applied to seemingly intractable
problems.

'Against stupidity, the Gods themselves rage in vain,' Schiller
wrote. True: but the finest generals demonstrate extraordinary
movements of swift and applied intelligence.

1

Alexander the Great (356–323 BC)

Alexander the Great is a legend among humankind. It is, however, as well to examine the facts: is the legend justified or justifiable? Essentially, his inspiration came from four sources. There was his father, King Philip II of Macedonia, a wise ruler and a good, sensible general. There was his mother, Olympias, a remarkable woman who imbued him with the spirit of paganism. The great Greek philosopher Aristotle was Alexander's personal tutor for twelve years (342–336 BC), and the works of the former are still studied with respect in the finest of Western universities. Finally, there was Alexander himself, who united his will, mind and imagination and his remarkable gifts for synthesis in achieving what most would call an impossible dream.

King Philip II dominated events by the sheer force of his personality. Restless and energetic, far-seeing and crafty, he won lands 'by wiles rather than arms', according to Polynaeus. Welding together the various feuding tribes, he created, as D.G. Hogarth states (in *Philip and Alexander of Macedon*, 1897), 'the first European Power in the modern sense of the word – an armed nation with a common national ideal'. Having established his authority over the turbulent Macedonian clans, he marched them east and west and south and north, by war creating a united

Greece under Macedonian leadership. His son, Alexander, fought with him to defeat an army of allied Greek states in 338 BC at the battle of Chaeronea; it was Alexander's command of the cavalry which shattered the Theban-Athenian flank. This victory enabled Philip to lord it over a Greek Confederacy.

Philip revolutionized militarism. Having seized the throne of Macedonia on the death of his brother Perdiccas III in 359 BC, he inherited the Macedonian cavalry or *Hetairoi* (king's companions), an ancient title dating back to Homer's *The Iliad*, and proceeded to reform the infantry, hitherto ill-disciplined bands of foot soldiers drawn from a disaffected peasantry. These were now drilled into a phalanx, a square of soldiers, each armed with a fourteen-foot spear, the *sarissa*, almost twice as long as the Greek spear. For defence, there was a light shield carried on the right arm. Both infantry and cavalry were divided into regiments of 1,500–1,800 men, sub-divided into battalions and companies and even sections of 16 soldiers, allowing Philip a flexibility in battle that had not been seen before.

Yet though he excelled at battlefield tactics, Philip also perceived strategic necessities. In 346 BC, marching on Thermopylae, the principal pass from Thessaly into Greece, he used bribery to buy the enemy's surrender and secure the pass. His subsequent mercy to his former opponents encouraged others to surrender also. He created a corps of engineers, which assisted his victories and those of his son. He grasped the importance of economics to successful warfare, eventually gaining control of the Hellespontine corn route and seizing the gold mines in Thrace. He realized that a good army cannot be put in the field unless it can be paid for. Moreover, he understood how to use the power of money to dictate the terms of a peace treaty.

Unfortunately, Philip quarrelled with Alexander upon marriage to a second wife, since his son feared for his position as legitimate heir. The King had expressed his intention of leading the Greek Confederacy against the traditional enemy, the Persian Empire. At a party, he tried to talk to his son, but he was so drunk that in crossing the room he tripped and fell before he could reach him.

'There,' said Alexander, 'lies the man who is preparing to cross from Europe to Asia, and he cannot even pass from one couch to another.'

Philip was stabbed to death by an unknown assassin in 336 BC. Thus, at the age of nineteen, Alexander became King of Macedonia.

Alexander's mother, Olympias, was the daughter of Neoptolemus of Epirus, who traced his descent from Achilles, hero of Homer's *The Iliad*, just as King Philip had traced his own descent from Heracles. The Queen was savage, mystical and domineering, although good to her son. She taught him that there are gods and goddesses, divine beings of a preterhuman intelligence beyond humanity's understanding, and that in order to evolve, mankind must make further contact with Them. She taught him also that there are demigods, hybrids between god and man who can lead the march of human evolution further.

As Bertrand Russell demonstrates expertly in his *A History of Western Philosophy*, there were two sides to Hellenistic paganism; and it was Nietzsche who originally – and brilliantly – analysed the matter. We find the two sides of the Sun God, called both Apollo and Dionysus. Apollo stands for Reason and veneration of the classical traditions of the past, extolling an harmonious civilisation. Dionysus, a demi-God who died and was resurrected as a God, is alleged to have introduced the fermented juice of the vine from Asia Minor into Europe, preaching an ecstatic revolution of human consciousness, as shown unforgettably by Euripides in his magnificent drama, *The Bacchae*. Here, King Pentheus, who stands for Reason in the Apollonian manner, is torn limb from limb by intoxicated Bacchantes when he visits them in the wilds; just before his violent death, he discovers that his killers are led by his own mother.

Alexander came to see himself as a demi-God, a Sun God. After all, it makes sense to worship the sun, which gives life to this our earth, rather than some gaseous invertebrate or some bloodthirsty father figure such as Jehovah in the Old Testament, forever roaring: 'Don't argue! Do as I say!' The influence of Alexander's mother, however, led him to command his soldiers never to harm women in any city they had captured, and in his personal life to treat women well.

King Philip, a man of reason and common sense, gave his son further benefit by employing the philosopher Aristotle (384–322 BC) as his tutor. Aristotle exemplified the use of reason. He had been the principal pupil of Plato, who had himself been the principal pupil of Socrates. Socrates had taught that the method of learning wisdom consists in asking questions all the time, seeking definitions for morally significant concepts. For this, this brilliant and innocent man was tried on charges of impiety and corruption of youth, and eventually condemned to death by the city-state of Athens in 399 BC: he exercised his right to commit suicide. Nevertheless, Plato and others continued the work that Socrates had started. However, there was one significant matter of variance between Plato and his pupil Aristotle. Plato held that if every quality is taken away from a table – its oblong or square nature, its woodenness, and all the things that go to make up a table – there would nevertheless remain the *idea* of a table. Aristotle thought that if you took away everything that makes up a table, there would be nothing at all.

Aristotle wrote books on Logic, Metaphysics and Ethics which are still of relevance today. He advocated a civilized society governed by individuals imbued with the ideal of 'the magnanimous man', one who is intelligent, cultured, gracious and genial, gentle to his opponents when he has defeated them, and keen to have a good and flourishing society around him. It can be successfully argued that he taught Alexander the use of reason both in war and in peace.

Alexander crystallized within his own heart the results of the various influences upon him.

Alexander had the good fortune to grow into a very handsome man, of medium height and fair complexion. Although he was a swift runner, he preferred hunting foxes or birds for his sport. As Plutarch relates: 'He was also by nature a lover of learning and a lover of reading.' This led him to enrol a corps of scholars on his campaigns, gathering many from conquered peoples, and some regard him as the founder of archaeology, since he had a passion for exhuming and examining the artefacts of every culture he had conquered, leaving the records enshrined upon papyrus or paper in libraries for the benefit of posterity. Although his age considered compassion to be unmanly, he was charitable to all who suffered misfortune.

Even so, the aim of Alexander was to conquer and rule a united Europe and Asia, as a demigod who would give humankind a pagan Paradise upon Earth.

It is hardly surprising that his fellow men and women accepted Alexander's conviction that he was a demigod, for he went to extremes in every affair he approached. His parental genes had given him natural intelligence and well-nigh inexhaustible energy. He had exceptional courage yet he could also be cunningly cautious. All who met him came away rejoicing in his extraordinary charisma. His ideas were astonishingly imaginative and at times, deeply mystical: yet he put them into practical effect by paying precise attention to the most minute of details. Many declared that he could not have been born without some divine influence.

As far as his methods were concerned, Alexander out-thought and out-fought everybody he faced. He understood that money is a vital weapon in the winning of wars, but that the essential wealth which supplies this money must be generated by the production of goods and services. Goods and services are tangible, and any money issued is based upon them. Alexander therefore emulated his father in encouraging manufacture, agriculture and commerce. He used the methods of peace whenever it suited his grand design, offering cities and city-states a much better deal than they had received under their erstwhile rulers, on condition that there had to be acceptance of his authority as Emperor and trade within his territories, not outside them. His regime proved, in fact, to be better for civilians than anything they had hitherto experienced. Before his conquests, military commanders had allowed or even encouraged their soldiers to kill the defeated enemy's men, rape the women and sell the children into slavery and prostitution. Alexander strictly forbade his soldiers to do this. In so doing, he secured the co-operation of the peoples of the lands he conquered, a vital piece of strategy.

As we shall see, this was a lesson ignored by Adolf Hitler when the Nazis invaded the Ukraine and the Baltic States. However, Mao Tse-Tung used Alexander's methods to excellent effect during the long campaign which ended with his conquest of China.

Marriage also formed a part of Alexander's strategy. In his endeavour to conquer the Persian Empire and beyond it, he saw it as obvious that the way to conciliate a conquered enemy was by way of marriage: no minor king wants to make war upon a territory where his daughter has married another minor king. In his desire to unite East with West, Alexander took a Persian wife, and also conducted a mass marriage between 10,000 Macedonian soldiers and the same number of Persian women.

When it came to warfare, Alexander proved himself to be one of the greatest military commanders who has ever lived. He used the intelligence gathered by his spies to employ a study of territory enabling him to position his troops effectively. He ensured that his soldiers were supplied with the finest weapons that the technology of his time could provide: for example, a light iron shield can render a heavy bronze sword completely useless. His personal charisma gave tremendous encouragement to his troops, for men do not fight well unless their confidence and morale are high. He told his soldiers – all the while ensuring that they had the necessary food, drink, equipment and all other requisite supplies – that they were fighting not just for the expansion of Macedonia, but also for the vision of a glorious human future. Given this stirring leadership, the men of Alexander's armies proceeded to fight as though they were demons.

Good generalship, as Alexander realized, consists of making the greatest gains with the smallest losses. (One criticizes First World War generals for making the smallest gains with the greatest losses.) Alexander had the ability to inspire confidence in his men by tackling a complex problem and making it simple.

There is, of course, the legend of the Gordian knot, which no man had ever been able to untie. Alexander could not do so either, and so shocked the pagan world by slashing through it with his dagger. He had reason in abundance, but the intuition he received from his mother caused him to take short cuts to victory which had not yet been seen upon the planet before.

Alexander was determined to conquer Asia Minor so as to fulfil the vision of his father, Philip, before he began to implement his own. With 30,000 infantry and 5,000 cavalry, and vastly outnumbered, Alexander landed near Troy, challenging King Darius of Persia in an act of supreme audacity. At the battle of Granicus, he personally led his elite cavalry to victory. Imbued with his belief in the vital importance of speed and timing, his forces sped across the land we now call Turkey.

There was, however, a problem of supplies and logistics. The

Persian navy was vastly superior to the Macedonian and would obviously beat it easily in any open-sea battle, leaving Alexander's army far from home and without anything to eat. Alexander solved this problem by sending his best troops on land to capture and thus blockade all key ports along the Mediterranean coast previously held by the Persians. This destroyed Persian supremacy at sea.

With the supply lines open, Alexander prepared to do battle with his foe, King Darius of Persia, at Issus in 333 BC. Darius had 100,000 soldiers at his command, thus outnumbering Alexander by 65,000. Undaunted, Alexander placed his phalanx of infantry in the centre and his elite cavalry on the right.

The Macedonian cavalry rushed swiftly to break the left wing of the Persians but Darius, a sound general who had the confidence of his troops, discerned a gap in Alexander's forces and commanded his division of dissident Greek mercenaries to break in between his foe's cavalry and infantry.

Alexander responded to the crisis by ordering his infantry to make a straight advance upon the King of Persia. His men were very good, spirited and seasoned fighters who slogged, sliced and cut their way through the Persian lines. Darius lost his nerve and was forced to flee the field. This was just as well for Alexander, because the Persian counter-attack had, through its ferocious Greek division, reduced his cavalry to a state of disorganized confusion. Nevertheless, Alexander had once again discerned the head and the heart of the battlefield in going straight for the king. The warriors of Darius fled once they knew that their king had done so.

This 'damn thing' of a victory, as Wellington said after Waterloo, laid open all of Syria, Palestine and Egypt to Alexander. The siege of Tyre took seven months, its citizens ignoring all appeals from the Macedonian king to come to peaceful terms. Here, perhaps, Alexander unworthily allowed his men to commit unjust actions.

The conquest of Tyre presented him with a problem. The city was positioned on a rock half a mile from the shore and defended by a 150-foot-high stone wall. Alexander approached the problem by having a causeway built from the shore to the island. His next move was a failure, for although he erected siege towers to destroy the walls of Tyre, these were in turn destroyed by Tyrian fireships. Consistent attack by battering rams, though accompanied by a high number of casualties, finally made a breach in the wall, and the Macedonian soldiers poured through it to kill every man they could find.

After that, Egypt surrendered to Alexander, who had now captured every single Persian naval base. King Darius of Persia regrouped his armies between Arbela and Guagamela for a final trial on land in 331 BC. By crossing the Syrian desert into Mesopotamia, Alexander was clearly resolved to put his fortunes to the ultimate test.

Figures concerning this combat vary. There is a general consensus that Alexander had some 47,000 men. As to Darius, according to Alexander's sources of intelligence, taken from captured prisoners, the enemy had 40,000 cavalry, 1,000,000 infantry, a number of war elephants and 200 chariots equipped with scythes on their wheel-hubs. These figures, taken from Arrian, are not reliable. Justin records 400,000 Persian infantry and 100,000 cavalry; Curtius claims 45,000 cavalry and 200,000 infantry (probably the most likely estimate); though according to both Diodorus and Plutarch, no fewer than 1,000,000 men were put into the field against Alexander's 47,000. In any event, no one can deny that Alexander was vastly outnumbered.

The presence of chariots was also a worrying factor for Alexander. As Lucretius writes in *On the Nature of Things*:

> Reeking with indiscriminate slaughter, they [the chariots' scythes] lop off limbs so instantaneously that what has been cut away is seen to quiver on the ground before any pain is felt. One man perceives not that the wheels and devouring scythes have carried off among the horses' feet his left arm, shield and all; another, while he presses forward sees not that his right arm has dropped from him; a third tries to get up after he has lost a leg, while the dying foot quivers with its toes on the ground close by.

How on earth was Alexander to win this battle: His leading general, Parmenio, had recommended a night attack. 'I do not steal victory,' Alexander had replied. In terms of man against man, this looked most unlikely, for the enemy outnumbered his forces by at least four to one. Darius duly placed a strong, straight reserve line and before it, three strong divisional groupings in straight lines; in front of them and on the left and the right – something of a technical innovation – he set groupings of at least a thousand men each in straight lines. He had chosen a flat plain for the battle, thus denying Alexander his customary use of geography. In a plain, straight battle, it seemed obvious to Darius that by sheer weight of numbers, he would win.

Alexander responded by positioning his troops at curves and angles. At the rear of his position he placed his supply unit and in front of that, angled slightly so as to confuse the enemy attack, his rear phalanx. Their job was to stand strong in defence should a retreat become necessary. Before them on the right wing, Alexander personally commanded his finest infantry and cavalry, arranging the former in a challenging straight line and the latter in a supporting curve to prevent any outflanking movement from Darius. He also held a group of cavalry in between the line and the curve, which would prove to be decisive in the forthcoming battle.

On the left wing, Parmenio commanded the Greek and Thessalian cavalry backed by infantry brigades. Alexander had placed these there to halt any outflanking manoeuvre by Darius. He had also worked out a way to combat the chariot attack.

Darius opened the battle with just such an attack. Alexander's soldiers replied with javelins and arrows. A chariot is no good without a charioteer, and the assault proved to be a disaster. The charioteers died and the horses clattered onward harmlessly.

Fierce fighting then took place, with the Persian cavalry, which included Scythian and Bactrian auxiliaries, trying to battle through Alexander's right flank. They were met, however, by his wing reserve, put there precisely to encourage the move of a general as easily deceived as Darius. Nevertheless, Alexander's right came under severe pressure by sheer weight of numbers. He responded with the intuitive leap of intelligence which characterizes military genius. Discerning that Persian cavalry movements, forceful though they were, had created a gap in their line, Alexander seized his chance and, with perfect timing, struck with speed and resolution.

The enemy army, now split in two, became confused. Once

again, King Darius lost his nerve and fled – appropriately enough, in a chariot.

On the left, that solid general Parmenio was having difficulties in stemming the assaults of the numerically superior Persian foe. The lack of men able to hold the line enabled Persian and their allied Indian cavalry to make a daring dash through to loot the Macedonian camp. Alexander had planned for such an eventuality, however, and sent in the reserves he had kept back for the purpose, composed of Greeks and Thracians eager to do battle. The Indians and Persians decided to disengage and retreat in good order.

Arbela was Alexander's greatest victory. It demonstrated beyond all reasonable doubt that his mind could always perceive the essential factors on any battlefield. It was his right hook which won the event, smashing through the gap in the enemy's line, which gap he had deliberately encouraged.

After Arbela, the power of Darius was broken and within the year, he was murdered by his own generals. From now on, the advance of Alexander was inexorable. The cities of Babylon, Susa and Persepolis were now easy meat for him, making him master of a vast Asian empire.

For the next six years, Alexander campaigned to expand his empire, all the while ensuring that there was peace and prosperity for the citizens already within its confines. Passing through Afghanistan and temporarily subduing it along his way, he resolved to conquer India, meeting King Porus in a battle which Fuller has described as being 'tactically the most brilliant of all'. Essentially, Alexander had crossed the River Indus and wanted to reach the Ganges, far to the east. King Porus tried to stop him at the River Hydaspes, sending in 200 war elephants. Alexander responded to the assault with typical intelligence, for he realized that a war elephant does not know what to do if its driver is killed by an arrow or a javelin: alternatively, one can chop an elephant's mobility at the knee with a quick swing of an axe.

This splendid victory opened India to him, but his army was tiring. Sensibly, Alexander decided on a temporary retreat to Persia prior to a future campaign in order to consolidate his well-gotten gains. Unfortunately for the world, in 323 BC he died from fever in Babylon. He was buried in Alexandria, the city he had wanted to make the centre of learning and scholarship, and of a civilization which united the cultures of East and West.

Unlike his father Philip, Alexander bequeathed no successor to humanity, and he died sighing that there were no more worlds for him to conquer. Certainly he left a deserved legend, but actually he left much more. Though no one person could maintain the empire he had conquered, there were nevertheless four great monarchies arising in its stead: Egypt under the Ptolemies, Asia Minor under the Seleucids, Macedonia under the Antigonids and, in India, the rule of the Chandragupts. These latter, according to Professor W.W. Tarn in his *Alexander the Great*, 'deduced the possibility of realizing in actual fact the conception, handed down from Vedic times, of a comprehensive monarchy in India; hence Alexander indirectly created Asoka's empire in India and enabled the spread of Buddhism.' A collage of quotations amply demonstrates the Macedonian King's achievements:

J.F.C. Fuller:

... his idea of world unity as the brotherhood of man was never extinguished. The fusing of races ... became a daily occurrence in the great cosmopolitan cities he had founded. In these the various races mingled and out of their mingling arose a common culture – the Hellenistic.

A.J. Reinach:

[Alexandria was] the meeting place of the world.... [Curiosity] drove mens' minds to multiply enquiries and information in every direction. They wanted to know everything, to explain everything. They interrogated old texts.... They travelled over the inhabited earth.... They carried to a very high pitch the study of the sciences properly so-called, which tended to become definitely separated from philosophy.... What is all this, if it is not the very principle of the scientific spirit?

Furthermore, Alexander had tremendous influence on the reform of the banking system, which can both win wars and preserve peace, having seized the hoarded wealth of Persia and having minted it into coins for circulation.

Athenaeus: '... the sun of "wealth, with far-flung might", as Pindar has it, verily rose.'

Fuller: 'Not only did he [Alexander] issue coin, but he unified the financial system by introducing a uniform standard. After his death the Ptolemys monopolised the whole of the banking business in Egypt....'

Ulrich Wilcken:

[Through] their central bank at Alexandria they ... transacted business in money with foreign countries.... In Alexander's wars, the previous barriers between East and West were removed, and in the next generation thousands of Greek traders and artisans entered the new world, to seek their fortunes in the new Greek cities, which shot up out of the ground like mushrooms. In this way the two previously detached circles came more and more to coincide and form a single economic circle; and when the Western Mediterranean was attracted into the orbit of the great revolution that occurred in the East, there was finally created a world commerce, which embraced the whole inhabited world, and extended from Spain to India, and beyond through Central Asia to China. This development was completed only under the Roman Empire, but its basis was the conquest of Asia by Alexander.

Professor Tarn:

Hardly was he dead when legend became busy with his terrible name.... Around him the whole dream-world of the East took shape and substance; of him every story of a divine world-conqueror was told afresh.... He lifted the civilized world out of one groove and set it in another; he started a new epoch; nothing could again be as it had been.

Alexander had virtually achieved that which all men desire: to make one's dream come true; though he had done so on a grander scale than anyone could envisage. It is hardly surprising that Plutarch stated of him: 'God is the father of all men but he makes the best ones peculiarly his own.' The idea of a civilized Empire, with its Emperor as a god-king was later adopted by Augustus Caesar, who created the *Pax Romana*. Still later, in the medieval days of the Papacy, this ideal became the guiding light of the Holy Roman Empire, though in its decline it became neither holy nor Roman and not even an empire.

Curiously enough, the Islamic Empire was only rendered possible by the connections of Muslims with the Hellenism Alexander had established in Egypt, Syria and Asia Minor.

By means of war, Alexander brought peace. By means of war, Alexander brought culture, commerce and civilization. 'War! What is it good for? Absolutely nothing!' This is certainly not true of this incredible man who lit a torch which was to ignite the Ancient World and thereby fructify human evolution.

2

Hannibal (247–183 BC):
Scipio Africanus (237–183 BC)

Alexander the Great had conquered an empire greater in territory than that of our contemporary United States of America. This empire broke up in the wake of his death, leaving a power vacuum. Two nations arose to pursue the imperial idea: Rome and Carthage. Initially, Rome, by its conquest of Italy, was supreme on land, while Carthage, from its situation in North Africa, in what is now Tunisia, held command of the Mediterranean Sea. Rome resolved to become a naval power and by the use of novel tactics demonstrated its superiority at sea in the victory over the Carthaginian at Mylae 260 BC; the decisive victory at the battle of Heraclea where the Carthaginians lost ninety-four ships to the Romans' twenty-four, gave Rome command of the central Mediterranean, although subsequent Carthaginian victories and attrition on both sides led to exhaustion and an uneasy peace.

Hamilcar Barca conquered Spain for Carthage, but died in 229 BC. War broke out again and Hamilcar's son-in-law, Hasdrubal, continued his campaigns, which led to another peace treaty whereby the River Iberus (Ebro) was fixed as the boundary between Carthaginian and Roman interests in Spain. Hasdrubal was assassinated in 221 BC, and his successor as General-in-Chief was his brother-in-law, Hamilcar Barca's son Hannibal. He resolved to take the Punic Wars (the wars between Carthage and Rome) right into the heartland of the enemy.

Hannibal is legendary for his celebrated crossing of the Alps with elephants, and for inflicting one of the worst defeats the Romans ever sustained at Cannae in 216 BC. His victory there was so spectacular a piece of generalship that his strategy was virtually copied by the Germans at Kiev in 1941, using tanks instead of elephants. The secret of such victory in battle can possibly be summarized in the acronym STOMT: Speed, Timing, Organization, Morale and Technology.

Given the fact that Hannibal won the battle of Cannae, in particular, so brilliantly, why did he eventually lose the war to generals far less innovative or imaginative? The purpose of this chapter is to try to answer these intriguing questions.

Hannibal was a charismatic leader whose troops were devoted to him. He had a strong constitution which could endure every form of hardship to which he subjected his soldiers, although he was of light but firm build. Well educated in Greek, his quick and calculating brain enabled him to act swiftly in estimating the nature of any given situation. Physically, he excelled in riding, running and fencing. His private life was quite austere for his times, for he was remarkably restrained in his use of wine and women.

His Roman critics were, obviously, somewhat hostile. According to Livy: 'To his reckless courage in encountering dangers, he united the greatest judgement when in the midst of them ... [yet he had] no regard for truth, and none for sanctity, no fear of the gods, no reverence for an oath, no religious scruple.' Polybius declares him to have been 'extraordinarily cruel ... [and] exceedingly grasping for money.' 'These vices,' Fuller comments, 'we think, may be largely discounted ... his "perfidy" was no greater than that of his great adversary, Scipio, and his cruelty in no way abnormal in his age.'

The intention of Hannibal was to reinstate the supremacy of Carthage over Rome. The position of ancient Republican Rome was then fraught with difficulty. The Romans had pushed the Gauls, their old enemies, into northern Italy; they had established an uneasy confederacy of Italian states; and their navy controlled both the Adriatic Sea and the supply routes via the Mediterranean to their territories in northern Spain. Moreover, from their naval base in Sicily, they could land an army at Carthage.

However, Hannibal had perceived, and was determined to exploit, the various weaknesses of the Romans. His strategic object was to break up the Italian confederacy and unite the Gauls behind his flanks, for, as he declared: 'I am not come to fight against Italians, but on behalf of Italians against Rome.'

Tactically, he had further advantages. The Romans relied almost wholly on infantry, formed in the phalanx or square of spears developed by Alexander. They drilled their soldiers to become mindless killing machines, who would go forward, go backward or stand still, according to command. They neglected the use of cavalry.

Hannibal had learned from the campaigns of King Pyrrhus of Epirus, a second cousin of Alexander, who had trained elephants for battle. Initially, the Romans had been defeated by this innovation (280–279 BC); they had subsequently made a series of counter-attacks, cutting off supplies and forcing Pyrrhus to withdraw, with heavy casualties, even though he had won a number of victories. Consequently, humanity came to call battles which are won, but in which the victor's losses are as great as those of the defeated, 'Pyrrhic victories'.

Hannibal was determined to surmount the particular problems that had confronted Pyrrhus, but also to use elephants. In the spring of 218 BC, therefore, Hannibal set out from southern Carthaginian Spain at the head of 90,000 infantry, 12,000 cavalry and 37 elephants, to defeat the power of Rome. According to Polybius, his men were 'highly efficient, and in an extraordinary state of physical training'.

Initially, the Romans seemed to have no answer to the imaginative tactical moves of Hannibal. Having crossed the boundary formed by the River Iberus, he took the Roman north of Spain by sheer force of arms and advanced swiftly through southern France to the Alps, throwing his enemy into confusion all the way. It was his hope to rouse the local populations in revolt against Rome, and to make an alliance with Cisalpine Gaul (that part of Gaul bounded by the Alps, the Rhine, and the Pyrenees) which would increase the forces he could send into battle.

Hannibal's invasion of Italy over the Alps from Gaul took a mere fifteen days, according to Livy, a considerable feat of movement. Nevertheless, the crossing was fraught with difficulties. One was the problem of extended supply lines in difficult country. The other was the savaging of Hannibal's rearguard by the Allobroges tribe, mountain men acting in alliance with Rome. Hannibal had left 22,000 men behind him to hold Catalonia in northern Spain, so that his crossing of the Alps was undertaken with 50,000 infantry and 9,000 cavalry in addition to his elephants.

'From that time the mountaineers fell upon them in smaller parties,' Livy wrote,

> more like an attack of robbers than war, sometimes on the van, sometimes on the rear, according as the ground afforded them advantage, or stragglers advancing or loitering gave them an opportunity. Though the elephants were driven through steep and narrow roads with great loss of time, yet wherever they went they rendered the army safe from the enemy, because men unacquainted with such animals were afraid of approaching too nearly.

Hannibal entered the plains of Italy with just 20,000 infantry and 6,000 cavalry, having lost 30,000 and 3,000 respectively during the crossing of the Alps. Fuller argues for a loss by desertion of 21,000 men. Even so, and despite the horrendous wastage of men, this handsome and romantic hero, just twenty-nine years old, proceeded to win three astonishing victories. The first was his luring of Sempronius into battle on the banks of the River Trebia (Trebbia), in northern Italy. According to Polybius in his *The Histories*, Sempronius put 36,000 infantry and 4,000 cavalry into the field, giving him a numerical superiority of 14,000 warriors. Nevertheless, Hannibal outmanoeuvred him by holding the centre with a perfect infantry formation while the Carthaginian cavalry outflanked him to savage his rear, causing the Romans to flee the field.

The second victory came in April of 217 BC, by the northern shores of Lake Trasimene, when Hannibal used swift movement and surprise to position himself between the armies of Servilius and Flaminius. Again according to Polybius, although the Romans outnumbered the Carthaginians by 2,000 men, they were driven from the field with losses of 15,000 killed, and 15,000 prisoners.

Cannae, a Roman supply depot, in southern Italy on the River Aufidus (Ofanto), is considered to be Hannibal's greatest victory; the battle was fought on 2 August 216 BC. Hannibal drew up his battle line in a crescent formation, putting his Spaniards and allies from Gaul dead centre with his Africans on their flanks, and a powerful division of cavalry on each wing. The Romans opposed him in straight lines. According to Polybius, the Romans had 80,000 infantry and 9,600 cavalry, although *The Cambridge Ancient History* calculates their strength at 48,000 men.

Hannibal's first move was to rout the enemy's cavalry, whereupon the Roman infantry attacked. Hannibal therefore commanded his troops to retreat in good order, thus forcing the Romans from a convex into a concave formation. Abruptly, the Carthaginian pushed forward his two divisions of African infantry, wheeling them both inwards so as to seal the pocket he had deliberately engendered. The cavalry then took the Romans from the rear, falling upon both flanks.

'The Roman army was swallowed up as if by an earthquake,' Fuller states. According to Polybius, the Carthaginians lost 5,700 men, and the Romans 70,000 infantry killed, 10,000 prisoners, and all of their cavalry bar 370 men – though if the numbers given in *The Cambridge Ancient History* are accurate, this can hardly have been the case. No one, however, can doubt the devastating nature of Hannibal's victory.

Valour, discipline and drill determined Roman tactics at that time, with the strategy being somewhat mechanical. Most Roman generals were little more than masters of drill, able to win, through discipline against a barbarian rabble, but they had learned nothing from Alexander's campaigns, leaving them open to exploitation of their blunders in tactics and ignorance of strategy by the imagination, insight and foresight of Hannibal.

Tactically, Hannibal was brilliant; yet one must concur with Field Marshal Montgomery's view that his 'strategy in Italy was a failure'. His fine general of the cavalry, Maharbal, strongly advised Hannibal to move directly upon Rome, but he dithered in southern Italy, arguing that the uprising of the Italian states, which he had fully expected, had not yet occurred; and that he lacked the troops to mount a lengthy and expensive siege of Rome. 'In very truth the gods bestow not on the same man all their gifts,' Maharbal protested painfully: '*You know how to gain a victory, Hannibal; you know not how to use one.*'

Livy thought that the delay of Hannibal saved both the City and the coming Empire. The opportunity which could not only have given Hannibal Rome, but would also have brought Carthaginian domination of all Spain, Sardinia and Sicily into the bargain, was now lost. Rome regrouped its forces and put in a new general, Quintus Fabius Maximus who, ironically, was soon to earn for himself the nickname 'Cunctator' – 'the delayer' and was the quintessence of the dull but effective general. He frustrated Hannibal by always retreating in good order and never giving him the satisfaction of the pitched battle which Fabius knew he would lose. For year after year, Hannibal campaigned fruitlessly in Campania. (It is not for nothing that at the turn of the twentieth century, British socialists formed the *Fabian* Society and spoke, in Sidney Webb's words, about 'the inevitability of gradualness'.)

Hannibal was unable to create the alliances with the Italian states within the Roman Confederacy that he had so deeply desired. As Fabius kept him occupied in campaigns that were more or less futile, Roman maritime supremacy ensured that the supply lines by sea from Carthage to Spain, and thence to his troops, were cut. Meanwhile, Rome had produced a new general to take the fight to the Carthaginians. This was Publius Scipio, called Africanus (237–183 BC).

At the tender age of twenty-one, Scipio had been present at Hannibal's devastating victory at Cannae. He came from a noble military family, and both his father and his uncle had won victories against the Carthaginians in Spain, before suffering appalling defeats there at the hands of Hannibal's brother, Hasdrubal. The Roman Senate sent Scipio to Spain, while Fabius was occupying Hannibal by resisting his assaults, then departing in good order to fight again. Scipio's task was to attack; in that, he was in every way a worthy opponent for Hannibal. Probably the best verdict on Scipio is that of Theodor Mommsen in his *The History of Rome*:

He was not one of the few who by their energy and iron will constrain the world to adopt and to move in new paths for centuries.... Yet a special charm lingers around the form of that graceful hero; it is surrounded, as with a dazzling halo, by the atmosphere of serene and confident inspiration, in which Scipio with mingled credulity and adroitness always moved. With quite enough of enthusiasm to warm men's hearts, and enough of calculation to follow in every case the dictates of intelligence, while not leaving out of account the vulgar; not naive enough to share the belief of the multitude in the divine inspirations, not straightforward enough to set it aside, and yet in secret thoroughly persuaded that he was a man specially favoured of the gods – in a word, a genuine, prophetic nature; raised above the people, and not less aloof from them; a man steadfast to his word and kingly in his bearing ... so confident in his own greatness that he knew nothing of envy or hatred, courteously acknowledged other men's merits, and compassionately forgave other men's faults; an excellent officer and a refined diplomatist without presenting offensively the special stamp of either calling, uniting Hellenic culture with the fullest feeling of a Roman, an accomplished speaker and of graceful manners – Publius Scipio won the hearts of soldiers and of women, of his countrymen and of the Spaniards, of his rivals in the Senate and of his greater Carthaginian antagonist.

As Hannibal charged and Fabius retreated in Italy, Scipio prepared for war in Spain, a war which would lead to a tremendous confrontation with Hannibal. Rather than give open battle in the field, Scipio marched swiftly on the port of Nova Cathagio (Cartagena), using speed to move between the three Carthaginian armies opposing him. Leaving the Carthaginian armies ten days' march from the strategic objective, an effective assault by land and sea saw Scipio capture Cartagena, bringing him a vital port the loss of which denied the Carthaginians their base through which they received reinforcements and supplies from Africa.

Scipio also a major arsenal of weapons, the silver mines, and local Spanish chieftains to be held as hostages. In the winter of

209–8 BC, he trained his soldiers in methods he had learnt by a study of Hannibal generalship. He took from his enemy's tactics, and proceeded to improve upon them. Providing his soldiers with the finest Spanish iron swords, Scipio also had them trained in the handling of weapons, and encouraged his officers to exercise individual initiative. Formerly, the Romans had fought in a formation of three straight lines, which unimaginative tactic had caused their colossal loss at Cannae. Roman victories had been based on strength rather than intelligence, since their units lacked the mobility necessary for the execution of a successful flanking movement, even if their commanders had ever decided upon such a manoeuvre. Scipio learned the lesson of Cannae by placing a solid field of legionaires in the centre, accompanied by light infantry who were mobile in attack, and placing his veterans and cavalry on the wings.

Time brought a slow but steady vindication of Scipio's views. He won the battle at Baecula 208 BC, though not completely. As planned, the Roman centre stood firm as its flanks assaulted Hasdrubal's forces. The latter declined to move into the trap Scipio had laid for him and withdrew in good order. Hasdrubal then fled to Italy in order to support his brother Hannibal. Scipio proceeded to take a number of Spanish fortresses after successful sieges which employed superior Roman technology in order to smash down the walls.

The battle of Ilipa, near Seville, was crucial to the control of Spain. Scipio, having captured a town, would establish terror in his enemies' minds by sacking it. He would then behave with the utmost kindness to the prisoners he had taken, who would be released, 'the girls with ear-rings and bracelets, the young men with daggers and swords', according to Polybius; this explains why Scipio was able to win Spanish allies. Even so, Ilipa presented him with considerable problems, for he had 40,000 troops to the Carthaginians' 50,000. It proved to be a very interesting battle.

Scipio placed his Spanish allies in the centre, with Roman legions and cavalry on the flanks. The Carthaginians, by contrast, put their Spanish allies on the flanks with their finest troops from North Africa in the centre. Perceiving this, Scipio ordered his men to take the enemy's flanks, which they duly did; meanwhile, his Spanish allies held the Carthaginians in the centre. Scipio, having learned from Hannibal, had cleverly enveloped the Carthaginians on each wing, forcing them to flee in bad order and effectively giving Rome mastery of Spain.

Encouraged by victory, in 204 BC Scipio invaded North Africa and attacked Carthage. By threatening Hannibal's homeland, he hoped to draw the Carthaginian away from Italy, having himself trained a Roman army in Sicily and secured an alliance with Masinissa of Numidia (roughly corresponding to modern Algeria) for the use of his excellent cavalry. Once landed, Scipio was initially held by a powerful Carthaginian defence; he therefore proposed peace negotiations as a delaying tactic. Eventually, once reinforcements and supplies had reached him from Italy, he chose battle at Bagbrades, near Utica. This time Scipio positioned a solid front of infantry, the *hastati*, at the centre; behind them were the *principes*, who were to hold the line should the first line of *hastati* give way. Behind them stood the *triarii*, whose job it was to act as reserves and to follow up a victory by slitting the throats of all enemies wounded upon the field of battle, since a dead man can do no harm. On his wings, Scipio placed Roman and Numidian cavalry. These forces between them completely smashed the armies of Hasdrubal.

Scipio had now gained his principal strategic objective: Hannibal had to withdraw from Italy in order to face him in pitched battle. The crucial battle was fought at Zama in Numidia in 202 BC. 'The two most famous generals and the two mightiest armies in the world advanced in battle, doomed either to crown or destroy the many triumphs each had won in the past,' Livy stated.

The terrain was a North African plain, south-west of Carthage by some five days' march. Hannibal had 45,000 infantry and 3,000 cavalry, Scipio 34,000 infantry and 9,000 cavalry. The latter had spent weeks prior to this battle in capturing ports and harbours so as to block all possibility of Hannibal's army being resupplied by sea. The Carthaginians proposed peace, but Scipio declined the offer. He was sure of winning, even though Hannibal had eighty war elephants. Even so, and as Livy remarked, his soldiers had little in common in terms of language, customs, arms and dress and were lacking in motivation. It seems as though the dull but effective tactics of Fabius Cunctator had caused Hannibal to neglect the very matters at which he had originally excelled: STOMT – Speed, Timing, Organization, Morale and Technology.

Hannibal gambled on the potential success of a quick knockout. Establishing light infantry of Ligurians and Gauls on the front line, he instructed his elephant cavalry in the centre to charge. His second line of Carthaginians and other African heavy infantry were relied upon to hold the position in the event of initial failure. His third line, the Bruttians, were to hold the defence in the event of regrouping or else mop up the enemy if the tactics succeeded.

By contrast, Scipio instructed his first line of light infantry, the *hastati*, to guide the elephants through the gaps between the Roman lines, leading them into the shooting ground which constituted his second line: the *principes*, who had been trained in using the javelin. Scipio also used blasts of horns and trumpets deliberately to increase the animals' panic, elephants' ears being extremely sensitive, thus further increasing the terror of these otherwise noble beasts, especially when their riders were expertly speared.

At the same time on the second line, and on each wing, Scipio had skilfully trained groups of horse cavalry, the Italians under Laelius and the Numidians under Masinisa – the latter were fighting as rebels against the Numidian cavalry which Hannibal had recruited. Scipio ordered an assault which routed the enemy on both wings. It was owing to the disparity in numbers of cavalry – the Roman advantage of horse was 9,000–3,000 – that Hannibal had initially proposed peace. Scipio had declined the offer since he was sure that he would win.

In case the initial assaults did not succeed, Scipio had established the *triarii*, heavy infantry trained to hold the line for purposes of regrouping or retreat.

The Carthaginian cavalry was chased from the field on that day: Hannibal therefore endeavoured to win the battle with his infantry. The Roman legions broke through the first Carthaginian line and then smashed their way through the second; however, Hannibal's third line of battle-hardened veterans held strongly in defence. According to Polybius, when the infantry had surmounted the piles of corpses, 'the two lines charged each other with the greatest fire and fury'.

The disciplined training Scipio had imposed upon his troops paid dividends when he ordered an organized retreat. His forces regrouped in the centre of the field, carrying away their wounded.

Then they gave defensive battle. 'Being nearly equal in numbers, spirit, courage and arms,' as Polybius writes, 'the battle was for a long time undecided, the men in their obstinate valour falling dead without giving way a step.'

Scipio was in fact gambling on his well-trained troops holding the centre while his equally well-trained cavalry wheeled from their pursuit of the horsemen they had routed: and Masinissa and Laelius did indeed return to assault the Carthaginian rear. These two moves from the flanks completely destroyed Hannibal's forces, the attacks from the rear on both left and right breaking up his infantry formations.

Livy states that at Zama, the Romans lost 1,500 men killed and 4,000 wounded. By contrast, the Carthaginians lost 20,000 dead with the same number captured: there is no known reliable figure for their wounded.

Perceiving that a siege of Carthage would be a difficult proposition in view of its substantial fortifications, Scipio proposed to employ his impressive victory in order to make peace terms which, among other things, would acknowledge that Rome, not Carthage, was the leading power in the Western world. These terms were:

1. The handing over of all ships of war and all elephants
2. Agreement to carry on no future war without the consent of Rome
3. The reinstatement of Masinissa in his former kingdom
4. The payment of 10,000 talents of silver spread over fifty years

These terms were accepted by the Roman Senate and people.

Hannibal, who had been forced to flee to Hadrumentum, accompanied by a mere handful of horsemen, eventually came to terms with Scipio Africanus, for these two generals had considerable respect for each other, as Livy demonstrates:

... when Africanus asked who, in Hannibal's opinion, was the greatest general, Hannibal named Alexander, the king of the Macedonians, because with a small force he had routed armies innumerable and because he had traversed the most distant regions, even to see which transcended human hopes. To the next request, as to whom he would rank second, Hannibal selected Pyrrhus; saying that he had been the first to teach the art of castrametation; besides, no one had chosen his ground or placed his troops more discriminatingly; he possessed also the art of winning men over to him, so that the Italian peoples preferred the lordship of a foreign king to that of the Roman people, so long the master in that land. When he continued, asking whom Hannibal considered third, he named himself without hesitation. Then Scipio broke into a laugh and said 'What would you say if you had defeated me?' 'Then, beyond doubt,' he replied. 'I should place myself both before Alexander and before Pyrrhus and before all other generals.'

Scipio had used against Hannibal the tactics which, as a youth, he had learned from the Carthaginian at Cannae. Moreover, Scipio had learned and employed lessons of strategy which, being beyond the ken of the vainglorious Hannibal, left him without the weapon of flexibility.

After this peace, Hannibal endeavoured to rebuild the power of Carthage, but after 193 BC the Romans accused him of breaking the treaty and circumstances forced him to flee to Ephesus and thence, eventually, to Bithynia in Asia Minor. The vision of Carthaginian supremacy possessed by this bold and brilliant general, so strong in tactics and so weak in strategy, found its fate in his tragic suicide by poison in 182 BC, at the age of 64.

Curiously enough, his opponent Scipio died in the same year, albeit from natural causes. But his defeat of Hannibal at Zama had lasting global consequences. Mommsen wrote that it was probable that:

> ... the two great, on whom the decision of the political question ... devolved, offered and accepted peace on such terms in order to set just and reasonable limits on the one hand to the furious vengeance of the victors, on the other to the obstinacy and imprudence of the vanquished. The noble-mindedness and statesmanlike gifts of the great antagonists are no less apparent in the magnanimous

submission of Hannibal to what was inevitable, than in the wise abstinence of Scipio from an extravagant and insulting use of victory.

So ended, on honourable terms, the Second Punic War. Livy, however, discerned the significance of Scipio's victory over Hannibal at the battle of Zama: '... before nightfall they would know whether Rome or Carthage should give laws to the nations.... For not Africa ... or Italy, but the whole world would be the reward of victory.' Polybius saw it in similar terms: 'To the Carthaginians it was a struggle for their own lives and the sovereignty of Libya; to the Romans for universal doination and supremacy.' The former part of Libya is now Tunisia.

The magnanimity of Scipio was not displayed in later years by the writer and Censor, Marcus Porcius Cato in the Roman Senate. Having fought in the Second Punic War, and visited Carthage in 175 BC, he used to end his every speech, no matter what its subject, be it on sewers or bread, on war or peace, with the climax: 'Carthage must be destroyed!' In 146 BC, during the Third Punic War, it was, the site was razed and dedicated to the infernal gods.

The Romans, having won supremacy in the Mediterranean; having united Italy; having conquered all Spain, Sicily, Syracuse and various islands; were now poised to extend their dominion. In his defeat of the handsome hero Hannibal, Scipio unwittingly opened the way for his own successor in generalship, Julius Caesar.

3

Julius Caesar (100–44 BC)

Hannibal had been an imaginative general, defeated in the end by the more sensible strategy and tactics of Scipio. With the exception of Alexander the Great, Gaius Julius Caesar was the most intellectual of commanders up to his time.

Initially, Julius Caesar had simply been a politician from the patrician gentry, as in later centuries was true of another great general, England's Oliver Cromwell. Although some military experts have criticized Julius Caesar as lacking tactically, the skills as an innovator which distinguish the greatest commanders, no one can deny that his grasp of strategy brought about the conquest of Gaul, the invasion of Britain, and the end of the Roman Republic and the foundation of the Roman Empire.

Earlier Roman commanders, in their endeavours to increase Rome's Republican might, had razed Corinth and Carthage to the ground, doing it so completely that a plough could be drawn over the sites. As John Terraine rightly remarks: 'Not even Ypres, after four and a half years of bombardment, nor Hiroshima, after an atomic bomb, was so utterly wiped out.' Fuller states: 'The obliteration of cities had now become the seal of Roman power.' 'To destroy that for which a war is undertaken seems an act of madness,' Polybius rightly declared, 'and madness of the very worst kind.' Caesar discerned the truth of this matter, winning success in Spain by promising, from a position of strength, decent treatment to the citizens of any city which surrendered peacefully – and then keeping his promise. Once surrender had been declared, Julius Caesar imitated Alexander in forbidding his soldiers to kill the men, rape the women, sell the children into slavery, or set all the buildings ablaze.

Returning to Rome in triumph in 60 BC, and heaped with praises, Julius Caesar now joined a triumvirate consisting of the three most influential men of the expanding Roman Republic: himself; the international banker, Marcus Licinius Crassus, later killed in a vainglorious endeavour to win the Middle East for Rome; and another good general, celebrated in Rome, Gnaeus Pompeius, of which the anglicized form is Pompey. The First Triumvirate, as it came to be known, effectively ruled Rome during the last years of the Republic.

Pompey had done wonderfully well in the years 67–61 BC, when he had destroyed the pirates of the Mediterranean, brought the Jews under Roman rule by his abrupt entry into Jerusalem, and, by marching up the Euphrates, established a strong Roman position on the shores of the Caspian Sea. In the First Triumvirate, Caesar had to cede the principal position in Rome to Pompey, though he himself was given spheres of influence in Cisalpine Gaul (Northern Italy), Illyricum (Yugoslavia) and Narbonese Gaul (Southern France) as 'Governor'.

Julius Caesar proceeded to demonstrate both his legendary courage (as a youth, he had laughed and joked with the pirates who had kidnapped him for ransom), and his intelligence. He was popular in Rome for his speeches, which established him as a first-class orator and demagogue. Since he realized that an army's morale is vital for victory, he used to speak to his soldiers before a battle, a bottle of wine in one hand and a hunk of bread in the other, spitting out obscenities, talking to the troops in the ordinary language they used and understood. The men loved him for that: and also for the fact that whenever Caesar saw that he could not win a battle, rather than sacrifice soldiers in the cause of personal vanity, he would command a retreat in good order to a safe line of defence. He was also most attentive to matters like the supply of food and medical care for the wounded.

Physically, he was a man of slender build but obvious vigour. There is no reason to doubt his own third-person description of his actions at a serious moment during a battle:

> The situation was critical and as no reserves were available, Caesar seized a shield from a soldier in the rear and made his way to the front line. He addressed each centurion by name and shouted encouragement to the rest of the troops, ordering them to push forward and open out their ranks so they could use their swords more easily. His coming gave them fresh heart and hope. Each man wanted to do his best under the eyes of his commander despite the peril.

There is not a military expert who does not respect the success of Julius Caesar in conquering the land we now call France during the Gallic Wars of 58–51 BC. To quote Plutarch: '[Caesar] took by storm more than eight hundred cities, subdued three hundred nations, and fought pitched battles with three million men, of whom he slew one million in hand-to-hand fighting and took as many more prisoners.'

Julius Caesar instantly grasped the use of developing technology, especially in the use of artillery. The *catapulta* could hurl a stone, with deadly effect, up to 500 yards, more accurately than the flintlock musket's shot of the eighteenth century AD. The *ballista* could throw stones weighing between 50 and 60 lb. These weapons enabled Caesar to smash down a fortress from a distance. He also ensured the safety of his men in defence, pioneering trench warfare. At the siege of Alesia aka Auxosis, he commanded his men for their own safety to shift cubic metres of earth, and thereby ensure that casualties were kept to a minimum.

Strategy was the masterpiece of this slender, intelligent man of slight build. He recruited to his armies not only Roman citizens, as before, but also mercenaries, criminals and foreigners. He realized that those men whom the Duke of Wellington, nineteen centuries later, would call 'the scum of the earth', could be used effectively if well commanded. Nevertheless, he could be merciless, and never more so than when tribes refused his usually generous terms of peace: at a site near what is now Maastricht, presently a place of

European unity, Julius Caesar sent in his men to slaughter what is said to have been 430,000 people.

Caesar's policy in Gaul consisted of dividing and ruling the various warring tribes. His principal enemy was Vercingetorix, a notable Gallic chieftain who incited the Celts to rebellion against Roman rule. The Venetii tribe particularly resisted Roman domination, but they were defeated at a sea battle in the Loire estuary which broke their hold on the Atlantic harbours. Caesar now held northern and western central Gaul, with added support from the Audui tribe, but there remained the problem of the Belgae, linked with Britain, on his northern flank.

It was for this reason that Britain was invaded by the Romans under Caesar in 55 BC and again in 54 BC. Too much has been made of these expeditions. They were not those of conquest: they were punitive and deterrent in intention and in effect. The British tribes agreed to make peace and not to interfere in the Gallic Wars, and the Romans therefore withdrew.

In 52 BC, having secured his flanks, Caesar headed for the decisive battle with the Avernian chieftain Vercingetorix, at Alesia in central Gaul, so that he could take control of the heartland of the country. He had always achieved his successes by striking swiftly at his enemy's weakest point. Now, in order to secure Gaul, and having gradually surrounded this last pocket of resistance, he had to take his opponent's strongest point.

It was not an easy proposition. Vercingetorix had repulsed Caesar back at the hill fort of Gergovia. Now, at Alesia, near Dijon, a fortified city which stood high on a hill, he defied the Romans to do their worst. To add to the Roman difficulties, Caesar had 55,000 men to the 90,000 of Vercingetorix.

Caesar responded to these problems with extraordinary generalship. He cut off all supplies to the Gauls by having an encircling line constructed, ten miles in length, protecting his siege engines. In front of this line, he had his men dig a 20-foot trench to deter a sortie by Vercingetorix's men. The fort could now be starved into submission without the loss of a single Roman.

Seeing the Roman preparations, Vercingetorix hoped for reinforcements. These indeed duly arrived in the form of an army of Gauls, said to number no fewer than 250,000, to besiege the besiegers. However, Caesar had already planned for such an eventuality by setting up wooden towers at 130-yard intervals along the entire circuit of his fortifications for purposes of observation and defence. Moreover, Caesar had had constructed yet another circuit of fortifications, fourteen miles long and deftly engineered, outside his original lines. To the approaches to this line he added pit traps filled with stakes.

Vercingetorix had hoped that he would succeed by attacking from both the front and the back, yet despite his numerical superiority, he was soundly defeated. Roman traps and artillery on both inner and outer circuits reduced the Gauls to a rabble, in spite of their repeated assaults. Julius Caesar had indeed shown himself to be a defensive genius.

Perceiving that the Gauls in the rear of the Roman position were in disarray, Caesar himself donned a scarlet cloak and led a cavalry charge against them, routing them and thus tightening his grip on the siege. Vercingetorix was a sufficiently good general to discern the nature of the situation. Caesar had managed to repel the assaults he had ordered from both front and rear. Starvation would now be the fate of one and all at Alesia. This was unacceptable to Vercingetorix, who decided to surrender.

'Here I am,' he said to Julius Caesar. 'You, O most strong, have conquered the strong.'

Now Julius Caesar, having conquered Gaul, was determined to take Rome itself. Rifts were developing between the ruling triumvirate. There was a quarrel between Crassus, whose power was based upon money, and Gaius Pompeius, whose power depended upon military might. There was increasing tension between Pompey and Julius Caesar, who disobeyed orders from Rome in 49 BC and instead crossed the Rubicon to march upon Rome, defying the command to disband his legions, 49 BC.

Julius Caesar was assisted in his astute moves by the fact that Crassus, aiming for a similar military glory to that of his rivals, had been killed in Parthia, 53 BC. He defeated Pompey's legions at Ilerda, Spain, 49 BC, in order to secure his rear. Rome promptly offered him the post of Dictator; but Caesar declined, declaring that he was happy to be elected Consul. The ensuing war between Caesar and Pompey proved to be a difficult matter.

In crossing the Rubicon, the small river marking the boundary between Cisalpine Gaul and Roman Italy, Caesar had secured

Italy to his cause. Pompey lost his nerve and retreated to Greece.
Civil war between him and Caesar now raged. 'I set forth to fight
an army without a leader,' Caesar said, 'so as later to fight a leader
without an army.'

Defying Pompey's boasted command of the sea, Caesar
managed to transport seven legions over the Adriatic to besiege his
rival at Dyrrhachium, now known as Durrës in Albania. The tactic
of trying to cut away Pompey's access to the sea was a failure,
mainly because Pompey had twice as many soldiers. Caesar was
wise to retreat in good order.

However, on 9 August 48 BC at Pharsalus in Thessaly, Greece,
Pompey gave battle to Caesar and the former was utterly confident
of his eventual victory. Pompey had 40,000 soldiers to Caesar's
22,000. Moreover, Pompey intended to use his numerical
superiority in cavalry to smash Caesar's right wing. The latter,
anticipating such a move, placed six cohorts of javelin-wielding
warriors in support of his horsemen, a cohort numbering between
300 and 600 men, with ten to a legion.

At first it looked as though Pompey was winning, for his
infantry pressed forward by sheer weight of numbers against
Caesar's centre, while his cavalry pushed back the Consul's
horsemen. It was at this crucial point that Caesar's reserves,
obeying their general's orders, used their javelins as spears for
stabbing, rather than hurling them as missiles. As horses reared
and their riders were speared, this infantry reserve pressed forward
to assault Pompey's left flank. As this too broke up in confusion,
Julius Caesar personally led his third line of infantry to storm and
smash the disordered enemy.

It was a sensational victory. Caesar had lost 1,200 men; Pompey
had lost 6,000, not to mention the greater number who simply
surrendered to Caesar. He was forced to flee to Egypt, leaving
Greece to his rival. Caesar pursued him, only to find on arriving
there that someone eager to curry favour had already assassinated
his opponent. He consoled himself for the lack of a fight by having
a love affair with the young and beautiful Queen Cleopatra.

Cleopatra, the subject of a subsequent chapter, became
pregnant by Caesar. He won a battle for her with ease, which
confirmed her on the hitherto disputed throne. Then, having won
Egypt by sex rather than fighting, he proceeded to destroy the

supporters of the late Pompey, using an alliance with Mithridates of Pergamum, and in 47 BC going on to Asia Minor to defeat King Pharnaces II at the battle of Zela (Zile, northern Turkey). It was after that battle that he is alleged to have said '*Veni, vidi, vici*' – 'I came, I saw, I conquered'.

In 45 BC, Julius Caesar returned to Rome, having also crushed the remaining Pompeian leaders in North Africa, thus stamping out the last flames of civil war, made conquests in Syria, and extended Roman influence everywhere by his use of diplomacy. Essentially, he persuaded rulers of other nations that they would benefit from a close alliance with Rome. On his return he was appointed Dictator for a ten-year period; and the Senate converted this into a lifelong office.

Julius Caesar was a brilliant administrator and his faith in his own genius and destiny could not be shaken. Realizing the nature of warfare in his era, he led men, money, trade and political aspirations towards one single-minded goal. He understood the importance of propaganda. At times his moves were astonishingly bold and amazingly rash, but they were based on the coldest of calculations. In common with Alexander, he brushed aside his own inner fears and stormed ahead, with his enemies sometimes being defeated by their own fears. He also had a unique ability to predict his enemy's intentions.

For once this failed on the Ides of March, the fateful fifteenth, 44 BC. Julius Caesar failed utterly to realize how much hostility he had aroused among men such as Marcus Junius Brutus and Gaius Cassius Longinus, supporters of Pompey who were honestly sworn to preserve the virtues and *virtus* of Republican Rome. Brutus, one of the leaders of a violent conspiracy pledged to ending dictatorship and restoring the Republic, was among those who assassinated Julius Caesar on the steps of the Senate.

Even so, and despite his dramatic death, Julius Caesar brought an end to the Roman Republic and gave the Western world the Roman Empire.

4

Mark Antony (82–30 BC)
and Queen Cleopatra (69–30 BC)

Julius Caesar's will named his great-nephew Octavian (Gaius Julius Caesar Octavianus) as his heir. Octavian, however, could not consolidate his position without the aid of the late Caesar's lieutenant, Mark Antony – whose demagogic oratory had aroused the crowd of Rome against the assassins of Caesar in a manner immortalized by Shakespeare – and of Marcus Aemilius Lepidus, a banker. These three formed the Second Triumvirate. In 42 BC at Philippi in Thrace (north-eastern Greece), Octavian and Mark Antony defeated Brutus and Cassius, who had fled Italy after killing Caesar, the two arch-conspirators dying by their own hands.

It is not surprising, given the legacy of Alexander, that although the civil war that was to break out between Octavian and Antony, and their supporters, in 32 BC, affected every aspect of Roman dominion, Macedonia was the chief area of war. Lepidus was now edged out of the picture by Octavian and Mark Antony, who managed to coexist uneasily until 33 BC, having agreed to divide up the spheres of influence, Octavian to rule over Italy and the West, Antony over Africa and Asia. In Egypt, however, Antony fell in love with Queen Cleopatra, a wonderful enchantress who had already cast her spell over Julius Caesar, and who, even today, is still renowned for her beauty, courage, and intelligence. He left her in 40 BC to marry Octavian's sister, Octavia; when he divorced her in 32 BC, having meanwhile openly become Cleopatra's lover (he had three sons by her), war broke out between him and Octavian.

In examining Antony as a general, it is clear that he was prone to excessive impetuosity. As Octavian endeavoured to consolidate his gains around Rome, Antony sought control of the Middle East. In 36 BC he invaded Parthia an ancient empire, successor to the Seleucids, which reached from the Euphrates to the Indus, and which was Rome's main rival for power in the east at this time. The Parthian cavalry's habit of retreating and then suddenly firing a volley of arrows backwards as they did so, gave rise to the expression 'a Parthian shot', utterly underestimating Parthian generalship and technology. Florus takes up the tale:

> The Parthians, who were crafty as well as confident in their arms, pretended to be panic-stricken and to fly across the plains. Antonius immediately followed them, thinking that he had already won the day, when suddenly a not very large force of the enemy unexpectedly burst forth, like a storm of rain, upon his troops in the evening when they were weary of marching, and overwhelmed two legions with showers of arrows from all sides. No disaster had ever occurred comparable with that which threatened the Romans on the following day....

Fortunately, on this occasion, Mark Antony had the sense to retreat in good order. Retiring to Egypt, a land of great wealth, he plotted a grand strategy with Cleopatra, a strategy which amounted to nothing less than replacing Rome with Alexandria as the principal centre of power. Antony proclaimed Caesarion, Cleopatra's son by Julius Caesar, to be 'King of Kings', to rule, in association with his mother, as Ptolemy XIV. Commercially and strategically, Alexandria was a better site from which to command the empire that both Alexander and Julius Caesar had envisaged.

And it was an empire that Octavian wanted, too: an empire ruled from Rome.

Antony's audacity had won the victory at Philippi, wiping away the last flowerings of the old Roman Republic. Octavian now perceived that there was an empire at stake. He had to take Egypt, or else, without the treasures of the Ptolemys and the wealth of the granaries, he could not provide his supporters and soldiers with the wealth that he had promised them. Antony and Cleopatra wanted a cosmopolitan world empire cast in the mould of Alexander the Great. Octavian wanted a Roman empire. The decisive encounter came in 31 BC at the naval battle of Actium, off the entrance to the Gulf of Amvrakia in western Greece.

Curiously enough, a fine analysis of this battle is that of William Shakespeare, who had clearly studied all the available chronicles of his classical predecessors. As Antony dallied with Cleopatra, Octavian 'so quickly cut the Ionian sea' from Tarentum and Brundusium (Taranto and Brindisi) also taking Toryne. 'Celerity is never more admired than by the negligent,' Cleopatra comments acidly.

Unfortunately, Cleopatra then insisted that the principal battle be fought at sea, completely ignoring the advice of their best general, Enobarbus.

ENOBARBUS   Your ships are not well manned.
Your mariners are muleteers, reapers, people
Engrossed by swift impress. In Caesar's fleet
Are those that often have 'gainst Pompey fought;
Their ships are yare; yours, heavy. No disgrace
Shall fall you for refusing him at sea,
Being prepared for land.
ANTONY   By sea, by sea.
ENOBARBUS   Most worthy sir, you therein throw away
The absolute soldiership you have by land,
Distract your army, which doth most consist
Of war-marked footmen, leave unexecuted
Your own renownèd knowledge, quite forgo
The way which promises assurance, and
Give up yourself merely to chance and hazard

From firm security.
ANTONY   I'll fight at sea.
CLEOPATRA   I have sixty sails, Caesar none better.
ANTONY   Our overplus of shipping will we burn,
    And with the rest full-manned, from th'head of Actium
    Beat th'approaching Caesar. But if we fail,
    We then can do't at land.

Just as Enobarbus predicted, dreadful morale and sloppy admiralship fell at Actium before the speed and determination of Octavian.

ENOBARBUS
    Naught, naught, all naught! I can behold no longer.
    Th'*Antoniad*, the Egyptian admiral,
    With all their sixty, fly and turn the rudder.
    To see't mine eyes are blasted.
                    Enter Scarus
SCARUS   Gods and goddesses,
    All the whole synod of them!
ENOBARBUS   What's thy passion?
SCARUS
    The greater cantle of the world is lost
    With very ignorance. We have kissed away
    Kingdoms and provinces.

Antony's preference for his affair with Cleopatra, rather than risking his life in battle at the head of his men, was blamed by some.

SCARUS
    … I never saw an action of such shame.
    Experience, manhood, honour, ne'er before
    Did violate so itself.
ENOBARBUS   Alack, alack!
                    Enter Canidius
CANIDIUS
    Our fortune on the sea is out of breath,
    And sinks most lamentably. Had our general

Been what we knew himself, it had gone well.
O, he has given example for our flight
Most grossly by his own.

Antony and Cleopatra had in fact broken every important rule
of battle. They dithered and dallied as Octavian sped. They failed
to train and inspire their troops. Their ships were simply not
equipped for a naval battle. They ignored good advice. Although
they had put together a formidable coalition of kings against
Roman rule, the political and strategic result of the Battle of
Actium is impeccably summarized by Shakespeare in the pithy
sentences of King Canidius:

... To Caesar will I render
My legions and my horse. Six kings already
Show me the way of yielding.

When Octavian, whose generalship was sound, dull and
effective, landed in Egypt, Antony and Cleopatra had little left to
put against him: the result might have been different if they had
declined a naval battle and held close to their allies in order to fight
an engagement in which they would have outnumbered Octavian's
forces. Both committed suicide rather than fall into enemy hands.

Octavian promptly annexed Egypt, including the divine
honours and titles of its Ptolemaic kings. In 27 BC, the Roman
Senate gave him the semi-divine name of 'Augustus' – 'the
Consecrated'. The victory he had won at Actium ushered in a
Roman Empire which stretched from the Atlantic to the Euphrates
and from the North Sea to the Sahara Desert. Augustus, a cold but
clever man, succeeded in establishing both internal peace and in
making secure the frontiers. By his unimaginative but sound
moves, the Roman Empire and the *Pax Romana* came into being.

5

Boudicca (?–61 AD)

Her age is unknown but Cassius Dio, a Greek historian, described Boudicca as being 'possessed of greater intelligence than often belongs to women'. Cassius Dio added:

> In stature she was very tall, in appearance most terrifying, in the glance of her eye most fierce, and her voice was harsh; a great mass of the tawniest hair fell to her hips; around her neck was a large golden necklace; and she wore a tunic of divers colours over which a thick mantle was fastened with a brooch. This was her invariable attire.

In estimating her age, we know only that Boudicca had two daughters, in an era when girls married at a very young age; and that as *Boadicea* (a copying error), she established an English myth, which is still commemorated (in London, at least) by a statue strategically placed in Highbury Fields, and by another at the north end of Westminster Bridge. What is the truth of the matter?

'Neither before nor since has Britain ever been in a more disturbed and perilous state,' declared that excellent Roman historian, Tacitus. He is probably our most reliable guide to these events since he was the son-in-law of Gnaeus Julius Agricola, a fine Roman governor, from 77–87 AD, of what had become the province of Britain, which had been annexed to Rome by the Emperor Claudius after his invasion and conquest in 43.

The Romans were endeavouring to master this unruly island, following in the footsteps of Julius Caesar, and had made some headway. Under Claudius, they had taken most of the country up to the border with Scotland, and had captured the noble King Caractacus, chief of the Catuvellauni, who was taken to Rome and led before Claudius in chains and who, dazzled by the splendours of Imperial Rome, asked the Emperor: 'Why, when you had all this, did you covet our poor huts?'

It was under the Emperor Nero (37–68) that the most severe revolt by the Britons took place against Roman colonization. Boudicca's husband, Prasutagus, king of the Iceni tribe, from what is now Norfolk, tried diplomatically to engender harmonious relations with the Roman invaders, making the Emperor of Rome joint heir to the kingship of the Iceni upon his own death, provided that the rights of his wife, Queen Boudicca, and those of their two daughters, to that particular throne were recognized and honoured.

Upon the death of King Prasutagus by natural causes, the Romans under Nero promptly broke this agreement and, banishing all possibility of female rule from their world as had been done in the case of Cleopatra, declared that the royal line of the Iceni was extinguished. Murder, robbery and rapine were then visited upon the Iceni by the Romans. As Tacitus has it:

> Kingdom and household alike were plundered like prizes of war, the one by Roman officers, the other by Roman slaves. As a beginning, the late king's widow Boudicca was flogged and their daughters raped. The Icenian chiefs were deprived of their hereditary estates as if the Romans had been given the whole country. The king's own relatives were treated like slaves. And the humiliated Iceni feared still worse, now that they had been reduced to colonial status. So they rebelled.

A neighbouring tribe, the Trinovantes (from what is now Essex), were subjected to taxes and conscription and slavery; and insult was added to their injury by Roman demands that they support the huge temple at Camulodunum (Colchester), erected at great expense to honour the memory of the 'divine' Emperor Claudius. Again, Tacitus, though a loyal Roman, saw the truth here:

> They [the Trinovantes] particularly hated the Roman ex-soldiers who had recently established a settlement at Camulodunum. The settlers drove the Trinovantes from their homes and land and called them prisoners and slaves.... Moreover, the temple erected to the divine Claudius was a blatant stronghold of alien rule, and its observances were a pretext to make the natives appointed as its priests drain the whole country arid.

In addition, there was the presence of the loathed provincial procurator, Decianus Catus, a model of ruthless greed and, in military terms, utter incompetence. 'War is usually a catalogue of blunders,' as Winston Churchill declared: for the British, this particular war contains more blunders than most. Initially, Boudicca aroused the Iceni, formed an alliance with the Trinovantes, and marched upon Camulodunum, scene of a British surrender seventeen years before.

The ineptitude of the Romans in this instance is quite beyond belief. They had neglected to build walls, ramparts or trenches. The greedy Decianus Catus sent just 200 men to relieve the town's small garrison which, on the appearance of the tribesmen, had withdrawn into the temple, and the Roman soldiers' weapons were inadequate and too few. The angered hordes of Britons, led by Boudicca, razed the town to the ground and besieged the temple, seizing it by storm after two days.

The Ninth Legion now marched to relieve the town. The victorious Britons fell upon this outnumbered force and slaughtered the infantry. Boudicca now held East Anglia: but she had to face a formidable Roman opponent in Suetonius Paulinus, an accomplished and sensible general who had earlier distinguished himself by campaigns won in the Atlas Mountains of Morocco, and who had taken that most difficult terrain of Wales. It was rare indeed in Roman annals for barbarians to win against a

Roman legion, as Boudicca had done, and there followed a most interesting contest.

'Suetonius, undismayed, marched through disaffected territory to Londinium [London].' Tacitus writes. Suetonius Paulinus seems to have been a rather cold and calculating man. Deciding that his numerical inferiority left him incapable of giving battle to Boudicca, he abandoned Londinium, a developing town of merchants, and marched north. Boudicca's forces promptly took Londinium (which, then, was by no means the important centre it was to become), slaughtered its each and every citizen, and razed it to the ground. Suetonius had meanwhile withdrawn to a much more important city, Verulanium, now St Albans, marching his men up Watling Street, the road to the north that the Romans had built. Boudicca and her tribes pursued him. 'Verulanium suffered the same fate [as London],' says Tacitus.

Now Boudicca was determined to drive the Roman invaders out of Britain for ever, and set off in hot pursuit of Suetonius, sending in guerrillas to harass his rear troops and supply lines, and leaving him with no choice other than to give battle. And there was further bad news for Suetonius Paulinus. He had been expecting reinforcements from the Second Legion, based in tranquil Exeter. Unfortunately for him, the commander was away on leave and his deputy, Poenius Postumus, an administrator rather than a military commander, chose to play safe and keep the troops in the west. Suetonius therefore had to put his 12,000 men against Boudicca's 100,000.

How could this Roman commander possibly achieve a victory against such appalling numerical odds? He reacted with his customary coolness and common sense. To begin with, he chose his ground carefully. Historians disagree as to the precise location, but it seems to have been at Mancetter, near modern Atherstone, about ten miles north of Coventry. The troops were ordered to leave Watling Street and position themselves before a steep escarpment of rock, with a thick wood behind them and a wide plain in front. As was customary in Roman generalship, the infantry was massed in close and disciplined order, with the lightly armed auxiliaries at their flanks and the cavalry judiciously assembled on each wing. With the escarpment at their backs they could not be taken in the rear, nor could they easily be outflanked.

For her part, Boudicca, possibly still aching from the whipping that she had so unjustly received, now showed her ineptitude as a general. Her idea of strategy and tactics was to stand up in her chariot, look at her horde – which included so many women in carts who had come to see the victory that it could hardly be called an army – and shout 'CHARGE!'

It was spectacularly bad generalship. Although the Britons were noted for their skill in using chariots (and later firmly established that reputation at the Roman games), it did not occur to Boudicca to position them as cavalry. It is said of primary schoolboys who play football that one boy kicks it and the other twenty-one run after it. Such was Boudicca's idea of winning a battle: 'CHARGE!' – and that was all.

By contrast, Suetonius Paulinus had a force of trained, disciplined, and battle-hardened men. He had deliberately chosen terrain which would favour the throwing of javelins so as to disable the British charioteers, and that would be followed by close-quarter combat with short swords, at which the legionaries excelled. Suetonius was a master himself of the clever use of retreat as a tactic, and he had chosen his ground well. Tacitus describes the matter:

Suetonius confidently gave the signal for battle. At first the regular troops stood their ground. Keeping to the defile as a natural defence, they launched their javelins accurately at the approaching enemy. Then, in wedge formation, they burst forward. So did the auxiliary infantry. The cavalry too, with extended lances, demolished all serious resistance. The remaining Britons fled with difficulty since their ring of wagons blocked the outlets. The Romans did not spare even the women. Baggage animals too, transfixed with weapons, added to the heaps of the dead. It was a glorious victory, comparable with bygone triumphs.

The British army fled the field. The casualty figures given by Cassius Dio, that the British under Boudicca lost 230,000 warriors, excluding non-combatants, is absurd, especially when one considers that she had at most 100,000 men in the field.

Tacitus, as usual, has the most reliable figures, putting Roman deaths at 360 and British at 10,000.

How could 12,000 men beat 100,000 men? The question is as easy as the answer is obvious. As was shown in our own time in the battle to preserve Twyford Down from obscene road development, twenty men from the Commandos and the Paratroopers, hired as unemployed ex-soldiers, can go through 2,000 well-intentioned environmentalists 'like a knife through butter.'

Boudicca and her daughters committed suicide rather than fall into Roman hands again: and Britannia became a Roman province. Whatever her bravery, the Queen of the Iceni is a classic example of a general who allowed her toughness to get ahead of her intelligence.

Boudicca should also have borne in mind that Suetonius Paulinus ensured that all his soldiers had shields – unlike her own men.

6

Attila the Hun (c. 406–453 AD)

'Who are those hooded hordes swarming
Over endless plains, stumbling in cracked earth
Ringed by the flat horizon only'
                  T.S. Eliot: *The Waste Land*, V,
                     'What the Thunder Said'

In the time of Attila, these 'hooded hordes' were the Huns, bent
upon the destruction of the civilization of Western Europe. Attila
has been portrayed as the self-proclaimed scourge of Christianity.
As Sir Edward Creasy has it in his *Fifteen Decisive Battles of the
World*:

His own warriors believed him to be the inspired favourite of
their deities, and followed him with fanatic zeal; his enemies
looked on him as the preappointed minister of Heaven's
wrath against themselves; and, though they believed not in
his creed, their own made them tremble before him.... It was
during the retreat from Orleans that a Christian hermit is
reported to have approached the Hunnish king, and said to
him: 'Thou art the Scourge of God for the chastisement of

Christians'. Attila instantly assumed this new title of terror, which thenceforth became the appellation by which he was most widely and most fearfully known.

Attila, who had become chieftain of the Huns in 445 AD by murdering his own brother, had a further claim. Standing before his troops, he raised an ancient iron sword, proclaiming that it had been darted down into the earth from Heaven and that he was the only man fit to wield it. This sword, he proclaimed, personified the Spirit of Death, and he added that it was destined to destroy the world as known. Attila declared that he was: 'Descendant of the Great Nimrod. Nurtured in Engaddi. By the Grace of God, King of the Huns, the Goths, the Danes and the Medes,' thus proclaiming himself to be chief of all: and hence future, self-proclaimed ruler of all of Europe and Asia Minor and; as he further announced, 'The Dread of the World'.

Who were the Huns, and where did they come from? A convincing explanation is provided by M. Deguignes in his *Histoire Générale des Huns, des Turcs, des Mongols, et des Autres Tartares Occidentaux* ... (four volumes, 1756–8) with which John Bury concurred in Appendix VI to his edition of Gibbon's *Decline and Fall of the Roman Empire* (seven volumes, 1896–1900). Monsieur Deguignes, a French scholar of Chinese, was of the etymological opinion that 'Hun' derived from the tribes of Northern China, the Hiong-nu or Hsiung-nu, marauding in the Altai, Kuen-lun and Khingan Mountains, and that it was on this account that in 258 BC the Emperor of China, Hwang-te, initiated the magnificent Great Wall, the only human feat of structural engineering which can be seen by astronauts from outer space.

The Great Wall forced the marauding nomads to move on, bringing their wagons, using their horses as mobile meat and dairy food; such a nomad was quite happy, if occasion required it, to make a small slit in his horse's throat and refresh himself with a little of the animal's blood. Thus the Great Wall of China inadvertently brought about the fall of a Roman Empire already in decline.

The Huns migrated westwards, in what the Germans call *Völkerwanderung*, the wandering of the nations. Wherever they went, they carried all before them; like a plague of locusts, they stripped all the ground before them of everything that had life. They were excellent horsemen and expert with the bow and arrow. Using mobility, speed and mass, for their numbers have been estimated at up to half a million men, they plundered and pillaged every town or village in their path, slaughtered the men, raped the women and sold the children into slavery.

These Asiatic hordes fell upon the Goths – the Germanic peoples, probably originally from Scandinavia, who, after the first millenium AD, had migrated eastwards the Ukrainian Steppes – and appalled them with their barbarism: it is worth remembering that at that time the Romans regarded the Goths as being the worst of barbarians. The Visigoths and Ostrogoths (Western and Eastern Goths) in consequence initially allied themselves to the fading Roman Empire with a plea for protection, promising to fight with the Romans against the common threat posed by the Huns. The Romans, whose power was waning, promptly agreed, and also sought to make alliances with other invading tribes – the Vandals, Franks, Angles, Saxons and Jutes – in order to preserve their increasingly enfeebled empire, which had already been divided between east and west, with capitals at Rome and at Constantinople. The migrating tribes, pursued by the Huns through Eastern and Central Europe (who then wheeled around to assault the Eastern Roman Empire), were dominated by the coalition of Goths, who sacked Rome itself in 410 AD. From then on, the Western Roman Empire, such as it was, had to deal in alliances with the Goths and other tribes.

What can be said about the Huns?

> In order to make a whole oasis liable to tribute, they need only seize the main canal; and the nomads often blindly plundered and destroyed everything. A single raid was enough to transform hundreds of oases into ashes and desert. (T. Peisker, *The Cambridge Medieval History*)

> ... from the Caspian to the Indus they ruined a tract of many hundred miles which was adorned with the habitations and labour of mankind, and five centuries have not been sufficient to repair the ravages of four years. (Gibbon, *The History of the Decline and Fall of the Roman Empire*)

They all have compact, strong limbs and thick necks and are so monstrously ugly and misshapen, that one might take them for two-legged beasts or for the stumps, rough-hewn into images, that are used in putting sides to bridges.... Roaming at large amid the mountains and woods, they learn from the cradle to endure cold, hunger and thirst.... They are not at all adapted to battles on foot, but they are almost glued to their horses.... In truces they are faithless and unreliable, strongly inclined to sway to the motion of every breeze of new hope that presents itself, and sacrificing every feeling to the mad impulse of the moment. Like unreasoning beasts, they are utterly ignorant of the difference between right and wrong. (Ammianus Marcellinus)

For by the terror of their features they inspired great fear in those whom perhaps they did not really surpass in war. They made their foes flee in horror because their swarthy aspect was fearful, and they had, if I may call it so, a sort of shapeless lump, not a head, with pin-holes rather than eyes.... Though they live in the form of men, they have the cruelty of wild beasts. (Jordanes)

Their emerging leader, Attila, was of short stature, with swarthy skin, and small beady eyes, according to Jordanes and Priscus. As a man he was vain, superstitious, cunning, covetous, arrogant and cruel, although simple, frugal and parsimonious in his private life – which did not prevent him from marrying his own daughter. He proceeded to establish absolute rule by terror over the Huns, abolishing tribal obligations, demanding oaths of unconditional loyalty to himself personally; and establishing a powerful and threatening Confederacy.

Under Attila, this Confederacy moved westwards and southwards like a whirlwind. 'Fury, surprise, elusiveness, cunning and mobility, and not planning, method, drill and discipline were its elements,' Fuller states. The principal weapons of the Huns were the horse and the bow, which latter was usually made out of bone, since the steppes from which they came were devoid of trees. They attacked swiftly, laid waste to the lands and annihilated entire populations, then withdrew rapidly in the event of a counter-attack by superior forces. These tactics worked brilliantly, but there was a deficiency in strategy. Attila made war on civilization and on human nature but, knowing nothing of agriculture, he was no more than a plunderer. His tactics meant that the Huns could not consolidate any area for long since all supplies were swiftly consumed. Moreover, the Huns lacked the siege engines and sundry equipment required for the storming of walled cities and fortresses.

Nevertheless, the lightning campaigns of 441 and 447 gave Attila an empire that made him supreme lord of Eastern and Central Europe, with his rear secured by victories, and by tribute paid by the Romans in Asia Minor. Attila resolved to add Gaul to his conquests. Here, however, he found himself opposed by Flavius Aetius, who has been called 'the last of the Romans'. Aetius (c. 390–454) stood in complete contrast to Attila. According to Gregory of Tours in in his *The History of the Franks*:

Of middle height, he was manly in appearance and well made, neither too frail nor too heavy; he was quick of wit and agile of limb, a very practised horseman and skilful archer; he was indefatigable with the spear. A born warrior, he was renowned for the arts of peace, without avarice and little swayed by desire, endowed with gifts of the mind, not serving from his purpose for any kind of evil instigation. He bore wrongs with the utmost patience and loved labour. Undaunted in danger, he was excelled by none in the endurance of hunger, thirst and vigil. From his early youth he seemed forewarned of the great power to which he was destined by the fates.

For twenty-five years, Aetius had been the supreme Roman military commander in Western Europe. The son of a Scythian soldier and a Roman noblewoman, he had in his early years been taken hostage by the Visigoths, which experience enabled him, later, to deal with them through comprehension of their mentality. Once ransomed, Aetius rapidly became the favourite of the Western Emperor Valentinian III and his formidable mother, Placidia, rising to police Gaul and control the errant ways of the Visigoths in southern France. In 437, the Burgundians threatened

Gaul's border on the Rhine. Aetius allied with the Huns under
Attila's brother Bleda and won a sensational victory.

There was no hope of an alliance, though, once Attila had had
Bleda murdered in 445: and West prepared for battle against East
as Attila invaded northern Gaul in 451. Initially, both sides
essayed the weapon of diplomacy, aptly described in later years by
Ambrose Beirce as 'the art of lying for one's country'. The Goths
would be crucial to the forthcoming, climactic struggle for mastery
within the West. Both generals sought the aid of Theodoric I, the
most powerful of the Gothic kings. According to Jordanes, Attila
was 'a subtle man ... [who] fought with craft before he made war'.
He urged Theodoric to ally with him against the Romans: and the
Emperor Valentinian to ally with him against the Goths.
Meanwhile, his hordes, perhaps half a million men in all, left their
customary trail of rapine, smoke, fire, murder and devastation as
they razed to the ground Rheims, Metz, Cambrai, Trèves, Arras,
Tongres, Tournai, Cologne, Amiens, Beauvais, Worms and
Strasbourg, then advanced upon Orléans.

The Bishop of Orléans, St Aignan, visited Aetius and informed
him that this strategically crucial city could not hold out beyond
14 June. Meanwhile, however, the emissary of Aetius, the future
Western Roman Emperor, Senator Avitus, had finally persuaded
Theodoric's Goths to ally with Rome. Attila besieged Orléans for
five weeks, took the suburbs, massacred the citizens and
repeatedly assaulted the city centre. Just when it seemed that all
was lost, the armies of Aetius and Theodoric appeared on the
horizon – on the fatal day of 14 June.

Fierce and brutal fighting followed in the suburbs. The narrow
streets increased the Romans' advantage with their short swords at
close quarters, the Huns being unable to deploy their superior
horsemanship to greater effect. Attila sounded the retreat and
withdrew by night. Aetius fell upon his rearguard, and Jordanes
opines that this cost Attila 15,000 casualties in addition to those
already slain in street fighting.

On 20 June 451, Attila, having retreated to the Plains of
Catalaunia (in Champagne, eastern France), proceeded to give
battle at a spot near what is now Châlons-sur-Marne. He
positioned his finest troops at the centre, with his tribal allies on
the left and right, intending an attack to strike right through the

middle of the Romano-Gothic force. Aetius responded by placing his *weakest* troops, the Alan tribe in the centre, taking command on the left with his Romans; and placing the Goths under Theodoric on his right flank. His idea was to draw the Huns into the centre and then outflank them on both sides.

> Hand to hand they clashed in battle [Jordanes writes], and the fight grew fierce, confused, monstrous, unrelenting – a fight like no ancient time ever recorded. There such deeds were done that a brave man who missed this marvellous spectacle could not hope to see anything so wonderful all his life long.

King Theodoric was slain but this only incited the Visigoths to greater fury, for they assailed the Huns in a ferocious determination to avenge the loss of their leader by slaughtering Attila, who fled to the fortifications of wagons he had earlier prepared. That day belonged to the Romans and the Visigoths, yet on the following morning Attila 'was like a lion pierced by hunting spears, who paces to and fro before the mouth of his den and dares not spring, but ceases not to terrify the neighbourhood by his roaring,' again according to Jordanes. Meanwhile, Aetius commanded his archers to give the Huns no peace with a constant shower of vicious arrows.

Unfortunately for Aetius, he had to take into account the political consequences of the death of King Theodoric, who was succeeded by his son Thorismund. Aetius did not trust the latter and feared that if the Huns were totally destroyed by the Goths, then the Goths would overwhelm the Western Roman Empire, or what remained of it. Calculating the consequences, he decided to preserve a balance of power. Making a temporary peace with Attila, he advised Thorismund to attend to his own dominions. Attila withdrew to beyond the Rhine. Jordanes states that 165,000 men were slain on both sides and Idatius puts the total at 300,000. Fuller remarks that 'All these figures are fantastic', but obviously there were very heavy losses. Moreover, Attila's plan to take Gaul had ended in failure.

Attila tried again in 452 by invading Italy, boldly taking Aquilèia, Padua, Vicenza, Verona, Brescia, Bergamo, Milan and

Pavia, visiting slaughter upon all their unfortunate inhabitants. Aetius, initially taken by surprise, responded with the tactics of Quintus Fabius Maximus against Hannibal, retreating in good order and cutting the enemy's supply lines whenever he could. Even so, by sheer weight of numbers the Hunnish horde marched relentlessly on Rome.

At this point, it is essential to distinguish between myth and fact. The myth is that Pope Leo I vanquished Attila the Hun and, though unarmed, vanquished him by the power of Jesus Christ and of St Peter's Church. This is arrant nonsense and Attila had no interest whatsoever in the Christian religion, and so was incapable of being swayed by its doctrines. The Pope was merely a useful diplomatic intermediary.

Attila was turned away by sound, natural reasoning. In a bold stroke, another general called Aetius (no relation) routed the Huns at a principal base camp by the Danube, cutting the wagon routes that formed Attila's main supply lines. Moreover, his depleted troops were now perishing through the famine and pestilence of which they themselves were the origin. Attila realized that he could not risk further heavy losses, especially without supplies, and so ordered a prudent retreat.

In 453, Attila took another wife called Ildico and drank so much at the marriage feast that the blood vessels of his nose burst and he died choking on his own blood.

His empire was swiftly torn apart by squabbling factions. Tribes which the Huns had conquered rebelled, and within three generations, this people which had once so terrified the world had become one of merely marginal significance.

It cannot be claimed that the fate of Attila's opponent, Aetius, and of the Western Roman Empire was any happier. On 21 September 454, in an insane fit of jealousy, the Emperor Valentinian stabbed Aetius to death, and in revenge was himself assassinated a year later. The Western Roman Empire, which Aetius had saved from total destruction, now proceeded to collapse utterly.

Nevertheless, the conflicts of Attila and Aetius had considerable consquences for Western civilization. The attempt by Asia to conquer Europe had indeed been defeated, but the slaying of Aetius by the Emperor Valentinian sounded the death-knell of the

Western Roman Empire. 'The Emperor has cut off his right hand with his left,' one astounded courtier commented. The collapse of Roman imperial authority left a vacuum of power and this was rapidly filled by the Roman Catholic Church, using its literate and bureaucratic efficiency to promote its own potential power. Everywhere, people were told that Pope Leo (known as 'the Great', and later as Saint Leo) had turned back the dreaded Attila by the power of Christ, when in fact he had come to the Hun leader as a mixture of humble suppliant and skilled negotiator. As Thomas Hodgkin rightly says:

> ... thus it is no paradox to say that indirectly the King of the Huns contributed more perhaps than any other historical personage, towards the creation of that mighty factor in the politics of medieval Italy, the Pope-King of Rome.

Alexander the Great had conquered an empire and had endeavoured to bring civilization wherever he went. Attila the Hun had conquered an empire, and had visited to bring barbarism on anything that survived in his wake. Aetius had tried to conserve what was left of civilization, only to be stabbed in the back by his own kind.

The Western victory in the conflict between Attila and Aetius preserved European from Asian domination; ironically, however, it also brought about the tyranny of the Church, and hence the Dark Ages.

7

Genghis Khan (1162–1227)

Ghengis Khan, also known as Jingiz Khan and Chingiz Khan, and originally as Temujin, had a devastating impact upon the world of his time. According to Gabriel Ronay, 'it was a progression that made the savagery and destruction brought upon the world by Attila the Hun look like reasoned acts of statesmanship'.

This is a fair comment in terms of the effects of Genghis Khan's assaults upon his enemies and innocent civilians: yet he was a far better general than Attila could ever have dreamed of being.

He was born, as Temujin, into a noble Mongol family, learning early how to ride and shoot a bow, which youthful training was to help to make him the greatest commander of horsed archers ever witnessed. However, upon the death of his father, who was poisoned in a feud when Temujin was nine, the tribe refused the right of the boy to rule. One chronicler even writes of the young Temujin being treated as a slave, with a steel-studded collar around his neck. If this is so, it could explain much about his own subsequent violations of human life and dignity.

Temujin was eventually ransomed by his late father's ally, Toghril, and being a natural leader, soon established a following of his own amongst the Mongols. He made alliances with Toghril and another childhood friend, Jamuka. Together they won a local campaign. Temujin was proclaimed Ghenghis Khan, meaning 'universal chief', by the Mongols in 1194. From the point of view of those who supported him, this was a wise decision.

The astonishing victories of this astoundingly cruel yet brilliant man have been ascribed by his enemies and critics to overwhelming weight of numbers, as if his generalship were no more than that of Attila. It is certainly true that Genghis Khan relied upon swift movements by massed cavalry archers, as did Attila, but there is rather more to it than that. His planning and organization were meticulous. He began a campaign by sending a corps of spies among his opponents. Once Genghis had received all relevant information, passed back from his spies by a relay of swift riders, he would strike in rapid and devastating fashion at the enemy's weakest point.

In 1202, he defeated the Tatars, fierce and savage warriors, to take western Mongolia. As the *Cambridge Medieval History* states:

> Unchecked by human valour, they [the Mongols] were able to overcome the terrors of vast deserts, the barriers of mountains and seas, the severities of climate, and the ravages of famine and pestilence. No dangers could appal them, no stronghold could resist them, no prayer for mercy could move them.

Small wonder that this man was therefore called by the Mongol riders 'the Perfect Warrior', and in 1206 (perhaps more appropriately) 'the Mighty Killer of Man'.

This new title came about because of a brutal civil war with his former allies, Toghril and Jamuka, whom he defeated for supremacy over the Mongol tribes. Genghis was a very cruel man but he could nevertheless inspire extraordinary loyalty in his troops. Once, when he had been badly wounded in battle and was bleeding from the neck, his loyal retainer Jelme lapped up the blood and refreshed his commander with milk he had surreptitiously stolen at great personal risk from the enemy encampment. Genghis did not want the enemy to know that he was badly wounded, even though, according to a tale related by

Arthur Waley, 'the ground was flowing with a regular slush of blood'.

'I swallowed as much of the blood as I could,' said Jelme, 'and only spat out the rest. Still, I did manage to swallow quite a lot!'

'Once before ...' Genghis replied, 'you saved my life; and now you sucked the blood out of my neck. When I was thirsty, you risked your life to get me buttermilk to drink and so brought me back to my senses. These three good deeds that you have done to me will remain forever in my heart.'

Genghis Khan was good to his loyal supporters. He was terrible beyond belief to his enemies. As he instructed his sons: 'The merit of an action lies in finishing it to the end.' His victories were usually impressed on human memory by the ghastly towers of skulls that the Mongols erected in the wake of their winnings.

He turned his attention towards China, the world's oldest continuous civilization, then divided into three kingdoms, each of which was well schooled in fortifications and, furthermore, was armed with artillery and gunpowder. Typically, Genghis chose to attack the weakest of the three, the Tangut kingdom of Hsia Hsi on the upper reaches of the Hwang Ho river. In 1207 his forces swept the Chinese defenders from the battlefields, but could not break through the fortifications of the city of Volohai. Genghis solved this problem in characteristic fashion, as described by Gabriel Ronay:

> He offered to withdraw if he was given by way of tribute one thousand cats and one thousand swallows. The startled Tangut complied. But instead of withdrawing Genghis set them alight and released them in one great rush of living fire. The hapless cats and birds set the city on fire in hundreds of places and, while the garrison fought the flames, the Mongols breached the walls.

Genghis was assisted in smashing down the defences by the Chinese engineers he had recruited, and whom he would employ upon all future campaigns. By 1212, he had conquered the Tangut empire, and he took particular pleasure in forcing the golden bit of slavery into its emperor's mouth.

The next campaign was against the Chin empire, with its

well-fortified capital of Yenking (later Peking, and now Beijing). According to Gabriel Ronay, there were 'battles of gigantic scale and atrocities of terrifying proportions'. After an arduous and prolonged siege, Genghis finally took Yenking in 1215 and crushed the power of the second kingdom. It says something about his generalship and the behaviour of his troops that according to a Persian chronicler, no fewer than 60,000 Chinese virgins committed suicide rather than endure the ensuing rapine.

Now Genghis turned his attention to the third Chinese kingdom, having taken Yenking, now Beijing, and holding the lands of North China to the Yellow Sea whilst consolidating his hold over the centre of the land. The reasons for his extraordinary success so far are, of course, obvious: STOMT – Speed, Timing, Organization, Morale and Technology. Genghis Khan was a master of the art of delegation, choosing excellent subordinate generals, most notably Subedei, but also his highly talented sons, Jochi and Chagatai; though his eventual successor, Ogedei, was probably the most intelligent among them. His fighting men, composed almost exclusively of cavalry, were welded to their horses and expert in using the short bow while moving constantly. These light cavalry were supported strongly by heavy cavalry, skilled horsemen with leather armour, sabres and lances.

Genghis promptly proceeded to take the west of China in 1218 and in a series of dazzling and devastating strikes, expanded to take Bukhara and Samarkand in 1220, establishing control between the principal trade routes of East and West. He occupied Central Asia, establishing an empire greater in territory even than that conquered by Alexander. The proud princes of Muscovy (Russia) had to bow the knee to him.

In terms of peace, surprising good sense was accompanied by utterly hideous barbarism. Surrender was often treated generously: native-born administrators were placed in charge of the new regimes Genghis Khan established, since he believed, rightly, that such men were more acceptable to the local population. The Muslim Turks were conquered and conciliated by laws allowing them freedom of worship and granting their mullahs exemption from taxation. By contrast, any city or land that resisted the advance of Genghis Khan was visited with genocide, fire and the sword. The men were slaughtered, the women were raped and the children were enslaved in the cruellest conditions.

By 1224, Genghis Khan had conquered Asia and ruled over a vast land empire from China in the east to Turkey in the west. However, two of the kingdoms of China arose in rebellion: the Chin empire, formerly based in Yenking; and the Tangut kingdom of Hsia-Hsi. Genghis Khan smashed back at the latter in 1226, when aged well over sixty. At the battle of the Yellow River in the winter of that year, fought deliberately in bitter weather with the river frozen over, Genghis Khan enticed his antagonists to cross the ice, then ordered his archers to shoot the horses of the enemy's cavalry. This was followed by a devastating attack by his heavily armoured horsemen, who speared their foes or chopped at limbs at close quarters.

China was now subdued, and this extraordinary empire was secure. Typically, the will of Genghis Khan stated that whilst he named Ogedei his successor, he demanded that the entire population of Ning-hsia be put to the sword. He died of natural causes before this had been duly done.

Genghis Khan, although a brilliant general, created no cities; he only destroyed them. Before him, flowers grew: after his hordes had passed, they did not. Although he excelled in the craft of warfare, he contributed absolutely nothing to the rather more important causes of human civilization and human evolution. It is fitting, perhaps, that his body was buried in a secret tomb. It is difficult not to concur with Voltaire when he compares and contrasts Alexander, Genghis Khan and the latter's descendant, that ferocious conqueror, Tamerlane. Voltaire argues that:

> Alexander, to whom the Orientals are so fond of comparing [Tamerlane]; but otherwise far inferior to the Macedonian, being born in a barbarous nation, and having, like Genghis Khan, destroyed a multitude of cities without having built one; whereas Alexander, during the course of a very short life, and in the midst of his rapid conquests, built Alexandria and Scanderoon, and rebuilt this very city of Samarcand, which afterward became the seat of Tamerlane's empire, as likewise a number of other cities in India; he also established several colonies of Greeks beyond the Oxus, sent the astronomical observations of the Babylonians into Greece,

and entirely changed the commerce of Asia, Europe, and
Africa, making Alexandria the magazine of the universe; so
far then, in my opinion, Alexander surpasses Tamerlane,
Genghis, and all the conquerors who have been put up in
competition with him.

Even so, the empire established by Alexander crumbled quickly
after his death. What was the legacy of Genghis Khan? Was it
merely the terrible towers of human skulls? It is arguable that the
principal legacy to humanity of this savage man was not the
Central Asian empire which collapsed in due course, but
ultimately the civilization of China under Genghis's descendant,
Kublai Khan.

It was the visit of Marco Polo of Italy to Kublai Khan of China
that firmly re-established trade and information routes between
East and West. Marco Polo saw a society far more civilized than
his own, though this may well have been because the
Mongol-descended Kublai Khan had had the sense to adopt
Chinese customs. As the poet, Samuel Taylor Coleridge has it:

> In Xanadu did Kubla Khan
> A stately pleasure-dome decree:
> Where Alph, the sacred river, ran
> Through caverns measureless to man
> Down to a sunless sea.

It is easy to estimate the immediate effect which Genghis Khan
had upon the humanity of his time. It is harder, however, to
estimate his effect upon human evolution, for few have affected
the planet more. As Coleridge has it:

> Weave a circle round him thrice,
> And close your eyes with holy dread:
> For he on honey-dew hath fed,
> And drunk the milk of Paradise.

8

The Hundred Years War
and Edward III (1312–1377)

Edward III of England succeeded to the throne at the age of fifteen in 1327. He was promptly faced with three problems: England, Scotland and France. In England, his mother, Isabella of France, had conspired with her lover, Roger Mortimer, to force his father, Edward II, to abdicate; the erstwhile king was later horribly murdered, legend holding that he was killed by a red-hot poker thrust up his anus as punishment for his homosexual activities, a view furthered by Christopher Marlowe in his play, *Edward II*.

Edward III tired of his mother's tutelage and of Mortimer's manipulations. In 1330, in alliance with the barons, he had his mother banished from the realm; and Mortimer was duly executed at Tyburn. Having consolidated his hold upon England, Edward marched north to do battle with Scotland's King David II, whose father, Robert the Bruce (Robert VIII), had routed King Edward II at the battle of Bannockburn in 1314, and had made 'the auld alliance' with France.

The battle of Halidon Hill in 1333 between the English and the Scots was essentially dictated by the tactics of Edward's grandfather, Edward I, known as 'the Hammer of the Scots'. In his campaigns of conquest in Wales, Edward I had learned the use of an excellent Welsh weapon, the longbow, and had employed it in winning his victories in Scotland against William Wallace. It was the failure of his son Edward II to deploy this weapon against Robert the Bruce at Bannockburn which had led to so disastrous a defeat. Edward III was determined to make no such mistake against King David.

At Halidon Hill, young King Edward III employed several tactical innovations. He commanded his horsemen to dismount and stand on foot, so that the horses would not confuse the course of battle, and he used skilled archers to demolish the Scots at range, thereby obtaining an astonishing victory. Peace having subsequently been made with Scotland on terms favourable to England, Edward now turned his attention towards France.

King Henry II, who ruled England from 1154–89, had by his marriage to Eleanor of Aquitaine brought that province – the Bordeaux region of south-western France – under English rule, albeit subject to French vassalage. The French King Philip VI now demanded that Edward swear his fealty and homage as a vassal. Perplexed by his problems with Scotland at the time, Edward agreed to do so, but this was in fact only a stratagem to buy time. As soon as Edward had subdued Scotland, he changed his tune and argued that his oath was invalid since Philip was not the rightful King of France. Diplomacy, in which the Pope, Benedict XII, became increasingly involved, grew increasingly convoluted, especially when Edward pressed his own tenuous claim to the French throne in addition to his possessions in Aquitaine, which, he argued, were his by right, not fiefdom.

Pope Benedict persuaded the Kings of England and Scotland to come to an uneasy truce, and requested that King Philip of France temporarily postpone his leadership of a renewed crusade against the infidels of the east to recover Jerusalem, which had been under Muslim control since 1187. An annoyed Philip responded by transferring the fleet he had assembled in the south, at Marseilles, to the north in order to dominate the Channel between England and France. He also declared that the town of Guienne in Aquitaine had been forfeited to the French crown. Edward decided to go to war.

This was a somewhat difficult proposition. France in the fourteenth century, although riven by factionalism, was a big and prosperous country inhabited by some 20 million people, compared with England's population of roughly 3.7 million. Edward began by using diplomacy, and by paying 30,000 florins, made alliances with John III, Duke of Brittany; Reginald, Count Palatine of the Rhine; and the Emperor Ludwig of Bavaria, among others. By thus drawing the battles towards the north and east, he hoped to avoid attacks upon English domains in Aquitaine in the south. His taking of the island of Cadsand from the French in 1337 started what came to be called the Hundred Years War – which would in fact last for 116 years.

Edward's next move was to adopt a policy of economic warfare, prohibiting the export of English wool to Flanders. This led the Flemings of the Low Countries to ally themselves with England, while the Emperor Ludwig denounced Philip as a usurper, recognized Edward as the rightful king of France, and appointed him Imperial Vicar for all the provinces west of the Rhine. Meanwhile, the French took control of the Channel, holding it so firmly that according to Sir Nicholas Harris Nicolas in his *A History of the Royal Navy*, 'no vessel could leave England without being plundered, and the crew taken or slain'. Notable English losses included the ships *Christopher* and *Edward*, laden with wool for renewed allies in Flanders. Between 1337 and 1339 the French proceeded to raid and raze towns in the Channel Islands and the Isle of Wight, as well as Portsmouth, Portsea, Southampton, Hastings, Dover, Sandwich, Winchelsea and Rye.

Undeterred, Edward crossed the North Sea to Flanders and, based in Brussels, commenced his first campaign in 1346. This was, on the whole, a disastrous failure. No pitched battle took place, no territorial gains were achieved, he retired £300,000 in debt, and meanwhile the army of Philip had captured Bourg and Blaye in the south and were now marching upon Bordeaux, the capital of Aquitaine. The sole gain was recognition of Edward as King of France by the Flemings.

Rather more was achieved at the naval Battle of Sluys (now Sluis) 1340, fought in the Scheldt estuary in what is now Holland. Here, 147 English vessels faced 190 French ships manned by 35,000 men-at-arms. In addition, they were backed by their ally, the mercenary Barbanero of Genoa, commanding a squadron of galleys.

The French were waiting for the English with heavy stones and crossbows. Edward's archers had longbows, much more accurate and powerful weapons than the short Norman bow, since arrows fired from longbows could penetrate two layers of mail armour. There has, however, for long been a debate about the merits of the crossbow versus the longbow, which latter was made from a 6-foot length of yew or elm and shot a 3-foot arrow over an average range of 200 yards. By contrast, the crossbow could deliver an equally powerful bolt, often iron-tipped, at 300 yards. Used efficiently, the crossbow was a much more deadly and accurate weapon. England's King Richard I, 'the Lionheart', had demonstrated its effectiveness during the Third Crusade against the Saracens under Saladin, which began in 1191. Richard had realized that the principal problem of the crossbow lies in the slowness of reloading. Troops armed with a short Norman bow or a longbow can shoot much faster. Richard's solution to this problem was, in place of a single archer, to set two men with two crossbows, one man loading each weapon as it was fired by the other, enabling his division to match the lethal archery of their Saracen adversaries.

The French failed to learn from the tactical innovation of King Richard I. The latter's descendant, King Edward III, however, was to employ massed formations of longbowmen to create a shock effect with a formidable barrage of arrows. Added to this, at Sluys the incompetence of the French generalship was quite astounding, though the valour of their men is not in doubt.

The French began by arguing with their ally Barbanero of Genoa, who wanted to take to the open sea immediately, but Admirals Hue Quieret and Pierre Béhuchet urged a defensive action in the harbour. Eventually it was agreed that Barbanero would take to open water while the French admirals drew up their ships in line of battle at the mouth of the harbour. In a further act of fatuity, they linked the ships of their front line together with iron chains and cables. This, of course, rendered impossible any chance of a retreat in good order should the day go against them.

The English naval assault was swift and the shower of arrows quite devastating, clearing the French decks and enabling the English to recapture the ships *Edward*, *Christopher* and *Rose*. Edward's Flemish allies from nearby Bruges and the vicinity now proceeded to assault the French in the rear and on land. Barbanero, deciding that the battle was lost, escaped with his twenty-four galleys. Edward ordered the slaughter to continue, urging his men-at-arms to engage the enemy in close quarter combat as they piled aboard their ships. Admiral Quieret was killed. Admiral Béhuchet was captured and later hanged from the yardarm, since he had been responsible for the burning of Portsmouth. One hundred and sixty-six French ships were annihilated. In tactical terms, the Battle of Sluys was one of the most devastating victories ever won by an English fleet. Command of the Channel returned to England.

Crossing again to Flanders, Edward could have chosen to exploit his victory to greater strategic advantage, but instead laid siege to Tournai in order to conciliate his Flemish allies. This siege, lasting nearly two months, proved to be yet another failure, further arousing the enmity of the Pope, Benedict XII, and with his own supplies exhausted, Edward was once more forced to withdraw.

The third campaign, to decide the successor to the Dukedom of Brittany took place in 1342–3, and was yet again a costly fiasco. The fourth, which Edward led in 1346, at last had some rather more decisive results.

In this campaign Edward III displayed somewhat greater strategic and tactical sense than many historians have given him credit for. Because his forces were also fighting in Gascony for possession of the English territory of Aquitaine, French troops were needed there which might otherwise have opposed him in the north; and he deliberately fomented a civil war in Brittany as another distraction for his enemy. His intention was not to occupy France, since that was impossible, given the country's size and much larger population, but to loot, pillage and plunder – and, in the end, take the French crown.

Landing near Cherbourg in 1346, Edward soon took Normandy by capturing Caen. King Philip's army came after him in hot pursuit, as Edward ravaged the country. The numerically superior force of the French king forced Edward to retreat eastwards along the River Seine. Although outnumbered by three to one, King Edward drew up his battle line when he found favourable terrain near Crécy, near Abbeville in northern France.

By then his force consisted of a mere 8,500 men, but he proceeded to position them well. His right flank was commanded by his son, the Prince of Wales, later to be known as 'the Black Prince', and his left flank by the Earl of Northampton, Constable of England, and the Earl of Arundel. Edward took command at the centre.

The Battle of Crécy was fought on 26 August 1346. Edward had chosen the site well, for his right flank was protected by a river, while his left flank was protected by a forest and also by the earthworks which he had ordered his men to dig. Having fed his men, Edward set them in the formation which he had learned from his grandfather, Edward I, and had proved against the Scots at Halidon Hill in 1333. This formation was:

ENGLISH ARMY

Cavalry (in reserve)

	archers		archers		archers	
RIVER	archers		archers		archers	FOREST
	men-at-arms				men-at-arms	

infantry (in phalanx formation)

The men-at-arms, heavily equipped, mounted troops, had been ordered to fight dismounted in the coming action since Edward thought that in the initial stages of the battle, the horses would only be a nuisance.

By employing this A-shaped formation, Edward discovered the way in which to deploy archers, cavalry and infantry so as to use all three arms to best advantage. He also took up his own position at a windmill on high ground, which enabled him to survey the entire field of battle.

By contrast, the French displayed utter incompetence. Although they had some Genoese crossbowmen, they despised them. Although they had infantry divisions, they despised them, too. According to the French at that time, the only men truly fit for battle were knights in shining armour; everyone else was scum. They had no notion of deploying troops for advantage at battle stations. Edward had drawn up his battle line in a deliberately chosen and carefully thought out formation. King Philip, on the other hand, did not know anything about battle except to yell

'Charge!' His infantry did charge, but then their king changed his mind. By that time it was too late.

The Battle of Crécy was fought under hideous conditions. At 6.00 pm, there was a fearful thunderstorm and an eclipse of the sun, according to the usually reliable French chronicler, Jean Froissart. When the sun came out again the English had it at their backs, while the French had it shining in their eyes. The Genoese charged and were deterred by a fierce volley of arrows from the English archers. They fell back, and so did the French infantry, as the English stuck to their formations. The French king ordered his heavy cavalry to attack, only to find its advance impeded by his retreating infantry and the continuing hail of English arrows.

'Kill me these scoundrels!' roared the King of France, 'for they stop our road ...': and so the French cavalry slaughtered their own infantry rather than the English enemy. Meanwhile, the English archers shot down the French horsemen. Night fell, but the battle continued. King Philip continued to order one wave after another of confused assaults, muddled all the more by retreating French troops.

'There is no man, unless he had been present,' Froissart declares, 'that can imagine, or describe truly, the confusion of that day.' According to his account: 'All the roads between Abbeville and Crécy were covered with common people, who, when they were come within three leagues of their enemies, drew their swords, bawling out, "Kill, *kill*" ...' The French kept charging in waves of confusion and the English stood still and shot or chopped them down. The men of the Welsh division, according to Froissart, who carried long knives in their belts, were 'falling upon earls, barons, knights and squires, [and] slew many, at which the King of England was much exasperated'. The King of England was annoyed for good reason. The flower of French chivalry had been put into the field and Edward wanted them captured alive so that he could ransom them.

Crécy was a devastating victory, proving that massed formations of foot archers could turn an armoured cavalry charge into a turkey shoot. The French lost 4,000 knights, including 1,500 nobles, among them the King of Bohemia. This blind man had asked his aides to take him to the field of battle so that he could wield his sword. This was duly done and he was promptly killed by English warriors. The fifteen chaotic French assaults were turned back by the numerically smaller but much more highly disciplined force of the English; and Edward had chosen his muddy terrain well, making matters doubly difficult for the advancing French horsemen. The pointed stakes he had commanded his archers to sink in the ground before them did nothing to assist the shambolic charges of the French cavalry, either.

Edward now held the north of France and moved freely to besiege Calais, delighted by the fact that his son, the Black Prince, had well and truly won his spurs at the battle of Crécy. Calais was not an easy city to take, defended as it was by a double wall surrounded by ditches filled with water. Edward, having secured command of the English Channel, had cut off all supplies by sea to Calais; now he cut off all land supplies. King Philip VI of France appears to have suffered a mental and moral collapse, and so did nothing to relieve the siege. His ally, King David II of Scotland, at Philip's request, marched his men south to Durham to threaten England, but was decisively defeated and captured at the battle of Neville's Cross on 17 October 1346. The Duke of Normandy approached Calais on 27 July 1347, exploring the possibility of relieving the city, but found Edward's position too strong to attack. On 4 August, the Governor of Calais, Jean de Vienne, surrendered and acceded to Edward's demand that six leading citizens be led before him, carrying the keys to the city, dressed only in their shirts and with rope nooses around their necks. It was the intention of Edward to hang these men *pour encourager les autres*, but Queen Philippa pleaded for their lives, kneeling down before her husband, and he agreed to spare the men, though England took Calais.

Calais was in fact the principal strategic gain of Edward's wars so far, though it was French incompetence that had proved to be the decisive factor. The port provided a bridgehead for any English excursion into France; furthermore, it became a laudably profitable commercial centre. Since it was in part defended by, and could be supplied by, the sea, this fortress on foreign soil was virtually impregnable. Edward ordered that all English exports should be routed by way of Calais. Moreover, as Major-General the Hon. George Wrottesley has rightly pointed out, invasion of

England would have been impossible, with Calais in English hands, until the invention of the steamship.

When, on 8 January 1558, the Duke of Guise finally took back Calais for France – England's Queen Mary I dying in November the same year, allegedly with the words: 'You shall find "Calais" lying in my heart' – the city was to become the base, thirty years later, for the Spanish Armada.

Edward was now aware that England had finally attained high international respect in terms of fighting prestige. Crécy? As Fuller declares of the French and the English: 'the former were stunned and the latter inebriated by it'. However, one victory in battle does not win a war, especially not if it may last over one hundred years. The French fought back by assailing English possessions in Aquitaine, Edward responded by sending his son, the Black Prince, to command the armies in the region. By following his father's tactics, the Black Prince won a tremendous victory at Poitiers in 1356. He took prisoner the French King John II, who had succeeded his father, Philip VI, on the latter's death in 1350, then chivalrously waited upon him at table pending a ransom. He also laid waste to the surrounding countryside.

Aside from the capture of Calais, it is difficult to discern just what the campaigns of King Edward III and the Black Prince achieved for the nation. Bertrand de Guesclin (*c*.1320–80) restored French morale by his campaign in Spain, where he defeated the English-backed Pedro the Cruel of Castile at Montiel in 1369, thereby bankrupting the English monarchy. In 1370 Charles V of France, who had succeeded his father, John II, in 1364, took advantage of these successes by appointing Guesclin Constable of France. Guesclin proceeded to recapture Poitiers, and having taken much of English Aquitaine, he also secured several towns in Brittany. Edward III promptly sent a strong English force to France.

'I do not say that the English should not be fought,' Guesclin said at a meeting in Paris, 'but I want it to be executed from a position of advantage. That is what the English did at Poitiers and Crécy.' Guesclin used the tactics that Quintus Fabius Maximus had employed against Hannibal when he confronted the marauding forces of Edward III. The English march through France was not opposed – at least not in pitched battle, but the baggage train of the invading army was annihilated, cutting off all supplies. Constant harassment left the English incapable even of foraging for food until, given his hungry and exhausted troops, Edward had no alternative other than to agree to a truce in 1375. Bertrand de Guesclin was buried at Saint Denis next to the tomb of his kind, and was celebrated by the French in later years as being among 'the Nine Worthies' – he was certainly in good company, for among those venerated were Alexander the Great, Julius Caesar, King Arthur and Charlemagne.

By contrast, King Edward III saw all his excellent victories disappearing in a puff of smoke, while his prosecution of a long continental war rendered the national treasury bankrupt. (In time this would cause his grandson, King Richard II, to introduce the poll tax among the poor of England, and so provoke the Peasants' Revolt.) For although Edward's tactics were good indeed, he appears to have had precious little grasp of strategy, except for his holding on to Calais.

The Black Death, a form of bubonic plague, swept through the lands of Europe at this time, 1347–1350, killing the Black Prince, father of Richard II, and at least a third of the population of Western Europe. Superstition now abounded as Western civilization sank into a state lower even than the depths of the Dark Ages. The papacy looked on unconcernedly and smiled, knowing that ignorance makes of people willing tools with which to increase potential power.

The campaigns of Edward III can be summarized by stating that although he deployed brilliant tactics, far in advance of those of his French adversaries, his only gain was Calais. The treasury was exhausted, and yet the largely pointless Hundred Years War continued.

9

The Hundred Years War and Joan of Arc (c. 1412–1431)

It is difficult to know precisely what to make of Joan of Arc. Essentially, there are five argued positions.

1. She was a witch and sorceress rightly burned at the stake in 1431, according to the Roman Catholic Church of her day.
2. She was a saint who genuinely saw visions and heard the voices of the angels, according to the Roman Catholic Church – which had had her burned alive – of five centuries later.
3. According to Voltaire, she was not a gentle shepherdess at all, but a robust publican's daughter 'who could ride without a saddle, and perform other manly exercises which young maidens are unaccustomed to'. (Monstrelet) Voltaire's somewhat cynical analysis alleges that for political reasons, a strong, decent woman was dressed up as a saint; and for political reasons, a strong decent woman was burned to death as a sinner.
4. Joan of Arc was a peasant girl, utterly sincere in her religion and dedicated to French nationalism, whether rightly or wrongly, who proved herself to be a good general.

5. She was a synthesis of all the above four factors.

First of all, and above all, the matter has to be seen in its context. The early fifteenth century witnessed civil wars in both England and France. In England, Richard II of the Plantagenet line was deposed by Henry IV (Henry Bolingbroke), son of John of Gaunt, of the Lancastrian line. Various civil wars, collectively known as the Wars of the Roses, followed the murder of the deposed Richard II. In France, the assassination of the Duke of Orléans provoked a civil war between the Orléanists (or Armagnacs) against the Burgundians. In 1412 the Armagnacs offered Henry IV of England the whole of ancient Aquitaine in return for his support, but a year later the English king died. John, Duke of Burgundy, instantly approached Henry's successor, his son, Henry V of England, to propose an alliance, encouraging the latter to press the old claim of Edward III to the throne of France. On 25 October 1415, Henry V crossed to France with 6,000 men, took Harfleur, and on 24 October, while in fact trying to shepherd an exhausted and starving army back to England, he faced the Armagnac faction of the French at Agincourt, Pas de Calais. Following the tactics of Edward III, Henry V chose high ground and encouraged his archers to set sharpened stakes in the ground before their positions. Their arrows could penetrate French armour; they were also able to shoot the enemy cavalry's horses, and slit the throats of an enemy heavily encumbered by unwieldy armour. In a shattering defeat, the Constable of France was killed, along with three dukes and seven counts, and the Duke of Orléans was taken prisoner. The French were slaughtered on the field, having made every mistake committed at the Battle of Crécy, while English losses were slight.

This victory enabled Henry to conquer Normandy in 1419 (with the exception of the island fortress of Mont St Michel). Now, John of Burgundy, who had taken Paris, was assassinated and his successor as Duke, Philip, negotiated the Treaty of Troyes with Henry V on 21 May 1420. By this, Henry was to retain Normandy and to share the government of France with the Duke of Burgundy, on condition that he married Catherine, daughter of the French King Charles VI. This dynastic marital alliance was duly concluded, and Charles VI disowned by treaty his own son, the Dauphin. However, this treaty, deeply unpopular in France, was arguably rendered null and void by the deaths of both Henry V and Charles VI in 1422.

The disinherited Dauphin now claimed the throne of France as Charles VII. As a result, the Duke of Bedford, brother of Henry V and Regent for the latter's infant son, King Henry VI, took command of the English armies in France. Charles VII proved himself to be a weak and incompetent king; conversely, by his victories at Cravant and Verneuil in 1424, the Duke of Bedford proved himself to be a very useful general.

In 1428, after a bitter and hazardous campaign, involving many losses, the English arrived to lay siege to Orléans. The capture of this city would have meant the fall of France to the coalition of Burgundy and England. It was at this point in time that Joan of Arc appeared.

The exact date and place of her birth are not known for certain, but the probability is that she was born in 1412 in the Duchy of Bar, on the border of Lorraine. At the age of thirteen, Joan had heard the voices of angels, and had seen them in visions surrounded by a cloud of brilliant white light. In 1429, at the age of seventeen, she donned male attire and managed to secure an interview with the Dauphin, who claimed for himself the title King Charles VII; she herself claimed to be inspired by a divine mission from God to save France. A desperate Charles allowed her some 3–4,000 men-at-arms and the able assistance of the Marshal of France, Gilles de Rais (in later years to be denounced as a child-murdering and molesting monster).

Joan proceeded to inspire the troops with her message of a divine mission. Nevertheless, she had a letter requesting peace sent to the English. It was rejected with jeering insults. Joan responded by taking 200 lancers on boats over the Loire. Initially, there were difficulties, since the wind from the north-east made it impossible to sail. '*Attendez un petit,*' Joan exclaimed irritably, '*car, en nom de Dieu, tout entera en la ville.*' ('Wait but a little time, for, in the name of God, all will enter the town.) Amazingly enough, the wind changed and the boats sailed. This 'miracle' had a profound effect upon the morale of her soldiers, and even Fuller notes: 'Joan, it would seem, possessed second sight; there are so many well-authenticated cases of her power to foresee and foretell coming events that are unlikely to apocryphal.' The inner city was held by the English.

Joan duly entered the outer suburbs of Orléans, where she was welcomed with warmth, and set about the siege of the inner fortress, once more sending a letter urging an amicable peace and once more receiving an insulting response. Joan responded by taking the fortresses of St Pouair and St Loup. She sent a third message appealing for peace to the English, and once again received insults in return.

Joan began her climactic assault on 7 May 1429. Although an arrow struck her between the neck and shoulders, penetrating her flesh to a depth of 6 inches, she merely had her wound dressed and returned to the battle. According to the *Journal du Siège d'Orléans* (1896) by Paul Charpentier and Charles Cuissard, an analysis of the comments of contemporary chroniclers, Joan rejected the advice of her male colleagues to retreat for the night in good order. '*En nom de Dieu*!' she exclaimed, 'you will enter the boulevard very soon; have no doubt of it, for the English have less strength than you.' She added: 'Why not rest a little and drink and eat?' As the soldiers did so, Joan retired alone to pray; then returned to renew the assault. Apparently, the English defenders 'shivered and were seized by a great terror'. Joan marched with her banner, declaring that when it touched the walls of the bastille, the fortress would fall. 'Jehanne, it touches it!' the soldiers shouted. 'All is yours!' she cried back. 'Enter!'

Her attack was made all the more likely to succeed because of another assault on the northern side, led by Nicholas de Giresmes of Rhodes, renowned as a valiant knight. This threw the English into such a panic that the governor of the fort and his men, desperate to escape, clogged up the drawbridge, which collapsed beneath them. They all perished, for their armour made swimming impossible, even in a shallow moat. The English subsequently withdrew in good order and the Maid of Orléans entered the centre of the city in triumph. It is difficult not to agree with George Bernard Shaw in his view that this was the first moment of European nationalism, a matter he puts exquisitely in his play *Saint Joan*.

'... There felle, by the hand of God, as it seemeth,' the Duke of Bedford wrote to the young King Henry VI, 'a grete strook upon your peuple ... called the Pucelle; that used fals enchauntments and sorcerie ...' Yet despite the tremendous nature of this victory, Charles, at least Dauphin, if not King, of France, did nothing; he declined even to visit Orléans. There was a meeting with Joan at Tours: and she proceeded to take Jargeau and Beaugency, while the victory she won at Patay consolidated her gains. One cannot say that Joan of Arc introduced any great innovations to the battlefields of her day, but when it came to morale, she was magnificent in inspiring her troops to do or die. Town after French town gladly opened their gates to her, including Châlons-sur-Marne and Rheims. On 18 July 1429, the dream of Joan, as foretold to her by the angels she claimed to have seen and heard, was duly fulfilled when Charles VII was anointed and crowned King of France in the cathedral at Rheims. Joan stood by him at the altar, clad in full armour and holding upright the banner of France. Shaw has the matter in a nutshell in his play, when one of the French lords tells her: 'But my dear girl, the voices that you hear are only in your imagination.' 'Yes,' Joan replies calmly, 'that is how God speaks to us.'

Joan now urged an immediate assault upon Paris, but Charles demurred. The war between France, on the one hand, and England and Burgundy, on the other, continued, even though, in the words of Sir James Ramsay in his *Lancaster and York*: 'It was admitted on all hands that a bold, prompt advance into the basin of the Somme would have raised all Picardy and brought the English dominion to a speedy close.' Joan nevertheless essayed an impetuous assault upon Paris. This failed because she had attacked without proper siege equipment.

By this time, Joan was weary of battle and wanted to go home. Charles VII wanted her to stay in the field and protect him as he endeavoured to negotiate an alliance against the English with the Duke of Burgundy, his former enemy. Meanwhile, the voices of Saint Catherine and Saint Margaret were informing Joan that she would be captured. This duly followed in a careless action of reconnaissance near Compiègne where, having become lost in a fog, she was taken by the soldiers of John of Luxembourg, and handed over to the Duke of Burgundy.

When England's astute Duke of Bedford heard the news, he instantly bought Joan from the Duke of Burgundy for 10,000 francs, and brought the papacy into play. His aim was to discredit Joan as a witch, harlot, and envoy of the Devil, thereby invalidating the crowning of Charles VII, overwhelming the French king with ridicule and, as Édouard Perroy states in his *The Hundred Years War*, 'his fleeting successes could be put down to an odious liaison between a criminal bastard and a shameless sorceress'. The former was, of course, the Marshal of France, Gilles de Rais. Bedford had a ready and willing ally in the Roman Catholic Church, which abhorred the idea of a woman warrior and was only too happy to charge Joan with the horrendous crime of *wearing male clothing*, in which lay the danger that such behaviour might give some women interesting and independent ideas. She was sent for trial by an ecclesiastical court, presided over by Pierre Canchon, Bishop of Beauvais.

There was a further serious matter, too, which Shaw pinpointed in *Saint Joan*. The Roman Catholic Church proclaimed that it was the one and only mediator between human beings and God. Joan was stating that her communion with the angels was direct, without the Church as intermediary. At her trial in 1431, she was sincere in stating that she believed that the Archangel Michael, Saint Margaret and Saint Catherine appeared toher in bodily form under a cloud of heavenly light. 'Clouds, wheels and flames of light are common phenomena with mystics, and with Yogis are experienced in the state of *Dhyana*,' states Fuller (who, in addition to his military expertise, was also the author of books on yoga and cabbala, and on that remarkable poet and mystic, Aleister Crowley). Essentially, Joan of Arc was stating that personal experience of the divine stood for more than obedience to the instructions of the Roman Catholic Church. Shaw is surely right to state that here we find the inception of what was to become the Protestant faith.

In fact, nothing that Joan of Arc might have had to say would have mattered to the court. Its members were all determined to find her guilty; and King Charles VII of France, whose crowning she had ensured, with his usual cowardice, would not lift a finger to save her now that she was herself in distress. The whole process of the court was a blasphemy against the noble name of justice. Under the laws of the time, the judges had no right to try her, since she was a prisoner of war. Voltaire writes:

> Such a person as the Black Prince would have honoured and respected her courage; but the regent, Bedford, thought it

necessary to detract from it, in order to revive the drooping spirits of the English. She had pretended to perform a miracle, and Bedford pretended to believe her a witch.... The university of Paris presented a complaint against Joan, accusing her of heresy and witchcraft. Therefore this university either believed what the regent would have it believe; or if it did not believe it, it was guilty of most infamous baseness. This heroine, who was worthy of that miracle which she had feigned [was] ... declared 'a superstitious prophetess of the devil, a blasphemer against God and His saints, and one who had been guilty of numberless errors against the faith of Christ.' As such she was condemned to perpetual imprisonment and to fast on bread and water. She made a reply to the judges, which, in my opinion, is worthy of eternal memory ...

This was portrayed wonderfully well by George Bernard Shaw in *Saint Joan*.

In the end, Joan gained even the respect of that excellent sceptical atheist, Voltaire, in being ultimately unable to deny that her visions and her voices came from God. She was promptly sentenced to the horrible death of being burned alive at the stake, and this sentence was carried out in the market place at Rouen on 29 May 1431. She was some centuries later declared to be a saint by the very Church that had burned her – and much good may this do her.

Some years later, the Church, ever eager to increase its power, moved against Joan's compatriot and former ally, Gilles de Rais, a brave warrior, Marshal of France and possibly the richest man in the kingdom. The charges were ludicrous in the extreme, namely, that he had abducted, tortured, sexually abused and mutilated at least 800 local children for purposes of foul satanic and alchemical experiments. The trial proved to be another grisly triumph for the Church. Gilles de Rais confessed under torture – as anyone would – to every crime of which he was accused. In Nantes in 1440 he was burned at the stake, just like Joan of Arc, and down the centuries has been held up as a model of infamy, inspiring the legend of Bluebeard. The *Encyclopaedia Britannica* doubts the legitimacy of the charges and the process of the trial; and in 1994, the Académie Française conducted one of its characteristically thorough investigations into the matter and concluded that Gilles de Rais was the innocent victim of trumped-up evidence. Perhaps, in a hundred years' time, the Roman Catholic Church will declare 'Bluebeard' to be a saint.

Though her body might have been consumed by the flames that brought her a death more painful than anyone can truly envisage, Joan's legacy outlived her terrible end. The matter is put well by John Payne, in his Introduction to *The Poems of Master François Villon of Paris*:

> The heroic peasant girl of Lorraine ... created the French people. Until her time France had been inhabited by Bretons, Angevins, Bourbainnais, Burgundians, Poitevins, Armagnacs; at last the baptism of fire through which the land had passed and the breadth of heroism that emanated from the Maid of Orleans had welded together the conflicting sections and had informed them with that breath of patriotism which is the basis of national life. France had at last become a nation. (Introduction to *The Poems of Master François Villon of Paris*).

'Pucelle de Dieu'; that is what they started calling Joan.

In 1456, the investigations of Pope Calixtus III declared Joan's trial to be irregular both in constitution and in procedure. From then on, people began more and more to call her 'la Pucelle de Dieu' – 'God's Virgin'. The inspiration she had given to her country demonstrated the vital importance of morale in military matters. As has been said, Joan was not in fact a particularly innovative strategist, though she followed an old rule of generalship in ensuring that her troops were well looked after, and, of course, in routing the enemy by taking his strongholds through boldness and daring, rather than by weight of numbers or long-drawn-out sieges. Tactically, she sometimes had the sense to assault a position from two angles at once. She realized also, as, later, Napoleon would declare, that 'one good soldier is worth ten bad soldiers', and employed the crucial factor of morale to instil courage and tenacity in her soldiers. If a man genuinely believes that he is fighting for God, is inspired by the voice of God through a prophet or prophetess, he will fight to the end for victory, and will gladly die in battle.

The burning of Joan of Arc did England precious little good. Even in death, she had saved France from being carved apart by England and Burgundy. The subsequent messy campaigns under King Henry VI of England were not very successful. Then, in 1454, the long series of English civil wars, known as the Wars of the Roses, broke out, as the two rival houses of the Plantagenet succession, York and Lancaster, fought for the throne. As the barons battled, the French took advantage of the situation to seize one English possession in their country after another.

After the Lancastrian-Tudor alliance finally won the English civil war at the Battle of Bosworth Field in 1485, both Henry VII and his son, Henry VIII, made occasional raids upon northern French territory, usually accepting tribute paid to them in order that they would go away in peace; by then, however, the *first* British Empire was fast being eaten away by the rise of French nationalism. In the reign of Mary Tudor, the French broke the heart of the Queen of England by retaking Calais. Joan of Arc is probably responsible for the fact that though the English won most of the major battles, they nevertheless lost the Hundred Years war. However, better skills in battle would be demonstrated under England's Queen Elizabeth I against the Spanish Armada.

10

The Spanish Armada and Queen Elizabeth I (1533–1603)

Queen Elizabeth I was certainly a most remarkable woman, and the same could be said for her mother, Anne Boleyn. This lady of the court, later accused of witchcraft, had attracted the amorous attentions of King Henry VIII of England, causing him to seek a divorce from his first wife, Catherine of Aragon. This resulted in a quarrel with the Pope, Clement VII, then the prisoner of the Holy Roman Emperor, Charles V, and when papal permission for the divorce was refused, King Henry VIII divorced Catherine anyway, married the beautiful Anne Boleyn in 1533, and repudiated papal authority by having Parliament declare that he was the Supreme Head of the English Church. His daughter by Anne, Elizabeth, was born in September 1533.

Suspicions of adultery, probably unfounded, led Henry to have Anne Boleyn beheaded in 1536; the truth was that he had tired of her. It cannot be said that he was a kindly father to his daughter, Elizabeth, and this perhaps explains her subsequent frigidity. Henry VIII proceeded to confiscate at least one-quarter of the lands of England then owned by the Roman Catholic monasteries, which he shut down and sold to the highest bidders. Meanwhile, the Act of Supremacy of 1537 made the King head of both State and Church. The national religion, according to the Act of Six Articles, was Catholicism without the Pope.

The sixteenth century was dominated by wars of religion. People killed one another for the alleged crime of not sharing a doctrinal belief. Henry's son, Edward VI, took the throne on the former's death in 1547. The young king favoured the Protestant cause, and in consequence Catholic churches were plundered under the somewhat vandalistic regime of the Regent, the Duke of Northumberland. Edward died, aged sixteen, in 1553, and was succeeded by his sister Mary, daughter of Henry's first wife Catherine of Aragon. Mary endeavoured to restore Roman Catholicism to England and had Protestants burned at the stake, including the Bishops Ridley and Latimer and the Archbishop of Canterbury, Thomas Cranmer, who supervised the production, and in 1552 the revision, of the beautiful Book of Common Prayer, the first prayer book of the Church of England. Mary tried to protect the nation by her marriage of dynastic alliance, in 1554, to King Philip II of Spain, then the most powerful country in the world, but she proceeded to lose Calais to the French. During much of her reign she had been misadvised by the ghastly Cardinal Reginald Pole, whom she had appointed to succeed Cranmer as Archbishop of Canterbury, and who had sought vainly to reconcile Mary's realm with the Church of Rome. He died in 1558, on the same day as Mary.

Elizabeth I now came to the throne of England. 'Be well assured I will stand your good Queen,' she stated to the nation before her coronation in January, 1559. The people responded. 'She is much attached to the people,' the Spanish Ambassador wrote, 'and is very confident that they are all on her side; which is indeed true.' Elizabeth now had to solve a series of appalling problems. The Hon. J.W. Fortescue puts the matter of her temperament quite well in his *A History of the British Army* (1910): 'She hated straight dealing for its simplicity, she hated conviction for its certainty, and above all she hated war for its expense.'

At the time when her grandfather, Henry VII, had taken the throne for the Tudor family, England had no standing army and virtually no navy. Henry VII had made peace with Scotland by a dynastic marriage of his daughter, peace with Spain by a dynastic marriage of his son, and peace with France by a lightning raid followed by a profitable peace through the Treaty of Étaples. The father of Elizabeth, Henry VIII, had smashed the Scots at the Battle of Flodden in 1513, and furthered peace with France by his meeting with King Francis I on the Field of the Cloth of Gold, near Calais, in 1520, all the while maintaining the Spanish alliance and building up a British navy. The latter became increasingly important to Elizabeth now that the English had lost Calais, for she realized that the defence of the realm from abroad lay in control of the English Channel.

Elizabeth began with an attempted consolidation of her queendom. By the issue of the Thirty-Nine Articles (1558), she tried to reconcile both Catholics and Protestants to the idea of a broad Church. This sensible policy worked with many but not with a few fundamentalist extremists of both the Catholic and Protestant persuasions. There was, too, the problem of Mary, Queen of Scots, who had been driven out of Scotland by the Protestants and who had sought refuge in England. Elizabeth had her cousin imprisoned in honourable captivity in a castle as she pondered what to do. Mary was in alliance initially with the French, whose power was expanding.

At first, Elizabeth through it best to preserve the Spanish alliance. She toyed with the idea of marriage to Philip II, the husband of her late sister, Queen Mary, but employed her tactics of delay in response to his proposals. Perhaps the unwelcome sexual advances of her uncle had made her forever frigid. In any event, relations between England and Spain rapidly worsened. Elizabeth, her treasury short of money, ventured into the slave trade with the licensed privateer, John Hawkins (until he was eventually killed by the Spaniards off Puerto Rico for preying upon a monopoly in West Africa which they regarded as their own). Elizabeth also backed the voyages of other licensed English pirates such as Sir Richard Grenville and Sir Francis Drake, who robbed Spanish galleons of treasure the Spanish had looted from their colonies in Latin America.

France collapsed into the dirty and disgusting Wars of Religion (1562–98) as relations between England and Spain grew increasingly acerbic. King Philip of Spain encouraged plots to put Mary, Queen of Scots upon the English throne through the assassination of Elizabeth. The Queen responded by sending troops to assist the Protestant Dutch in their revolt against Catholic Spain. Philip's answer was to take Portugal, which gave him the whole of that country's possessions in Latin America, including Brazil. Elizabeth, frightened by the Babington Plot (1586) which had been fomented by Spanish agents, had Mary, Queen of Scots put to death in 1587, thus eliminating the only viable claimant to the crown.

King Philip responded by building a great fleet of warships, the Armada, packed with armed soldiers and intended to be the greatest marine force the world had ever witnessed. Historians still dispute the precise purpose of this force, and it has been argued that Philip's primary aim was to frighten the English out of their interference with Spanish trade in the West Indies and South America, and their intervention in the war between the Dutch and the Spaniards in the Low Countries, rather than to invade England. It is impossible to sustain this position in view of King Philip's letter to his chief admiral, the Duke of Medina Sidonia:

> When you have received my orders, you will put to sea with the whole Armada, and proceed direct for the English Channel, up which you will sail as far as the point of Margate, then open communications with the Duke of Parma, and ensure him a passage across.

(Captain Caesero Fernandez Duro, *La Armada Invincible*, 1884.) Parma commanded the Spanish army in the Low Countries, and was to command the troops that sailed with the Armada.

Philip II was utterly confident of victory, believing himself to be the divinely chosen instrument of God, and Spain to be empowered as God's own nation. Masses were said in 50,000 churches, the Spaniards fully believing in their own invincibility and godly mission. To many a neutral foreign observer, England seemed to have as much chance of success as it would, today, if the United States of America were to launch its military might against Britain. But King Philip had also gone beyond the belief that God was on his side, in favour of the conviction that he was on God's side.

The chief admiral, the Duke of Medina Sidonia, did not share his king's confidence. Nor did the chief general on land, the Duke of Parma. One commander opined that those who believed the Armada would triumph were hoping for a miracle. King Philip remained convinced that God would supply it, the ultimate aim being to bring England back into submission to the Roman Church and the Pope, and to do it by fire and the sword and the tortures of the Spanish Inquisition. In any event, there seems to have been no divine hand in the logistics, although Medina Sidonia was a more experienced seaman than most of his captains and a capable administrator, which King Philip was not. In the event, although the English army was negligibly small, the Spanish Armada carried neither enough troops for effective occupation nor enough ships to carry the reinforcements from the Duke of Parma's troops. Shortly after it put to sea in 1588, it was discovered to be short of gunpowder, the fish aboard went rotten, the wine turned sour, the water became brackish, and men began to die by the score before a single battle engagement.

The Armada consisted of 130 ships, a total displacement of 57,868 tons, armed with 2,431 guns, manned by 8,050 sailors and carrying 18,973 soldiers in addition to 3,470 galley slaves. By contrast, the English fleet consisted of 197 ships. In point of fact, the largest English ships were as heavy as the largest Spanish galleons, though they sat lower in the water and could manoeuvre more easily. The Spaniards had 1,124 pieces of artillery compared to 1,972 on the part of the English. This artillery, which had come about via the invention and gradual adoption of gunpowder, had revolutionized warfare, and especially naval warfare, in a manner which had been realized by the English much earlier than the Spaniards. If the actual nature of the weaponry is analysed, then it is seen that the Spaniards had three times as many heavy-shotted medium-range pieces as the English: but the English had three times as many *long*-range pieces. It was Sir Francis Drake's grasp of this fact that was to have such a telling influence in the subsequent sea battles.

King Philip II was for once sensible in ordering Medina Sidonia to avoid giving pitched battle to the English fleet and, above all else, to ignore Sir Francis Drake. In view of Drake's history, this was a wise decision. In 1577, Drake had sailed in his *Golden Hind* at the head of a small fleet and remorselessly plundered the

Spanish treasure ships, which had themselves looted remorselessly from the riches of the New World. Drake's rapacious raids upon foreign plunderers led to his extraordinary and unprecedented circumnavigation of the globe, and although Magellan's ship had preceded him, Drake was the first captain to return alive to tell the tale, for which he was knighted by his secret partner in plundered treasure, Queen Elizabeth I.

In a superlative display of naval strategy, Drake had raided Cadiz in 1586, to sink thirty-three ships being readied to join the Spanish Armada as they lay at anchor; this celebrated 'singeing of the King of Spain's beard' delayed Philip's preparations by two years. Now Drake demanded ships with which to essay another rapid, pre-emptive strike. His intention was to use the superior swiftness of English ships and the greater range of English gunnery, as well as the better seamanship of English captains, to bottle up the Armada in harbour and destroy its ships. It can be argued that had these plans been followed, the Spanish Armada would never have sailed.

There was, however, another factor influencing Queen Elizabeth I. She wished to avoid a war at all costs; understandably, given the fact the eventual conflict would cost England the then colossal sum of £1.5 million. Ignoring the advice of her Privy Council, she sent emissaries to the Duke of Parma in the Spanish Netherlands to discuss peace, seemingly unaware that Parma's initial approach had been a ruse to buy time until the Armada had been fully assembled and was ready to set forth. She forbade Drake's audacious plans, and appointed Lord Howard of Effingham as Supreme Commander of the English fleet.

Fortunately, Lord Howard was a good commander, probably aware that he owed his appointment more to his rank in society than to any proven skills at naval warfare. He promptly appointed Drake as his Vice-Admiral and President of the Council of War, and wrote increasingly frantic despatches to Her Majesty, praising his captains and sailors but begging for more money, more food and more ammunition. Initially these pleas fell on deaf ears, until the fleet's commanders were in despair. Constant pressure eventually resulted in limited supplies. These would also help to determine the course of the forthcoming battle.

On 19 July 1588, the Spanish Armada sighted the Lizard, the

south-westernmost tip of the English mainland. Captain-General Don Alonzo de Levya urged Medina Sidonia to assault Drake's ships in Plymouth Sound. Within the sheltered confines of the Sound, the English vessels would have lacked all mobility, and the Spanish Armada would have destroyed them. Unfortunately for the Spaniards, Medina Sidonia had his irrevocable orders from King Philip II, who was, in turn, apparently in receipt of orders from God.

On 21 June, the English fleet sailed and engaged the Armada for the first time. The Spanish strategy was the old-fashioned one of engaging at close quarters, ramming ships and boarding them. Howard wisely agreed with Drake's strategy of keeping at a distance and trusting to superior long-range gunnery. The Spanish *San Salvador*, carrying the Paymaster-General of the Armada and his treasure chests, exploded, turning in seconds into a burning hulk, later captured by Drake. The Spaniards could not match English ships, seamanship and gunnery. Their morale fell, whilst that of the English had been encouraged by a magnificent parade and a rousing speech by Queen Elizabeth at Tilbury.

The Armada had expended much firepower to no effect and was running low on ammunition. It was proposed to establish a base on the Isle of Wight to replenish supplies, but Howard and Drake had anticipated such a move and a fortuitous wind allowed a renewed English assault on 23 July. 'The enemy's ships,' Medina Sidonia stated, 'were so fast and handy that nothing could be done with them.' This action saved the Isle of Wight but was otherwise indecisive. So were the skirmishes which followed as the Armada retreated in relatively good order and anchored between Calais and Cape Griz Nez, thus to some extent reversing the tactical position. Howard now found his own fleet to be without sufficient powder and shot to capitalize on the situation, and was also cut off from his supplies, while the Spaniards endeavoured to replenish theirs from the French mainland.

Howard and Drake replied by firing eight small ships and sending the blazing vessels towards the enemy fleet where it lay at anchor at Calais, throwing it into utter chaos and confusion. 'They dislodged us with eight vessels,' a Spanish officer wrote, 'an exploit which with one hundred and thirty they had not been able to do nor dared to attempt.' The fireships did not in fact succeed in doing any significant *physical* damage, but they added to Medina Sidonia's growing perplexity; above all, they forced the Armada to put to sea again. Moreover, Parma sent word that he was unable to embark because a rebel Dutch fleet, known as the 'Sea Beggars', under Justinian of Nassau was blockading the coast, a vital factor which is too often forgotten by some English historians.

The English now assaulted the bedraggled Spanish Armada. It has been estimated that in spite of 100,000 rounds of shot being fired by the Spaniards, only one captain and twenty – forty sailors from the English fleet were killed; and not one English ship was seriously damaged by enemy action. By contrast, in this encounter alone, Spanish casualties amounted to 600 killed and 800 wounded; with no ships sunk. A squall caused Howard to break off the battle and the wind soon became a gale. In the British Museum one may see the talisman presented to Queen Elizabeth to invoke the winds to save the realm by the most learned English mathematician and astrologer of his age, Dr John Dee.

In fact, there is no need to use magic to explain the unsettled weather conditions which are still found in the English Channel today. Fuller has even argued that the wind saved the Armada from 'inevitable destruction', since it meant that the English fleet could no longer pound this becalmed shambles to pieces.

But the wind also meant that Medina Sidonia could not possibly retreat back through the Channel to the Bay of Biscay. The Dutch had blocked any possibility of linking with Parma. His only hope of returning to Spain therefore, was flight to the North Sea, a long voyage around Scotland, and a return via the Atlantic. It might have been possible to land in Scotland and fire it to arise against England had the Armada been in a healthy state, but many of its ships had been rendered unseaworthy, provisions were short, as was ammunition, and Drake was in hot pursuit. Howard, in fact, sensibly called the chase off on 3 August – the weather did the work for him. As Fuller has it:

Of the 130 sail which stood out from Lisbon in May, 63 are believed to have been lost. Two were abandoned to the enemy; three were lost off the French coast; two were lost off Holland; two were sunk off Gravelines; 19 were wrecked off Scotland or Ireland; and the fate of 35 is unknown. The

English did not lose a ship.

When the survivors of this catastrophe finally arrived back in Spain, King Philip II remained unperturbed. 'Great thanks do I render Almighty God,' he declared, 'by whose generous hand I am gifted with such power, that I could easily, if I chose, place another fleet upon the sea.' He tried to do that twice more but, mysteriously enough, on both occasions violent storms drove the ships of these armadas back into port.

Sir Francis Drake, the nemesis of King Philip's Spain, used the English victory to continue his royally licensed piracy of Spanish treasure ships and general commerce until he died of dysentery in 1596. Nevertheless, he was more fortunate than either the Spaniards who took part in the Armada, 60 per cent of whom died in the campaign, or the English sailors, 50 per cent of whom died in the year after the Armada from poverty, disease and neglect. For this, Queen Elizabeth I must take the blame, since her notorious parsimony led her to ignore Howard's noble pleas for help for the men she had so deftly encouraged to do battle.

The defeat of the Spanish Armada, exquisitely analysed by Professor Garett Mattingly in his book of that name (1959), had far-reaching effects on both the international situations of England and Spain, and on naval strategy. Mattingly cogently argues that Drake's original plan to assault the Spaniards in their own harbours was too audacious and unrealistic, but that while Drake was perhaps wrong for all the right reasons, Queen Elizabeth I was right for all the wrong reasons. In this there lies a marked contrast between male intellect and female intuition. The strategy upon which the Queen insisted did indeed win the battle: yet her mean-spirited conduct towards the ordinary fighting men who had gained the victory cannot be ignored, any more than it can be excused. The war with Spain blundered on at great expense without either England or Spain gaining an acre of territory. After the death of Elizabeth in 1603, James VI of Scotland, now also crowned James I of England, made a tired peace with Spain that reflected little credit upon either side.

Even so, there were genuinely significant consequences flowing from this battle. Until 1588, Spain had enjoyed an international reputation, established firmly for a century, for invincibility. Her empire, political and commercial, included Central and South America, in addition to possessions in North America and enclaves dotted around the Indian Ocean. The defeat demolished international recognition of Spanish superiority, and a myth, which was not, in any case, warranted by the wealth, resources or population of Spain, was destroyed. For the Spaniards themselves, this loss of face was devastating, destroying the illusion that they were God's chosen which had so fortified their fanaticism. Slowly, having lost conviction in her mission to be tireless in enforcing her imperial and religious principles upon all whom she encountered, Spain declined into a second-rate power.

Spain's principal mistake was that she paid insufficient attention to taking command of the sea. Spanish captains were inspired more by zeal and greed rather than by sea sense. The English and the Dutch had demonstrated, moreover, and beyond all reasonable doubt, that small nations though they were, they could command their home waters sufficiently well so as to extinguish any naval threat. The English continued to raid, rob and harass Spanish trade routes. Within less than a century, rivalry for command of the seas would lead to wars between England and her former Dutch allies. Despite slender resources and small armies, both nations gained empires because of their supremacy at sea: Spain, lacking that command, could not hold its vast expanses of land territory once seriously challenged.

Of course, command of the sea depends upon the acquisition of appropriate naval bases, essential as supply points. The inability to secure such a base was one of the main reasons why the Spanish Armada not only failed, but would have been unable to succeed in the first place. Subsequent English naval thinking – at least, whenever such thinking was sound – consisted on the whole of denying an enemy any base near England's shores and, where possible, bottling up the enemy's ships in their own harbours, rendering it impossible for them to set sail.

There were further and necessary refinements made in the use of artillery as a result of what had been learned in the battles. The Spaniards had indeed possessed cannon sufficient to destroy an enemy vessel but only at close range, and manoeuvring to that range was beyond the capabilities of their captains. The English found that their culverins were neither powerful nor accurate enough at the long ranges upon which they relied. Eventually this led to further research into the use of the cannon.

The victory over the Armada greatly added to the myth of a God-given destiny for England which Queen Elizabeth was deliberately weaving, aided by poets such as Edmund Spenser. It was a myth of which she herself was the personification. She now claimed that God was on *her* side; indeed, she has sometimes been credited with the line: 'He made the winds and waters rise to scatter all mine enemies.' These words are, however, more likely to have been penned by her court astrologer and magus, the remarkable intellectual, John Dee, then accounted the most learned man in Europe. The medal made for Prince Maurice, commander-in-chief of the Dutch, whose role in the Armada campaign had proved so vital and decisive, bears a startling resemblance to the Dee talisman for Queen Elizabeth in the British Museum, and carries a Latin inscription, which translates as: 'God blew and they were scattered'.

It was Dr Dee who promoted to the Queen navigation and exploration, who urged the colonization of America which he called 'Atlantis', and which notion was further intellectually explored by James I and VI's Lord Chancellor, Sir Francis Bacon, in his book *The New Atlantis*, 1618, and who first used the phrase 'the British Empire' in a printed work. From these beginnings and from the defeat of the Armada, the notion of a grand British imperial destiny, wrested from Spain, was born.

11

Oliver Cromwell (1599–1658)

Oliver Cromwell emerged to bring order out of the chaos of the English Civil Wars of 1642–8. Had it not been for these, he would have lived a quiet life as an East Anglian country gentleman and Member of Parliament for Huntingdon – presently represented by John Major, the Prime Minister – and then for Cambridge, where he had enjoyed his further education. Up until the Civil Wars, he was no more than a country squire, a convinced Puritan of strong and sincere religious belief, a backbench MP interested in advancing the interests of his constituency but making little mark upon the nation.

The English Civil Wars were essentially a struggle between the dying feudal world, headed by King Charles I, who had, between 1629 and 1640, endeavoured to rule without Parliament on the basis of the Divine Right of Kings, and the newly emergent capitalist and mercantile classes, who believed that Parliament should have greater power. When Civil War broke out in 1642, Cromwell promptly took Cambridge Castle. Raising a troop of cavalry, and lacking all previous military experience, he received much military education at the battle of Edgehill, Warwickshire, on 23 October 1642. Here the Parliamentarian ('Roundhead') forces faced a formidable opponent in the twenty-three-year-old nephew of King Charles I, Prince Rupert of the Rhine, who had distinguished himself in Dutch campaigns during 1637–8, and who was commanding right wing of the Royalist ('Cavalier') cavalry.

Quarrels between Prince Rupert and the Earl of Lindsey were typical of the factionalism which disfigured the Royalist cause. Rupert, quite rightly, wanted to apply the infantry tactics which had been pioneered with great success by Sweden's King Gustavus Adolphus during the Thirty Years War, of 1618–48, a complex European struggle between the kings of France and the Hapsburg rulers of the Holy Roman Empire and Spain. Having seized the higher ground from which to give battle at Edgehill, Rupert insisted that the modern Swedish fashion be followed in placing pikemen and musketeers next to one another, with cavalry on either wing. Lindsey demoted himself from general to colonel and proceeded to sulk. (It brought him little profit, since he was mortally wounded in the subsequent battle.) Rupert knew also that his cavalry was scantily trained and short of firearms; it was vital, therefore, that it should achieve maximum impact with its first charge. The horsemen were consequently instructed to ride in the closest possible formation and to hold their fire until they had closed with the enemy.

The ensuing charge of Prince Rupert's force on the right easily routed the Parliamentarian cavalry that faced it. However, and as Cromwell, present at the battle, was quick to see, Rupert's cavalry hotly pursued their fleeing adversaries and did not return to regroup. The resolution of the Earl of Essex meant that the centre of the Parliamentarian infantry held. The resulting battle between the opposing infantry for the centre was inconclusive, though when the Royalist horse finally returned, Essex's army was forced to give ground. 'Both armies camped in the field, neither being willing to allow the other to claim sole possession,' C.V. Wedgwood writes. On the next day, both sides claimed a victory, though Essex decided to retreat with the Parliamentarian forces towards Warwick.

Rupert now seized his chance to harass the retreating army's baggage and equipment, forcing Essex to abandon cannon and blowing up four of his ammunition wagons. The coolness and tenacity of Essex in retreat had probably saved his army from disaster; now, however, Rupert discerned that the route to London, held by Parliamentarian forces, was wide open. If his strategy had been followed by King Charles I, it is possible that the Royalists might have won the war by the end of 1642. Charles, to his own subsequent cost, chose to prevaricate.

Prince Rupert, a vigorous and dashing general, won the Battle of Chalgrove Field, Oxfordshire, in 1643, enabling him to take Bristol and secure the west of the country for the King. Next he marched north, in the following year raising the Parliamentarian siege of York by forcing the enemy to face him at Marston Moor, a few miles west of York. This time, however, his opponent as cavalry commander was Oliver Cromwell, who had no fear of the legend which had grown up around Rupert, as told by Mark Bence-Jones:

> His [Rupert's] very name struck terror in Puritan hearts.... All kinds of legends grew up about him.... He was invested with diabolical powers.... He could prophesy, he could make himself invisible, he was endowed with the gift of languages....

Cromwell, however, in training the regiment of cavalry he had raised, the Ironsides, emphasized the importance of marshalling the cavalry *after* the initial charge; he also instructed them to engage the enemy at a fast trot, rather than a headlong gallop. Finally, and unlike Prince Rupert, Cromwell forbade undisciplined pursuit of a fleeing enemy.

The rival tactics were put to the test at Marston Moor on 2 July 1644. Prince Rupert, as Mark Bence-Jones states, 'in an hour's fighting on that damp July evening ... lost both his army and his reputation.... And indeed, after Marston Moor, Rupert's luck did not return.' The Ironsides Cromwell had selected and trained were well-equipped yeomen, self-disciplined, godly men of good character and high morale. As colonel of the regiment, Cromwell had won minor battles at Gainsborough and Winceby. At Marston Moor he proved his point that an ordered and disciplined unit can beat an untrained rabble, however dashing its leader, and as a result the north of England was secured for the Parliamentarian side.

Rupert retreated south with 6,000 men, yet was appointed to command all of the Royalist forces. Both sides had roughly 70,000 men and there were a number of skirmishes. Meanwhile, Cromwell, his reputation high after the victory at Marston Moor, spent the winter of 1644–5 in raising and training the New Model Army under the overall command of General Sir Thomas Fairfax, the first professional army that England had ever witnessed.

Do you think [Cromwell had asked] that the spirits of such mean base fellows will ever be able to encounter gentlemen that have honour and courage and resolution in them? ... You must get men of spirit ... of a spirit that is likely to go on as far as gentlemen will go – or else I am sure that you will be beaten still.

This was his grand idea [Fuller writes], that leadership is useless without disciplined followership, and that discipline demands not only that officers and men know what they are fighting for, but 'love what they know', for without affection discipline is sterile. He, therefore, sought out men who had the fear of God before them, 'and made some conscience of what they did.'

'I have a lovely company ...' Cromwell had written to Fairfax in September 1643, 'they expect to be used as men!' 'In these last seven words,' Fuller comments, 'lies the secret of the whole system of Cromwell's discipline.'

'It was this army,' John Terraine avers, 'well organised and equipped, soundly drilled, and clad in the red coats which would remain the British Army's standard dress until 1914, which won the Civil War.' At the battle of Naseby, Leicestershire, on 14 June 1645, Cromwell's disciplined troops routed the rabble of Rupert, allowing some of the Royalist horsemen to charge through so that they could be slaughtered on their disorganized return. As at Edgehill, Rupert had lost control of his impulsive and impetuous cavalry: Cromwell had *not* lost control of the New Model Army. Naseby was a devastating and decisive victory. Soon after, in September 1645, Parliamentarian forces recaptured Bristol, which Rupert had originally won, thus adding the west to their conquest of the Midlands which had resulted from Naseby. Rupert urged

King Charles I to make peace, and was rewarded for his loyalty, courage and skills by being dismissed from his command.

Cromwell's victory made him the most powerful figure in the Parliamentarian party. Regarded now as the leader of the Protestant sect known as the Independents (later the Congrega-tionalist Church), he no longer needed the support of his Presbyterian allies from Scotland and could now dominate Parliament itself. Prince Rupert was forced to flee the country in 1646, cursing the factionalism of the officers and the amateurish conduct of the men which had led him to lose. Subsequently he became an admiral and commanded a Royalist fleet-in-exile from 1649–53, which harassed the shipping of the fledgeling English Republic. On the Restoration of Charles II to the English throne in 1660, Rupert commanded the English fleet with some success in the Second and Third Dutch Wars of 1665–7 and 1672–4; he was also an early member of the Royal Society, a scientist and inventor, an artist, and one of the founders of the Hudson's Bay Company. He must be accounted unlucky in having commanded a sloppy force with incompetent officers when confronted by a general as determinedly single-minded as Cromwell.

King Charles I decided to give himself up to the Scots, of whose country, which then still had a separate parliament, he was still king, James I and VI's accession in 1603 having united the crowns of the two countries. The Scots promptly demonstrated their loyalty to him by handing Charles over to Parliament in return for payment of £40,000. Nevertheless, the King continued to intrigue, arousing a Scottish rebellion which was crushed by Cromwell at Preston on 16 August 1648. Realizing that there could be no security in the realm as long as Charles was alive, Cromwell ensured that the King was brought to trial. The latter, who behaved throughout with an admixture of arrogance and dignity, was found guilty of being a 'Tyrant, Traitor, Murderer and a public enemy'. On 30 January 1649, he was publicly beheaded in Whitehall, and England became a republic, with Cromwell at the head of its army, though he was gradually gathering the reins of executive power.

The murder of Charles I shocked Europe, as did Cromwell's next actions, the brutal repression of the members of a radical political movement known as the 'Levellers', and the yet more brutal 'pacification' of Ireland, still in Royalist hands. The man called 'brave Oliver' by Lord Macaulay, in his interesting poem, 'The Battle of Naseby', now proceeded to commit atrocities still execrated by the Irish people to the present day. At Drogheda on 17 September 1649, an estimated 4,000 defenders were put to the sword, not counting women and children. 'I am persuaded,' wrote Oliver Cromwell, 'that this is a righteous judgment of god upon these barbarous wretches, who have imbrued their hands in so much innocent blood; and that it will tend to prevent the effusion of blood for the future.' There is nothing like God to sanctify excuses for genocide; and this policy of massacre was repeated at Wexford in the same year. He reduced the remaining rebel garrisons, and outlawed the practice of Catholic worship. Scottish and English settlers were then brought in to take over confiscated lands in Northern Ireland. In consequence, the name of Cromwell will be forever execrated in Ireland; for Great Britain today, his policy then has resulted in appalling problems now.

But however abominable Cromwell's Irish policy, there is something to be said for the excellence of his generalship in the Second English Civil War, waged against Parliament by Charles, son of the executed King Charles, in alliance with the Scots. The Battle of Dunbar, south-eastern Scotland, on 3 September 1650 displayed Cromwell's gift for commanding infantry as well as cavalry. 'Let god arise, let His enemies be scattered!' Cromwell roared to his troops, having chosen and taken up position on higher ground. Once again, a disciplined professional army defeated a rabble of untrained amateurs. 'They run, they run – I profess they run,' Cromwell declared, 'I profess that they run.' Exactly one year later, to the day, Cromwell broke a further Scottish invasion (he had already captured Perth earlier in 1651) at Worcester, using to full effect the efficiency, discipline, flexibility and, above all, the conviction in the rightness of their cause, that he had imbued in his troops, and which was so conspicuously lacking in his opponents. The future Charles II had to hide in an oak tree, before fleeing to France, where he was to remain in exile for nine years.

Having defeated the Irish, the Scots and the Royalist rebels, there remained the subjugation of England. Initially, Cromwell endeavoured to negotiate with the various factions in what was known as the 'Rump' Parliament, the much-reduced House of Commons after it had been 'purged' in 1648 of 'presbyterian' elements. He was confident of the support of the New Model Army and essayed various constitutional expedients, all the while finding it increasingly impossible to deal with fanatical extremists. Eventually his patience snapped and he used his military might.

The House of Lords had been abolished; yet on 20 April 1653, Cromwell marched upon the House of Commons. 'Conceive, gentlemen, in your heart of hearts, the possibility that you may be mistaken,' he had urged the members; but there is no reasoning with a fanatic. Entering the House of Commons, Cromwell declared: 'You have sat too long here for any good you have been doing. Depart, I say, and let us have done with you. In the name of God, go!' He added to the Speaker as he regarded the Mace: 'Take away that fool's bauble....' Cromwell now became Lord Protector and military dictator, and in 1654 he dissolved Parliament, ruling alone just as his old antagonist, King Charles I, had tried to do.

As a ruler of England, Cromwell was capable, but intractable problems defeated a man of even his extraordinary abilities. In religious matters, he was tolerant, firmly believing that religion was a matter of conscience between human beings and God. He deplored religious persecution, and repealed all statutes against the Jews, once more allowing them to immigrate to England. Frequently he wrestled with his own conscience in bouts of fervent prayer. In 1655 he divided the country into twelve provinces, each governed by a major-general. Unfortunately, the major-generals he appointed under his dictatorship lacked his toleration and applied fanatical dogma to enforce their petty tyranny. A man could be fined ten shillings for going to the next village to hear a sermon on a Sunday; a girl could be put in the stocks for the hideous crime of mending a dress on the Sabbath. Christmas Day had been abolished in 1652, and it became a crime to hang decorations and eat mince pies and plum pudding. The theatre was proscribed, and so were old rites like dancing around the maypole. It is hardly surprising that when Cromwell died in 1658, one writer described his funeral as 'the joyfullest ... I ever saw'.

Even so, Cromwell did bring England a badly needed period of stability. The Jews, banned since 1290, began once more to make their customary contribution to the cultural and economic life of the country. The Quakers, too, emerged from the half-light of persecution, now that Cromwell had at last allowed them to hold their own services without penalty. Under Cromwell, there was at least freedom of worship; meanwhile, the commerce of England prospered.

When Cromwell turned to foreign affairs, he found himself embracing the idea of a British Empire as first formulated by Dr John Dee in the reign of Queen Elizabeth I. The Lord Protector rightly discerned that for such an enterprise, naval power was essential. He had begun his military career as a commander of cavalry, his dragoons armed with single-shot firearms and long swords. At Dunbar, he had displayed formidable abilities as an infantry commander in his skilful deployment of armoured pikemen and musketeers. Now he essayed naval command.

Ironically enough, it was Cromwell's late antagonist, Charles I, who had endeavoured to build up the British navy; his tax, known as 'ship money', had been a contributory factor in provoking the English Civil Wars. Cromwell had 207 new ships built during the eleven years of his rule. He was also very fortunate in his subordinate, Admiral Robert Blake, who led the fleet in the First Dutch War (1652–4), in a battle for commercial and imperial supremacy and control of sea lanes. The Dutch Admiral Van Tromp proved to be a formidable opponent and honours were roughly even when the war ended, though the naval prestige of England had soared, and there had been some small commercial gains.

Cromwell's second foreign war involved an alliance with France, whose power was growing, against the declining power of Spain. Tactically, it was successful, in that England gained the island of Jamaica. Strategically, it was a failure in the short term. The cost of the war inflicted economic depression upon England; raised the national debt to over £2.5 million; destroyed the confidence of the City of London financiers, who thereby became ready and willing to restore the monarchy; and returned captured English trade to the Dutch. Furthermore, whilst the war further reduced Spanish prestige, it left France the most powerful nation on the Continent.

When Cromwell died in 1658, it was as a deeply disappointed man who had ultimately failed to realize his ambitions in both domestic and foreign policy. For a short while Cromwell's son, Richard, ruled in his place; then, in 1660 King Charles II was duly restored to the throne, and the House of Lords and House of Commons were reinstated in the same year. However, the legacy of Cromwell was tremendous. In *European Civilisation, Its Origins and Development* (1937), Margaret James puts the matter succinctly:

> At home, the doctrine of an active faith helped to sanctify a growing industrialism. Abroad it helped to sanctify the shadowy beginnings of imperialism. In the same way as chosen individuals were held to glorify God by rising to a higher position than their fellows, so a chosen nation was thought to exalt Him by dominating its neighbours.

Oliver Cromwell was the first Englishman to create a truly professional British army. He was the first to advocate openly the notion that England had a noble and God-given imperial destiny. He realized that morale is crucial to the winning of any war, and he inspired his troops with the faith he himself held so fervently. His vision of a British Empire would, however, be promoted somewhat more cynically by a successor: John Churchill.

12

John Churchill, Duke of Marlborough (1650–1722)

Whether rightly or wrongly, Oliver Cromwell had honestly believed he was the divinely appointed servant of God, the instrument of a Divine Will far greater than himself. John Churchill did not believe in anything other than his own will and his own advantage. In consequence, he was excoriated for his personality by his critics during his time, and his posthumous reputation has been execrated by later historians: yet no military historian will deny that, in military terms, John Churchill was a genius.

He was accused of avarice, financial corruption, treason, opportunism and intrigue. All these charges have some substance, though he should be judged by the standards of his time. Had he not displayed the necessary talent for intrigue, it is doubtful if he could have risen to the position from which he won England its greatest land victory since Agincourt.

The son of a Royalist squire, he initially approached the Stuart court through the influence of his sister Arabella, then mistress of Charles II's younger brother, the Duke of York (later King James II), and consolidated his tenuous position by way of a liaison with

Barbara Villiers, Lady Castlemaine, the tempestuous mistress of King Charles II. The bedroom led to the battlefield. Churchill distinguished himself at Tangier in 1688(a possession brought to Britain by Charles II's marriage to Catherine of Braganza); in service with both the Duke of York and the French Marshal Turenne on land and sea against the Dutch in 1672–4; during the Duke of Monmouth's Rebellion against King James II in 1685; and against rebels in Ireland in 1690. Meanwhile he had married Sarah Jennings, a lady-in-waiting at Court and a close friend of the future Queen Anne.

When his patron, James II, proceeded by his politics, especially that of re-establishing Catholicism as the nation's faith, to upset not only his enemies but also his friends, 1685–8, it was John Churchill who turned traitor and who, as leader of the only viable land army in England, went over to the cause of William of Orange, supporting the claim to the throne of William and his wife, James's daughter Mary. As a result of this, the 'Glorious Revolution' of 1688, James II fled to exile, never to return to England.

All of which did not, however, prevent Churchill, created Earl of Marlborough in 1689, from intriguing with the Jacobites, putting forward a plan for the deposed King to return under a protectorate governed by Marlborough. His correspondence detailing the plot was discovered by agents of King William, and in 1692 Marlborough was imprisoned for a period in the Tower of London, though the punishment was designed to be only a warning. In 1701, King William III finally forgave him, appointing him chief of the English armed forces. This was a wise decision; and no one has put the matter better than Fuller, in his *The Decisive Battles of the Western World*:

> Whatever may have been his failings as a man, as a general and a statesman Marlborough stands high above his contemporaries. Courteous and patient, he possessed what so few men of genius are endowed with – ability to tolerate fools gladly. Though his courage was of the highest, his imagination vivid, and his common sense profound, his master characteristic was his self-control. Nothing unbalanced him, whether it was the stupidity of his allies, the

duplicity of the politicians, or the ability of his enemies. As a general he possessed the rare virtue of seeing a war as a whole, and of being able to relate sea power with land power and strategy with politics. Nothing escaped his observation, and no detail, tactical or administrative, was too minute to be overlooked. A master of stratagems, he consistently mystified his enemy; a master of detail, his men were never left in want. In the planning of a campaign he took infinite pains, and in its execution infinite trouble. In an age which believed that the defensive was the stronger form of war, he invariably sought to bring his enemy to battle, and proved conclusively that a vigorous offensive is usually the soundest defence.

Queen Mary II died in 1694, and in 1702 her husband, King William III, followed her to the grave. As their marriage had been without issue, the crown then passed to Anne, James II's second daughter. Anne had seventeen children by her husband, Prince George of Denmark, but all except one died in infancy, and that one lived only to his eleventh year. She attributed the tragedy of her child-bearing to an alleged betrayal of her father James II, though it is more likely that poor medical attention and the high incidence of disease and infection in those days were responsible. Queen Anne has often been depicted as a woman without qualities, dull, sleepy, utterly lacking in intelligence. Seventeen pregnancies resulting in seventeen deaths assuredly accounts for much of her physical behaviour. Moreover, her critics have often failed to realize that under the reign of this queen, England would excel in culture – the names of writers like Daniel Defoe, Jonathan Swift, Joseph Addison, Richard Steele, and Alexander Pope, spring instantly to mind – in commerce; and in continental military power, thanks to Marlborough (who, in December 1702, was created Duke of Marlborough). Architecture has rarely flourished as it did during the reign of Queen Anne. She had the intelligence to realize her own limitations, and the sense to summon excellent advisers. One of these was Sarah, Duchess of Marlborough, who, as a long-time confidante and attendant of the Queen, was able to persuade her that Marlborough's actions would be to the lasting benefit of England. Moreover, it was Queen Anne who gave the Royal Assent to the Act of Union of 1707, which brought about

the legislative union of England with Scotland. In terms of the
effect of her reign upon our country, Anne is probably our most
underrated monarch, and her short reign one of the most felicitous
England has ever enjoyed.

But if England prospered both commercially and culturally
under her regime, there were also horrendous problems
concerning foreign policy. Marlborough followed Cromwell in
that he laid down a strategy which still endures today. English
foreign policy is based upon commercial rivalry and the
maintenance of a balance of power in Continental Europe. War
will only be essayed if either of these factors is threatened. In 1701
war did indeed threaten.

King Louis XIV of France had embarked upon a programme of
expansionism in order to make his country the dominant power in
Europe. He wished to take the United Provinces' land now known
as Belgium from the Dutch; to crush the power of Austria; to put
his ally, Maximilian, Elector of Bavaria, on the throne of the Holy
Roman Empire, thus ensuring that control of German lands
passed from the Habsburgs to the Wittelsbachs as French puppets;
and to put his grandson Philip on the throne of Spain so as to gain
all the territory, power and influence of the decaying Spanish
Empire. So began the curious War of the Spanish Succession.

Former enemies united. France and Spain, which had fought
each other for Contintental supremacy during the Thirty Years
War, now established a solid alliance. They were opposed by a
Grand Alliance of two groupings. The first of these was Austria,
where the Holy Roman Emperor Leopold I had an ally in the
Margrave Louis of Baden, whose forces blocked one route into
Austria from France. However, Austria was still open to attack on
three sides. In the east, Hungary was threatening revolt. To the
south, the Spaniards had possessions in northern Italy, enabling
their French allies to take the Po Valley and advance upon Austria
from there. On the west Bavaria, neutral for a time, was now
willing to join the Franco–Spanish forces in order to wrest what is
now Germany from Austria.

In the north, the second grouping, England and France,
formerly enemies, formed an alliance. Marlborough's objectives
were to check French expansion and secure English trade routes
and ports. To these ends, he employed the strategies of

international diplomacy backed by might both on land and at sea. His intentions were to block French ambitions in the Netherlands, destroy the Franco–Spanish power that threatened Austria, and expand English command of the sea, to which end he placed Admiral Rooke in command of the fleet – a wise choice, as it turned out.

Rooke has to be one of the most underrated commanders in the Royal Navy's history, though it must be said that his first attack, an attempt to take Cadiz in August 1702, was a disaster. He more than made up for this, however, in October by an assault on Vigo, in which fifteen major French ships were captured or destroyed, as was a Spanish fleet. This daring attack caused Portugal to defect to Marlborough's Grand Alliance. (Portugal's King Peter II agreed to import English cloth and export port cheaply, thus temporarily ousting claret as the favourite drink of the cultured Englishman.) Rooke then, on Marlborough's orders, escorted the Holy Roman Emperor's son, the Archduke Charles of Austria, to Lisbon in 1704 and proclaimed him King of Spain, in opposition to the Bourbon claimant, Philip, the puppet of Louis XIV; the rivalry between these purported Habsburg and Bourbon kings provoked an eight-year war in the Iberian peninsula. Nevertheless, Admiral Rooke proceeded to capture Gibraltar, which had neglected its defences, and repulsed a French fleet of relief under Admiral Toulouse, thus giving England command of the Mediterranean. It is a pity that Rooke's memory is not publicly honoured, since the part he played in Marlborough's land victories was vital, as the latter fully realized.

When Marlborough embarked to fight the might of Louis XIV, he could not fail to be aware of the changes which had taken place in warfare, and was quick to make use of them. The matchlock musket (in which a slow-burning fuse ignited the priming powder when the trigger was pressed) had been replaced by the much more efficient flintlock (in which the spark from a flint striking steel when the hammer fell ignited the priming), enabling a faster rate of fire and surer ignition, while the cumbersome pike had been superseded by the bayonet, attached to the musket's muzzle; Marlborough thus arming his men with two deadly weapons combined in one. He was also minutely attentive to the conditions of his troops, always ensuring that they were watered, well-fed, clothed, equipped and cared for when wounded. This did much to raise morale in what was now a professional army. He also reduced the harsh discipline of the lash, favouring encouragement over punishment, though this would not always obtain. An unknown British soldier writing from Gibraltar, under siege by the French, in 1727 records: 'April 12th. A recruit who refused to work, carry arms, eat or drink, was whipped for the fifth time, after which being asked by the officer he said he was now ready to do his duty.' This was mild compared to a case cited by Trevelyan: in 1712 a private in the Guards was sentenced to no less than 12,600 lashes, and was on the verge of death after the first 1,800. Marlborough discerned that such punishments were stupid, pointless and counter-productive, ensuring instead that his soldiers were looked after well. The troops loved him in return, and nicknamed him 'Corporal Johnny'; the honour of a general being called 'Corporal' affectionately and with respect by his troops would not be seen again until the days of Napoleon. Marlborough's eminently intelligent policies were to bear redoubtable fruit.

Besides his care for his men, Marlborough's strategy and tactics were revolutionary, for he was the first to seize upon opportunities offered by the improved technology of modern warfare. Previously it had been thought that the defence will always win in the end, given a strong position, and adequate supplies. In the seventeenth century, this had often led to siege warfare and complex manoeuvres without any engagements ensuing, intended only to display the force disposed: the resolutions of many battles were often political rather than military, with a dynastic marriage sometimes providing a solution to a crisis. Marlborough, however, was determined to employ military force, and to defeat the enemy in the field.

Heading the Anglo–Dutch forces, he invaded the lands of what is now Belgium, then ruled by the Franco–Spanish alliance, and by his aggressive tactics seized French fortresses on the River Meuse, thus giving the Dutch access to this river as a trade route. The Earl of Marlborough was promptly created a duke. Unfortunately, he found his Dutch allies almost impossible to work with, and told them so, writing to Anthony Heinsius, Grand Plenipotentiary of Holland:

'The difference of opinions, I am afraid will encourage the enemy, for it is most certaine they know all that passes here; so that if I might have millions given me to serve another year and be obliged to do nothing but by the unanimous consent of the Generals, I would much sooner dye....

Fortunately, Marlborough had a potential ally in Prince Eugène of Savoy, a Frenchman opposed to Louis XIV on dynastic grounds and consequently commanding troops of the Holy Roman Emperor, Leopold I of Austria. Prince Eugène, later numbered by Napoleon as amongst the seven greatest commanders in history, had liberated Hungary from the Turks in a campaign lasting from 1684–88, and by his subsequent victory at Zenta in 1697, put a stop to all further Ottoman Turkish invasions beyond the Balkans. During the War of the Spanish Succession, Eugène, badly outnumbered, fought with varying degrees of success against the Franco–Spanish armies in Italy until urgently recalled by the Emperor to defend Vienna. The French and the Bavarians were now marching in full strength, aiming to capture that vital city and so destroy Austria as a combatant. If Vienna fell, the war would be over.

Marlborough proceeded to break all the rules of war in his time by taking a colossal and calculated risk. His intention was to protect Vienna by marching his men across Europe to the Danube so as to link up with his allies, Prince Eugène, commanding the Austrian Army, and Louis, Margrave of Baden, who controlled a strategic position on the Rhine. In an astonishing piece of military daring, the English general took the high risk of marching his men across the southern German lands, exposing them to attack either by the armies of Marshal François Villeroi in the Netherlands, or of Marshal Tallard, who had positioned his troops so as to deter any action by the Margrave of Baden. This was the most rapid military march ever essayed until this time, though it was made easy by Marlborough's constant study of maps, and by his attention to the health and welfare of his soldiers.

The great march was so swift, and its commander so secretive, that not even his Dutch allies were sure whether Malrborough had headed for the southern Rhine, the Moselle or the Danube. Neither his allies nor his enemies were able to guess what he was about to do, nor could anyone believe that an army could march so fast. The best comment is surely that of Robert Parker in his *Memoirs of the Most Remarkable Military Transactions from 1638–1718*: 'Surely never was such a march carried on with more order and regularity, and with less fatigue both to man and horse.'

Confounding his enemies by feeding them deliberate disinformation and by constant switches of direction, Marlborough moved south-eastwards up the Rhine and took Coblenz in May, his troops now being joined by 5,000 Prussian allies. On 10 June, at Mondelsheim, he was joined by Prince Eugène and Louis of Baden, with their armies. On 2 July 1704, in a brilliant setpiece of siege warfare, Marlborough took the Schellenberg fortress, at Donauwörth on the Danube, by attacking it at its strongest point, the western flank, where assault was consequently least expected. This swift and sensational march of 250 miles had opened the way to Bavaria, a state that Marlborough wanted to knock out of the war. Having gained the vital bridges, he finally gave pitched battle to the alliance of France, under Marshal Tallard, and Bavaria under its Elector Maximilian, at Blindheim, known better as Blenheim, on 13 August 1704.

His clever capture of bridges had secured Marlborough's lines of retreat in case of defeat, a distinct possibility in view of the position of the enemy who, according to Winston Churchill, had 60,000 men to the 52,000 of John Churchill, Duke of Marlborough. Moreover, the Franco–Bavarian armies possessed the advantage of high ground, and the cover of woods, and the defensive obstacle of a river. Marlborough chose to use surprise, attacking at 2.00 am, so throwing the unsuspecting and unready enemy into confusion. This did not, however, prevent Tallard, assuredly one of the world's worst generals, from sitting down at 7.00 am and writing to King Louis XIV, informing him that his excellence in military skills had forced the Grand Alliance to withdraw.

The Franco–Bavarians had ninety cannon to the sixty-six the English could muster: yet Marlborough had discerned a fatal flaw in their defence. The French and Bavarian armies were drawn up side by side, with cavalry on each wing of each army, and infantry in the centre. This meant that in the centre, where the two armies joined, there were two wings of cavalry, a hinge between two bodies of infantry. It was this hinge of two cavalry forces that Marlborough intended to exploit.

His first move was directly to attack the village of Blenheim on his right, the most strongly defended bastion and the last place that the French would expect him to assault. Although Blenheim successfully resisted two assaults, the matter forced Tallard to transfer eighteen more battalions to the garrison, thus weakening his centre. After some difficult hours but with the able support of Prince Eugène, Marlborough managed to entrap more men in a besieged state in Oberglau, two miles west of Blenheim. On Marlborough's right, with the bulk of the enemy bottled up in two garrisons, Eugène could now make progress towards Lutzingen, a mile west of Oberglau, preventing all possibility of reinforcements reaching the weakened enemy centre, which could no longer hold.

At 5.00 pm, Marlborough commanded a massive assault upon the centre, and the French cavalry was forced to flee by the intensity of the Allied musketry. Eugène now advanced, after an afternoon's stiff fighting, to render hopeless the position of the enemy on Marlborough's right. The Franco–Bavarian armies fled, the few remaining troops prepared to stand and fight being slaughtered by the Allied armies. The garrison of Blenheim surrendered.

The Allies lost 4,500 killed and 7,500 wounded (including 2,000 British). The Franco–Bavarian alliance lost 38,609 men killed in action, drowned trying to escape, wounded, or made prisoner, including deserters.

Writing to his wife, whom he called his 'dearest soul', on the following day, Marlborough termed Blenheim 'as great a victory as has ever been known'. And so it was, for, as his descendant Winston Churchill stated: 'it changed the political axis of the world.'

The Battle of Blenheim completely wrecked Louis XIV's grand design to make Europe part of a French Continental empire. Had Marlborough lost his gamble, Austria would have been pushed out of the international picture and the Bavarian capital Munich, not Vienna, would have become the centre of the Holy Roman Empire, controlling the German state, and directly in thrall to the King of France. In addition, the victory ruined the plans of Louis XIV to place a Stuart king upon the thrones of both England and

Scotland as the puppet of France. In addition, the assiduously cultivated legend of the invincibility of the French armies was shattered.

Marlborough proceeded to make a friend of his most able ally, Prince Eugène, inviting him to inspect his cavalry escort.

'My Lord,' said Eugène, 'I never saw better horses, better clothes, finer belts and accoutrements; but money, which you don't want in England, will buy clothes and fine horses, but it can't buy that lively air I see in every one of these troopers' faces.'

'Sir,' Marlborough answered smartly, 'that must be attributed to their heartiness for the public cause and the particular pleasure and satisfaction in seeing Your Highness.' Eugène had discerned Marlborough's astonishing effect upon morale; yet the English general was ever a diplomat, as he showed when he entertained the defeated Marshal Tallard, captured towards the end of the Battle of Blenheim, whom he treated with the utmost courtesy and consideration.

'I am very sorry,' said Marlborough, 'that such a cruel misfortune should have fallen upon a soldier for whom I have the highest regard.'

'And I congratulate you,' Tallard responded, 'on defeating the best soldiers in the world.'

'Your Lordship, I presume,' Marlborough answered drily, 'excepts those who had the honour to beat them.'

Louis XIV now sought a peace that would allow him some honour, though he stubbornly refused to surrender on terms unfavourable to France. His country was still paying for this useless continuation of the war in 1789, long after his death, and the taxes were a contributory cause of the French Revolution, which began in that year. Marlborough responded to the 'Sun King's' challenges with his customary alacrity. At Ramillies in Flanders on 23 May 1706, he used his right wing to draw away the French left and then his cavalry, moving at the slow trot favoured by Cromwell, smashed its way through the French centre and was followed by the infantry, which drove the enemy from the field. This victory gave England control of Antwerp and Dunkirk.

At Oudenarde, also in Flanders, in July 1708, the commander of the French forces, Marshal the Duke of Vendôme, expected Marlborough to repeat his earlier tactics and so assaulted the

English general's weak right wing. However, quarrelling among Vendôme's subordinate commanders made for a botched job, causing fatal delay, for Prince Eugène arrived with his troops to reinforce that flank formidably. Vendôme had prepared for Marlborough to attack through the centre, which he had reinforced. The latter, however, showing his astonishing talent for improvisation in the field, left the centre to defend itself and enveloped the French army from both wings. It was a crushing victory, in which the English and their allies suffered 7,000 casualties, and the French 18,000.

There followed a period of squabbling between the members of the Grand Alliance, and Marlborough was forced to expend his substantial energies on political rather than military affairs. The Dutch declined to capitalize on his victories, refusing to give money badly needed for the campaign, thwarting Marlborough's own grand plan to invade France in alliance with Prince Eugène. In all probability, the Dutch were playing the English at their own game of maintaining a balance of power, having no wish to let England become too dominant in Europe. Nevertheless, Marlborough captured the manufacturing city of Lille in 1708, and subsequently laid siege to Mons.

On 11 September 1709, the Marshal the Duke of Villars, commanding, with the Duke of Boufflers, a French army, offered him battle at Malplaquet, some 10 miles south of Mons, which city was under siege from Marlborough's Anglo–Dutch–Austrian army. This time, Marlborough employed the tactics of Blenheim, using infantry on his flanks to draw away the French strength from its centre, and following this with a direct assault there by the 30,000-strong Allied cavalry. Villars, however, had foreseen the possibility of this move; when the French troops in the centre began to stagger, he promptly sent reinforcements. Marlborough responded by throwing his own last reserves into the centre of battle, and superior morale and training ultimately caused the French centre to collapse, though Villars withdrew in good order. On 26 October, Mons surrendered to the Allies. Nevertheless, the Allies suffered 22,000 casualties at Malplaquet compared to the 12,000 suffered by the French. As a result of the high casualties, the Allies were forced to abandon their plan to march on Paris, and Marlborough's political enemies were to use these losses to discredit him. Malplaquet was his last great battle.

The next few years were difficult for this splendid general. Queen Anne, who had Tory sympathies; Sarah, Duchess of Marlborough, a Whig supporter, and Abigail, Lady Masham – a cousin of Sarah's – replaced the latter as Her Majesty's confidante. In 1711, the Tories took power from the Whigs and announced a foreign strategy based on a 'blue water' policy: that is, British naval supremacy, as gained by Admiral Rooke in concert with Marlborough, would be enough to protect the realm, and therefore no further foreign land expeditions were required. Marlborough, accused in that same year of misappropriating public funds, was forced to resign his command and all his appointments. Retiring abroad in disgrace, he continued to intrigue and on the death of Queen Anne in 1714, played a part in ensuring that the thrones of England and Scotland went to the brutish boor, George, Elector of Hanover, who, once crowned as George I, promptly rehabilitated Marlborough.

Between April 1713 and September 1714, a series of treaties between the rival European powers, known collectively as the Treaties of Utrecht, had been signed, bringing to an end the War of the Spanish Succession. Although the terms did not amount to all that Marlborough had wished to accomplish, they were far more favourable to England than anyone could have hoped at the outbreak of the war and this was on account of his victories, which fundamentally altered the balance of power in the Western world.

There were six principal consequences of the War of the Spanish Succession deriving from the Treaties of Utrecht, which can be summarized thus:

1. Louis XIV recognized the Protestant succession in England.
2. Both England and France recognized Louis XIV's grandson, Philip of Anjou, as King Philip V of Spain and the Indies, albeit upon the condition that the crowns of France and Spain would never be united. In fact this gave the French a strategic victory, since Hapsburg rule in Spain was now replaced by Bourbon rule.
3. By way of compensation, Hapsburg Austria was given the Spanish Netherlands (Belgium), to be known for a time as the

Austrian Netherlands, as well as the Italian cities of Naples and Milan.

4. The United Provinces of the Dutch were recognized, as were their various Barrier fortresses.

5. England gained Nova Scotia, Newfoundland and the region around Hudson Bay encroaching Quebec from the French; and also Gibraltar and Minorca and Spain, thus confirming British dominance in the western Mediterranean.

6. England received the exclusive right to import black slaves into Spanish America for thirty years. This was a term of the Treaties which was to prove extremely favourable to the furtherance of England's commercial prosperity.

These were not the only legacies of the war, however. The power of international banking increased. King William III had spent £30 million in ousting James II. In the reign of Queen Anne, the twelve years spent fighting the War of the Spanish Succession cost roughly £50 million. Half the total of £80 million was paid for by taxation; the rest was borrowed on the National Debt, never to be fully repaid. The poverty of the present was thus underwritten by the prosperity expected in the future. This enabled the bankers to increase their influence, while that of the landed interests declined. Soon enough, the sons of bankers would be purchasing feudal lands and marrying the daughters of feudal lords who found thesmelves in straitened circumstances.

'*Qui risque rien, n'attrape rien*,' said Napoleon a century later, and Marlborough is a shining example of the audacity the French Emperor had in mind. His grasp of politics, strategy and tactics was unfortunately not shared by his allies, though it was appreciated by his soldiers, who chanted a folk song popular in its day, 'Lord Marlborough':

I was beloved by all my men
And Kings and Princes likewise.

Marlborough broke all the rules of tedious manoeuvre and siege, forcing the enemy to give pitched battle, at which, through his attention to the smallest details, he excelled. It is assuredly fitting that he was given Blenheim Palace and that his eventual descendant, Winston Churchill, rallied the nation in the Second World War, over 200 years later. It is unfortunate that his strategy of suddenly attacking at the strongest point of the enemy was so unwittingly pursued during the First World War. One suspects that Marlborough would have found a far better way to break through the lines.

13

Frederick the Great (1713–1786)

Frederick II of Prussia has been called the greatest general of his era by a great many commentators, including his successor to that claim, Napoleon. It is a reputation perhaps surprising in a king who wrote to his friend Voltaire, one of the greatest writers of his age: 'Have you forgotten that war is a scourge, which ... adds to them [his soldiers] all possible crimes?'

It is not easy to understand this man who deplored war, not only in his letters to Voltaire but also in his other published works, writing in his Military Instructions: 'With troops like these, the *world itself* might be subdued, if conquests were not as fatal to the victors as to the vanquished ... we must not satirise war but get rid of it, as a doctor gets rid of fever.' In one of his many poems, he calls Bellona, the Goddess of War, 'that woeful, wild woman, beloved of ancient Chaos ...' and describes battle as 'this brazen-headed monster, the War Demon athirst for blood and for destruction'. But for all his dislike of war, Frederick was the most aggressive commander of his time.

Perhaps an understanding of this most paradoxical of men is to be found in his reaction to his father, King Frederick William I, an absolute ruler of great energy, violence, brutality, and boorishness. This brute used to spit in his son's food in order to stop him from eating too much; once, having sentenced the young Frederick to death, he was thwarted by his ministers, and therefore forced his son to watch as he shot and killed his own friend Katte for the 'crime' of interceding for the boy. On another occasion, he tried to strangle his son with a curtain cord. This ornament to Prussian royalty died in 1740, to the regret of absolutely nobody; he did, however, leave Frederick II with a substantial inheritance.

The parsimony of his father had resulted in there being a substantial surplus in Frederick's Treasury. Moreover, Frederick William had been fanatical in the drilling of his Prussian soldiers, so much so that his troops came to regard action in the field as being vastly preferable to peacetime life in the barracks. Nevertheless, the result was that Frederick II inherited an army of 80,000 soldiers, the best-trained in Europe. He commented, with the cynicism that would always mark his thinking: 'If my soldiers began to think, not one would remain in the ranks.'

Frederick's first move on his accession was to consolidate his father's kingdom by breaking all his father's rules. All religious sects were to be tolerated since 'everyone must get to heaven in his own way'. His cynicism is apparent, though, in his instructions to his soldiers:

> If we are in a Protestant country, we wear the mask of protector of the Lutheran religion, and endeavour to make fanatics of the lower order of people, whose simplicity is not proof against our artifice. In a Catholic country, we preach toleration and moderation, constantly abusing the priests as the cause of all the animosity that exists between the different sectaries....

Having freed the press, Frederick encouraged the arts, something which included his notable and long friendship with Voltaire, funded scientific study, abolished torture, fed the poor freely and gave accommodation to elderly widows provided that they were willing to weave cloth to adorn the backs of soldiers and civilians in the expanding Prussia he envisaged. As Fuller rightly comments: 'He would seem to have been a mixture of Puck and Machiavelli welded together on the anvil of Vulcan by the hammer of Thor.'

'I and my people have come to a satisfactory understanding,'

Frederick declared: 'They say what they like and I do what I like.' This promptly led to his involvement in the War of Austrian Succession. Frederick agreed to recognize the Hapsburg claimant, Maria Theresa, daughter of Charles XII, to the throne of the Austrian Empire, provided that she would cede Silesia, then an Austrian province, to Prussia. When Maria Theresa refused this demand, knowing that she had the support of Saxony, Frederick went to war.

'The whole strength of our troops lies in attack,' Frederick pronounced, moving to assault his enemies before they had even begun to think of defence against him; 'and we act foolishly if we renounce it without good cause,' he added. Initially he succeeded in his invasion; but at Mollwitz on 10 April 1741, where his troops were commanded by Field Marshal Schwerin, the Prussian cavalry was routed and it was his finely trained infantry that brought about the Prussian victory. Always willing to learn by his mistakes, Frederick reformed the cavalry and, in winning the Battle of Chotusitz on 17 May 1742, gained Lower Silesia, which was duly ceded by Austria to Prussia at the Treaty of Breslau later that year. With this success, Prussia withdrew from the war, though it was only to be for a short period.

When discussing the possibility of perpetual peace with Voltaire, Frederick remarked, with his customary cynicism: 'The thing is most practicable, for its success all that is lacking is the consent of Europe and a few similar trifles.' In 1744, perceiving that Austria was planning in due course to retake Silesia, Frederick promptly anticipated the move and began his second campaign.

'What distinguishes Frederick the most,' Napoleon wrote, 'is not his skill in manoeuvring, but his audacity. He carried out things I never dared to do. He abandoned his line of operations, and often acted as if he had no knowledge whatever of the art of war.'

Tactically, this particular campaign met with mixed fortunes. On 2 September 1744, a lightning march by Frederick's forces captured Prague from the Austrians, but the supply lines were over-extended and he had to retreat. Austrian pursuit under Prince Charles of Lorraine was nevertheless brilliantly routed at Hohenfriedburg in Silesia on 4 June 1745. A second invasion of Bohemia was driven back by the Austrians, but at Sohr on 30

September 1745, Frederick inflicted 8,000 casualties upon them. Prussian command of interior lines of supply and communication enabled Frederick to use rapid, stabbing assaults against the Austrians and the Saxons at Hennersdorf on 23 November and Kesselsdorf on 15 December. Maria Theresa, realizing that she faced defeat at Frederick's hands, sought terms with Prussia. The Treaty of Dresden, later in the month, confirmed Prussian possession of Silesia, and added 16,000 square miles and 1,000,000 new inhabitants to Frederick's realm.

Frederick disliked long wars on account of their cost and the inevitable deterioration of soldiers during extended campaigns. 'An army marches on its stomach,' Napoleon is reputed to have said in later years; but Frederick had inticipated him, writing in his Military Instructions: '... battles determine the fate of nations ... the first object in the establishment of an army ought to be making provision for the belly, that being the basis and foundation of all operations.' Feeding armies in the field, however, was (and is) both difficult and expensive. Frederick must therefore have felt dismayed by the 'Diplomatic Revolution' which ushered in the Seven Years War of 1756–63.

Prince von Kaunitz of Austria, Maria Theresa's Chancellor of State, discerned an opportunity in the war weariness of Frederick, who had said: 'Henceforth I would not attack a cat except to defend myself.' He proposed an end to hostilities between Austria and France, and an alliance against Prussia between those two countries, and with the Tsarina Elizabeth of Russia, who wanted East Prussia; Sweden, which wanted Pomerania; and Saxony, which wanted Magdeburg. This put an alliance of 70,000,000 people against the mere 4,500,000 of Prussia.

Frederick promptly allied Prussia with England, which was keen to protect Hanover against French incursions, and also to bite away at France's colonial territories in Canada and India. The King of Prussia prepared for war in his customary thorough fashion, as the British Prime Minister William Pitt the Elder declared in Parliament: 'We shall win Canada on the banks of the Elbe'. Horse artillery, light cannon that could be brought into action – or out of danger – at speed, was one of Frederick's innovations, as was the Prussian drill that enabled his soldiers to fire their muskets three times faster than the enemy. He also employed to devastating effect the most powerful long-range cannon of his time, the howitzer, for the shelling of reserves held back out of battle by the enemy. Curiously enough, though, Frederick never grasped the use of light infantry. Although he defeated the Austrians at Lobositz in October 1756 and Prince Charles at Prague in May 1757, he lost the battle of Kolin in June the same year because the Austrians deployed Croatian light troops against him. Prussia, a landlocked state, now found herself surrounded on all sides.

It has been said that the best form of attack is defence: for Frederick and his embattled kingdom, however, the best form of defence was attack. The essence of his generalship was simplicity itself. He employed speed and mobility as his main assets, frequently feinting to the enemy's strongest point, and then wheeling his troops around and marching swiftly to assault his opponent's weakest point. This move, which became known as the Oblique Order, was explained by Frederick:

You refuse one wing to the enemy and strengthen the one which is to attack. With the latter you do your utmost against one wing of the enemy which you take in flank. An army of 100,000 men taken in flank may be beaten by 30,000 in a very short time.... The advantages of this arrangement are (1) a small force can engage one much stronger than itself; (2) it attacks an enemy at a decisive point; (3) if you are beaten, it is only part of your army, and you have the other three-fourths which are still fresh to cover your retreat.

'It is an invariable rule of war to secure your own flanks and rear, and endeavour to turn those of your enemy,' he also wrote.

'... You are never to imagine that *every* thing is done as long as *any* thing remains undone.... Those battles are best into which we force the enemy ... to oblige him to do that for which he has no sort of inclination and as your interest and his are diametrically opposite, it cannot be supposed that you are both wishing for the same event.'

'His Oblique Order,' Napoleon commented, 'could only prove successful against an army which was unable to manoeuvre.' His enemies were indeed unable to manoeuvre effectively, even though Frederick was in a perilous and parlous position, outnumbered in the field by at least three to one. In the north, the Swedes, once they had gathered their forces at Stralsund, would be 130 miles from his capital, Berlin; in the south, the Austro–Saxon armies would be forty miles from Berlin; in the east, a Russian crossing of the Oder would leave them fifty miles from Berlin; in the west, a French invasion at Halle would leave them one hundred miles from Berlin.

Frederick switched rapid attacks from front to front, frequently using bribery to neutralize an enemy temporarily. At Rossbach, twenty-five miles west of Leipzig, on 5 November 1757 he won a sensational victory against the Franco–Austrian armies, skilfully using both the advantage of his interior lines of communication and his Oblique Order, which the enemy endeavoured to copy in vain. The Prussians lost 165 killed and 376 wounded: their opponents lost 3,000 killed and wounded, 5,000 prisoners (including 8 generals and 300 officers), and 67 cannon, as well as large quantities of baggage and supplies. This tactical victory had tremendous strategic consequences.

The French army, the myth of whose invincibility had previously been shattered by Marlborough, now became an object of general ridicule. England, which had grudgingly voted Frederick £164,000 in 1757, now gladly gave him £1.2 million for the protection of Hanover and for other operations to keep the French diverted while British forces slowly took France's colonial possessions in Canada and India. Meanwhile, the French ceased their attempts to take German territory.

Now Frederick marched his men eastwards to Leuthen, near Breslau (Wroclaw, in what is now Poland). At Rossbach he had won with 22,000 men against 41,000. On this occasion, setting out from Leipzig on 13 November and marching his troops 170 miles in an astonishing 15 days, Frederick had 35,000 men and 167 guns to the Austrian army's 65,000 men and 210 guns. He relied upon the efficient military machine built upon the Prussian rank and file, who were treated as robots, instructed to 'Obey! Kill!! Die!!!', and upon the individual initiative he encouraged in his senior officers.

The situation did not look appealing, especially since a Prussian army had recently been defeated at Breslau. However, on 5 December Frederick promptly assaulted the village of Borne, three miles north-west of Leuthen, and captured it; the Austrian General Nostitz, mortally wounded, was captured, as were 800 of his men. More important, Frederick now had a perfect vantage point from which to survey the deployment of the Austrian troops to the east.

What followed was a masterpiece of battle. Frederick knew the terrain well, for he had frequently conducted military exercises upon these very lands. Calculating coldly, he sent his advance guard forward against the Austrian right, instructing them to stay out of range of musket fire. Count Lucchessi, in charge of this wing of the Austrians, promptly decided that this was Frederick's major thrust and begged urgently for his commander-in-chief, Marshal Daun, to despatch strong reinforcements. Daun promptly sent his reserve cavalry and part of the cavalry from his left wing.

Discerning that he had fooled Daun, Frederick immediately ordered the main body of his troops to wheel right and go south from Borne to assail the weakened Austrian left. Daun was initially complacent. 'The Prussians are off,' he said happily, 'don't disturb them.' In fact the Prussians were marching directly across the Austrian front, concealed by the wooded hills that Frederick knew so well. Just after 1.00 pm, the Prussians burst upon the unsuspecting Austrian left wing and destroyed it.

Frederick had deployed his men in two parallel columns, each of four groupings. He did not have them engage the Austrians all at once, but in a series of stages, which meant that wave after wave of fresh troops fell upon the enemy. A desperate Austrian cavalry attack was repulsed, Daun's once orderly columns disintegrated, and his troops retreated to Leuthen itself, where they were bottled up in ineffective formations. At 3.30 pm, Frederick ordered a heavy artillery bombardment of the village, at what was effectively a sitting target, followed by an infantry assault. It has been said by some that the artillery secured the victory; whatever the truth of that, Leuthen was taken after half an hour.

Determined not to admit defeat, the Austrians bombarded Frederick's soldiers with their own artillery and Lucchessi launched a cavalry attack on what he suspected would be Frederick's weakened left wing. He had reckoned without the mobility of Prussian forces. He had also reckoned without the individual initiative of General von Driesen, commanding the Prussian left wing, whose timing was perfect. Suddenly Lucchessi found himself assailed from the south-west by Driesen's forty cavalry squadrons, the bulk of which struck him dead centre, while the Bayreuth Dragoons assailed his flank and the Puttkammer Hussars savaged his rear. Lucchessi was killed and his troops fled as the victorious Prussian cavalry launched itself on what remained of the Austrian infantry and scattered them like seeds of grass. By nightfall, with the enemy's retreat a rout, Frederick had gained his greatest victory.

The Prussians had suffered some 6,400 casualties. The Austrians had lost 10,000 killed and wounded, 21,000 prisoners, 116 guns and 4,000 wagons. Frederick promptly took the small town of Lissa, three miles east of Leuthen, which he found crowded with fugitives, including many Austrian officers. 'Good evening, gentlemen,' he said to them, 'I dare say you did not expect me here. Can one get a night's lodging along with you?'

Here Frederick displayed his chivalry, yet it is often difficult to resolve the peculiar paradoxes of his character, sometimes humane, on other occasions ruthless. He declared: 'To shed the blood of soldiers, when there is no occasion for it, is to lead them inhumanely to the slaughter ... though our wounded are to be the first objects of our attention, we are not to forget our duty to the enemy.' Splendid words indeed, yet during the First Silesian War, when Frederick had demanded that all lights be extinguished on pain of death, he had found one Captain Zietern writing a letter by candlelight to the wife he adored. 'Sit down,' said Frederick, 'and add a few words I shall dictate.' The officer obeyed and, at the king's dictation wrote: 'Tomorrow I shall perish on the scaffold.' Captain Zietern was duly executed on the next day.

Frederick the Great's ruthlessness also provoked him to pursue his advantage after Leuthen. Breslau, scene of an earlier Prussian defeat, was swiftly recaptured on 19 December along with 81 guns; the Austrians, who had already lost roughly a third of their army, now lost a further 17,000 men.

'A masterpiece of movements, manoeuvres and resolution,' Napoleon said of Frederick at Leuthen; after that battle no force would ever seriously threaten the existence of Prussia again until the time of Napoleon. At Rossbach, Frederick's opponents had lost the battle by endeavouring to emulate his tactics, but instead displaying only gross inefficiency and utter incompetence. At Leuthen, however, Frederick proved his right to be accounted among the greatest of generals. He had demonstrated beyond all reasonable doubt that, given an intelligent commander, a small force can defeat a larger one. As is so often the case, Fuller puts it perfectly: 'At Leuthen, Frederick moved, concentrated, surprised and hit.' Yes. He adds: 'Nevertheless, above all, what gave Frederick the victory was that his men had confidence in him as a general.'

Despite these splendid victories, the Seven Years War continued. 'In war the skin of a fox is at times as necessary as that of a lion,' Frederick wrote, 'for cunning may succeed where force fails.' Cunning was certainly necessary. Frederick defeated the Russians at Zorndorf on 25 August 1758, but could muster only 37,000 sorely wearied troops against the 90,000 gathered by France, Russia and Austria at Hochkirchen where, on 14 October 1758, he was defeated. Even so, he recovered and forced the Austrians to quit not only Silesia but also Saxony.

Disaster followed against the Russians at Kunersdorf on 12 August 1759, where the Prussian army suffered 20,000 casualties, and after which the Russians occupied the capital, Berlin. Frederick refused to admit that the war was lost, and managed to keep the French at bay; he also managed to rebuild and replenish his forces. Victories against the Austrians at Liegnitz on 15 August 1760, and at Torgau on 3 November 1760, bought him time as, meanwhile, the Russian supply lines began to collapse. Fortuitously for Prussia, in 1762 the Tsarina Elizabeth of Russia died and Frederick promptly made peace with her successor, Peter III, an admirer of the Prussian king, who was thus able to reoccupy Berlin. Sweden too decided to leave the alliance and make peace with Prussia. Frederick remained indefatigable and indomitable, even though his ally, England, abandoned him, also in 1762. (This proved to be a serious error on England's part, for she was left without European allies when, thirteen years later, the War of American Independence started.) Although he had always favoured the rapid offensive, he now turned his attention to defence, building strong fortifications which he termed 'the mighty nails which hold a ruler's provinces together'. His attention to base camps enabled him to make rapid strikes to the south and west, winning victories at Burkersdorf on 21 July 1762, and Freiburg on 29 October, enabling him to obtain favourable terms for Prussia under the Treaty of Paris, signed in 1763.

Prussia was now firmly established as a great Continental land power, despite all endeavours by numerically superior enemies to put an end to its very existence. In addition to the defeat at Hochkirchen, when he had been outnumbered by 90,000 troops to his 37,000, Frederick had nevertheless won at Zorndorf against 52,000 to his 36,000; lost at Kunersdorf against 70,000 to his 26,000; won at Liegnitz against 90,000 to his 30,000; and won again at Torgau, when his 44,000 men had defeated 65,000 Austrians. As a commander, he would never admit defeat while there was any hope of success, even when the military situation would have appeared hopeless to any neutral observer.

Frederick's desperate defence of his kingdom from 1756 to 1762 may perhaps be accounted a finer piece of generalship than his superb offensive victories at Rossbach and Leuthen. After the Seven Years War, he reigned in peace for another twenty-three years and was called 'an enlightened despot', who often chose to spend his time writing poetry and discussing philosophy. His countrymen called him 'the Great', and it is certain that the foundations of German nationalism were built upon the history of his reign, and especially upon his military success. In time, and because of his wars, the centre of political gravity in the German lands would shift from Austrian Vienna to Prussian Berlin; when Germany was finally united, it was Prussian militarism that was to inspire her ambitions.

The soldiers of the Prussian Army, which Frederick had made the finest in the world, venerated their king to such an extent that they would not, and did not, alter the tactics he had drilled into them, something of which Napoleon took brutal advantage in 1806. Nevertheless, it was Napoleon, thinking of what he called 'two o'clock in the morning courage', who wrote of Frederick: 'He was above all great in the most critical moments, this is the highest praise one can make regarding him.' The French Emperor added: 'It is not the Prussian army which for seven years defended Prussia against the three most powerful nations in Europe, but Frederick the Great.'

14

Napoleon Bonaparte (1769–1821)

Few men have affected the world as much as Napoleon Bonaparte of Corsica. Volumes have been written in analysis of his personality, his campaigns, his strategy and his tactics. Here it is only possible to give a succinct summary of the salient points.

From humble beginnings as a lieutenant of artillery – a weapon which he would later use to such notable· effect – in the French Revolutionary army, Napoleon became for a time master of the continent of Europe, and was hailed as the greatest general since Alexander. To what extent, however, is the legend which surrounds him justified or justifiable?

Most military historians agree that although he was an innovative master of strategy, Napoleon's tactics were baased on those of Frederick the Great. There appears to be some mistake in this analysis. Frederick drilled his troops to perform as automata; Napoleon demanded individual initiative. Frederick was as attentive to the needs of his troops as Napoleon, but relied upon supply lines and depots: Napoleon, whilst realizing that 'an army marches on its stomach', encouraged his soldiers to live off the lands through which they marched, thus obviating the need for depots and leaving the supply lines free for arms, ammunition and equipment. Napoleon had no patience with the formal gallantry of the early years of his training, in which infantry engaged infantry, cavalry fought cavalry, and artillery fired against artillery: he was fully prepared to use artillery to shoot down both cavalry and infantry. In 1793, his superb command of the guns at the major French port of Toulon, under siege by the British, broke the siege and brought him promotion to the rank of general.

It was as a senior commander that he proved himself to be quite outstanding. His brilliant grasp of propaganda and his own conviction that he was a man of destiny inspired his troops. Furthermore, he had good material to hand in the French Revolutionary armies. The mathematician and military engineer Lazare Carnot (1753–1823), member of the Revolutionary Convention and Minister of War from 1800, had mobilized an entire nation in an unprecedented manner. 'The young men will fight,' said Carnot,

> the married men shall forge weapons and transport supplies; the women will make tents and clothes and will serve in the hospitals; the children will make up old linen into lint; the old men will have themselves carried into public squares and rouse the courage of the fighting men....

This call to arms resulted in the recruitment of 1 million men who believed with passion in the causes of France and of 'Liberty! Equality! Fraternity!', rather than simply seeking a few coins a day.

Given this army, with its exceptionally high morale, and supported by a nation whose morale was also high, Napoleon proceeded to prove himself to be among the very greatest generals of all time. Like Frederick the Great, his field strategy in any battle was simple. He manoeuvred his divisions into a position of superiority at a *key point* on the enemy line, and struck there with all his strength. He held that the aim of battle was not primarily to conquer territory but to destroy the opposing force; after that, the taking of territory could be resolved by peace treaties advantageous to the victor.

Speed and surprise were the keys to Napoleon's victories. He possessed – usually – an uncanny knack for outguessing his opponents, anticipating their moves. His mastery of the topography of any terrain astonished his commanders, as did his astounding capacity for work and his attention to every detail, administered through a system of command, subjugated to him, which assisted his rise as much as it would contribute to his fall.

His belief that 'every private soldier carries a field marshal's baton in his cartridge pouch,' further raised the morale of his troops; he based promotion, not upon influence, wealth, or family connections, as was traditional at that time, but upon merit. In 1799, he had introduced the notion of the all-arms corps – a self-contained body combining infantry, cavalry, artillery, engineers, transport, supply, and medical services, as well as ancillary services such as those dealing with discipline and pay – consisting of two or more divisions, permitting deployment along several axes of advance, supported by squadrons or companies of skirmishes to harass the enemy's more formal, and therefore rigid, columns and lines. A collage of quotations from Napoleon probably displays the essence of these matters:

> In the art of war, as in mechanics, time is the grand element between weight and force.... One should never try to guess what the enemy can do.... It is an axiom in strategy, that he who remains behind his entrenchments is beaten; experience and theory are at one on this point.... In short, I think like Frederick, one must always be the first to attack.... A General requires two o'clock in the morning courage.... Truth alone wounds.... The fate of a battle is a question of a single moment, a single thought.... the decisive moment arrives, the moral spark is kindled, and the smallest reserve settles the matter.... There is a moment in engagements when the least manoeuvre is decisive and gives victory; it is the one drop of water which makes the vessel run over....

In 1795, Napoleon assisted the Directory, then ruling France, with a 'whiff of grapeshot' from the cannon he commanded to rout a disorderly pro-Royalist mob. The Directory responded by placing him in command of the Army of Italy; and Napoleon promptly crossed the Alps to win victories at Lodi in 1796 and Rivoli in 1797 against the Piedmontese and Austrians, giving France the dominant position in the Italian north. A bold strike against Vienna compelled the Austrians to make peace on terms favourable to the French.

Napoleon now perceived that the greatest enemy of his ultimate grand design was England, whose aims were incompatible with those of France. As Fuller rightly states: 'To remain prosperous and powerful, England had to export her manufactured goods, and to become prosperous and powerful, France had to protect her infant industries.' Napoleon began to ponder the possibility of invading England but meanwhile decided to strike at her Eastern trade. To this end he arrived in Egypt with an army in July 1798, defeating the native Egyptian force at the Battle of the Pyramids. As we shall see in the succeeding chapter, England's Admiral Nelson put an end to this audacious plan by his equally bold destruction of the French fleet at Aboukir Bay, close to the harbour at Alexandria.

Returning to France with his objective unattained, Napoleon nevertheless emerged from the *coup d'état* of 9 November 1799, which overthrew the Revolutionary government, as First Consul of France. The Austrians had again declared war, but although outnumbered by two to one, Napoleon won a narrow victory at Marengo on 14 June 1800, thus further consolidating the French hold on Italy. This victory forced an uneasy peace upon the Allied anti-French coalition in 1802. Napoleon used it to tighten his hold on France and *her* allies, and on 2 December 1804 had himself and his wife Josephine crowned Emperor and Empress of the French. As the Emperor, he formulated the *Code Napoléon*, still the basis of the modern French judicial system; reformed the civil service, centralizing all major administrative power in Paris; and concluded a Concordat with the Pope in Rome, thus winning over his Catholic subjects and providing his propaganda machine with a platform within every Catholic church in France and the territories under her rule.

His appetite for hard work, which led him to attend to the smallest details both civil and military, was prodigious. His soldiers thought that he was an infallible genius; and so did he. A growing fear among other European states of his increasing influence led to the formation of a Third Coalition against the expanding might of France: England, Austria, Prussia and Russia. Napoleon resolved upon invading England but, as we shall see,

Nelson put paid to this plan by his crushing naval victory over a combined French and Spanish fleet at Trafalgar on 21 October 1805, leaving England supreme at sea. Napoleon's response was his endeavour to become supreme on land.

'It is impossible to have too many men on a battlefield,' he maintained, yet when he moved into Moravia against Austrian and Russian armies, he was outnumbered. Mack, the Austrian commander, promptly threw away this advantage. Instead of waiting for the support of Kutusov, commanding the Russian forces, he adopted a careless and sloppy battle position on the erroneous assumption that Napoleon would be advancing through the Black Forest. As a result Napoleon won a slashing victory at Ulm on 20 November 1805, forcing Mack to surrender.

Napoleon now marched at the armies of Kutusov and the Austrian commander Weyrother. Sensibly, Kutusov retreated, falling back on his own supply lines, thereby shortening them while those of Napoleon became perilously extended. Weyrother now decided that it was time to strike and on 2 December 1805, the Battle of Austerlitz commenced. The Austro–Russian forces had 85,200 men and 278 guns compared to the 73,000 men and 139 guns of the French. Their plan was to assault Napoleon's right wing, turn the flank and roll it up to the north. However, an assault on his right, across the River Goldbach, was precisely what Napoleon wanted, since it would enable him to launch a counter-attack elsewhere. French defences on the right held strongly, forcing the allies to transfer reinforcements there from the centre, precisely as Napoleon had hoped. A blistering assault was promptly launched upon the Austro–Russian centre and after fierce fighting, the key positions on the Pratzen Heights were taken by the French.

Napoleon now essayed a push by his left wing and a savage cavalry battle followed. Slowly the French pressed forward – very slowly. This was not what Napoleon had originally intended, and he now showed his ability to improvise brilliantly. From the French positions, the Pratzen Heights were some distance forward of the River Goldbach, where Napoleon's right was being pressed. Using the Heights as a pivot, therefore, he wheeled his central corps around to take the allied forces attacking his right from the rear, as his right wing, till then on the defensive, suddenly flung its forces into an attack, catching the allied armies in a sandwich. The latter broke, variously opting for pell-mell retreat, or slaughter, or surrender. By the end of the day, there were 27,000 Austro–Russian casualties to 8,300 French. A few days later, Austria requested an armistice, which was granted on terms which temporarily but effectively negated her influence. 'Roll up the map, Mr Speaker,' Prime Minister Pitt the Younger lamented in the House of Commons, 'it shan't be wanted these ten years.'

This sensational victory was followed by a campaign against Prussia. Napoleon's mobility was astonishing. Whereas the Prussian armies, a worthy but somewhat pallid reflection of what they had been under Frederick the Great, marched an average of thirteen miles a day, Napoleon's corps managed distances of more than twenty-five miles in twenty-four hours. Nevertheless, unimaginative though the Prussian Army was, it numbered 200,000 men, the bulk of whom were drawn up at Jena and Auerstadt. Believing mistakenly that the main Prussian force was at Jena, Napoleon attacked there on 14 October 1806 and won a devastating victory through overwhelming numerical superiority. Meanwhile, he had sent Marshal Davout to Auerstadt, where he found his 26,000 men and 44 guns ranged against 60,000 Prussians with 230 guns. Incredibly enough, Davout exploited the mistakes made by an incompetent Prussian high command bedevilled by petty rivalries and won a dazzling victory, though he was never to receive his just share of the credit for it. Perhaps Napoleon felt that Davout was merely an extension of himself.

The French Emperor immediately consolidated the victories with a series of brilliant strokes, capitalizing on Prussian confusion, destroying all resistance and taking Berlin on 27 October 1806, having forced one fortress after another to capitulate. In just twenty-four days he destroyed Prussia and Saxony as military powers, killing and wounding 25,000 men, taking 100,000 prisoners, and in Berlin alone seizing 4,000 cannon, 20,000 horses and 100,000 muskets.

With Prussia defeated, Napoleon fully expected England to come to terms. Here, however, he was mistaken. England could not allow him to bestride the continent of Europe like a colossus; nor, moreover, would she let France threaten British exports. Napoleon therefore resolved to impose his Continental System by the Berlin Decrees of 21 November 1806, of which Article 1 declared: 'The British Islands are declared in a state of blockade.' From this moment on, any ally of France had to accept that. Any country that did not was thereby an enemy. Britain responded with Orders in Council promising confiscation of ships and cargo of any neutral countries trading between ports in the possession of France. Britain also used the power of the purse to subsidize and encourage her last leading land ally, Russia, whose Tsar Alexander I desired to continue mutually advantageous trade with the British.

After a harsh and savage winter campaign, Napoleon finally managed to bring the Russians to battle at Eylan on 8 February 1807. A raging blizzard did not assist either the soldiers or the calculations of the French Emperor and after a bloody, brutal but indecisive engagement, the Russians retreated calmly and steadily, allowing the winter to do its worst. This was the first time that Napoleon had not won a pitched battle outright, but remaining unperturbed, he besieged the Baltic port of Danzig and, by his skilled employment of artillery, forced its capitulation. The Russian commander Bennigsen then made a fatal error in deciding to attack, since Napoleon had by then replenished his army's supplies. On 14 June 1807, the French destroyed the Russian army at Friedland. The Tsar at once sought an armistice and an alliance with France.

The Treaty of Tilsit of 27 July 1807 between France and Russia, and on 9 July between France and Prussia, gave Napoleon the realization of his vision as Master of Europe. Having defeated Austria, Prussia and Russia, he could mould the Continent according to his heart's desire. Essentially, he wanted to create a United States of Europe under French hegemony, an object still sought, albeit through political and economic means, by some French politicians to this day.

It seemed as if Napoleon were invincible on land. He forced Prussia to cede all of her territory west of the Elbe and reduced her to half her former size. Poland, a weak kingdom which between 1772 and 1795 had been partitioned between Prussia, Russia, and Austria, was now the Grand Duchy of Warsaw ruled by a Franco–Russian alliance. Having earlier abolished the Holy Roman Empire, Napoleon created the Confederation of the Rhine, giving him domination of the western German lands and of northern and southern Italy; the Middle Papal States had been secured in alliance by his Concordat with the Pope. And the Russians agreed to close the Baltic Sea to English shipping. Like Napoleon himself, his soldiers thought him infallible.

It was this belief in his own infallibility that provoked Napoleon's future ruin. He became convinced that everything he did was right simply because he did it. Tightening his grip upon the Continental System, he warned Denmark to deny her ports to English shipping. When Denmark complied, the Royal Navy bombarded Copenhagen on 2 September 1807, without so much as a declaration of war, seizing seventy warships (the Danish fleet had already been decisively defeated by the English, under Nelson, on 2 April 1801). Since Denmark immediately declared war on England, Napoleon's strategy might be thought astute. On 12 December 1804 Spain declared war on England. Portugal, however, England's oldest ally, did not want the same fate to befall her own fleet; consequently her ports remained open to British shipping. Napoleon now made a serious error of judgement. He sent armies into the Iberian Peninsula with two aims: the first, to put his brother Joseph on the Spanish throne; and the second, to compel the submission of Portugal. French troops arrived in 1807–8, to be met with fierce resistance from Spanish guerrillas and from the Portuguese, to whom the English sent an army. The Peninsular War was to last six years and eventually tie down half a million French soldiers who could have been better employed elsewhere.

The power of English money remained. Austria suddenly arose and marched against him once more. Napoleon responded by defeating an Austrian army at Eckmuehl on 22 April 1809, inflicting 40,000 casualties on the Austrians. On 13 May, a bloody engagement against the Austrians at Aspern–Esseling brought Napoleon within an eyelash of defeat; not for nothing did he reply, when musing upon whether to promote a colonel to general: 'Is he lucky?' The Austrians hoped he might abandon Vienna, which he had entered on 13 May, but unexpectedly crossing the Danube, he attacked at Wagram on 5–6 June. In this stiff battle of attrition Napoleon employed the greatest barrage of artillery any soldier had ever experienced and though the losses on both sides were high, the Austrian armies under the Archduke Charles were eventually scattered. The resulting Treaty of Schoenbrunn forced Austria to cede territories to France, Russia, Bavaria and Saxony and to pay an indemnity of 75 million francs.

From the British point of view, Wagram and its consequences were an absolute catastrophe. Napoleon cemented his position by divorcing Josephine and marrying the Archduchess Marie Louise, daughter of the Austrian Emperor Francis I (in 1800, the Holy Roman Emperor Francis II, perceiving the approaching end of the empire, had himself proclaimed Francis, Emperor of Austria. The Austrian, later Austro–Hungarian, Empire dates from that proclamation). This dynastic alliance pleased Russia. A treaty was signed between France and Sweden, and in August 1810 the Swedish Diet (parliament) recognized Napoleon's man, Marshal Jean-Baptiste Bernadotte, as heir apparent to the throne of Sweden and declared war on England. Holland was annexed by Napoleon on 9 July 1809. This was an excruciatingly severe blow to English trade. Bankers like Sir Francis Baring and similar mercantile interests saw a real possibility of English national bankruptcy and made every endeavour to avert it by exerting the strongest possible financial pressure on Tsar Alexander I, who eventually relented of his support for Napoleon's blockade under the Continental System and, in 1810, opened Russian ports to English goods, which action led to increasingly acerbic relations between Napoleon and Russia.

'War will occur in spite of me,' Napoleon sighed – ruefully, since he desired peace with Russia, the country which held the key to the ultimate success of his Continental System and blockade of the British Isles – 'in spite of the Emperor Alexander, in spite of the interests of France and the interests of Russia.... It is all the scene of the opera and the English control the machinery....' He added later: 'Russia was the last resource of England. The peace of the whole world rested with Russia. Alas! English gold proved more powerful than my plans.'

Napoleon proceeded to assemble the largest army of invasion ever seen in the history of the world, 435,000 men with 165,000 reinforcements. The weather conditions, a combination of scorching sun alternating with driving rainstorms which churned the ground to mud once the River Nieman was crossed on 24 June 1812, rendered the invasion pitiably slow. It took three months for the advance guard to march just 560 miles. The Russians retreated, scorching the earth behind them as they did so, their irregular partisans continuously harassing French supply lines. Disease was already rife among the French Grand Army, and was to claim many more victims than battle. Nevertheless, Napoleon held to his conviction that he was a God-given man of destiny. Having reached Smolensk, he could not, as some military historians have claimed, have improved his army's situation by retiring into winter quarters, for he had no means by which he could keep his troops adequately supplied. He could either abandon the campaign, giving the strategic victory to England, or else march on to take Moscow and force the Tsar to come to terms. He had also to bear in mind that if the Tsar lost, he was still the Tsar: the position of Napoleon as Emperor depended upon his victories.

Napoleon undertook the gamble, but his Grand Army could muster only 120,000 men against roughly the same number of Russians, under Kutusov, at Borodino, seventy miles west of Moscow, on 7 September 1812. This battle, which lasted fifteen hours, was bitter, savage and indecisive. The French lost 28,000 men; the Russians 40,000. The latter retreated again, but not in rout, and over the next month were able to re-form. Napoleon pressed on in pursuit and, offered no resistance, took Moscow on 14 September. The Russians had abandoned the city; 80 per cent of the population had fled, leaving only beggars and criminals deliberately released from gaols. Fire broke out, by what cause is not known, but the Russians had thoughtfully provided for that eventuality by removing all hoses and pumps. In five days, three-quarters of Moscow was razed to the ground. As the ruins blazed, the Tsar sent word that he would not make peace at any price. On 19 October Napoleon, realizing that it would be impossible to hold these smoking ruins during a Russian winter whilst keeping his troops supplied and reinforced, called for a retreat, also ordering that the city should be stripped bare. The spoils included 150,000 horses and 40,000 carts, but the Grand Army's disciplined retreat soon declined into a disorderly rout.

At those depots, established during the advance into Russia, which still remained defended, most of the supplies had been consumed during the advance and subsequent operations. On 9

November, the first French troops reached Smolensk – which they themselves had burned down less than three months before – and in three days promptly ate supplies planned to last for two weeks. There was nothing left for those who came after them. It had begun to snow on 4 November, and on the 14th the temperature fell to minus 16 degrees centigrade. As the troops huddled together for warmth, lice jumped between them and typhus spread rapidly. On 28–29 November, the Russians launched a counter-stroke against the half-paralysed Grand Army as it attempted the crossing of the River Beresina, and the French suffered a further 25,000 casualties. By 14 December, the Grand Army had been reduced to just 10,000 effective troops as it limped back to France, its men dying as, starving, exhausted and sick, they fell out along the road. On 18 December, the Emperor's carriage took him through the Arc de Triomphe: it was, however, the first time in his reign that he had not entered Paris in triumph.

This catastrophe did not deter Napoleon from raising yet another army of a quarter of a million men. Such a force was essential to his survival, since England and Russia were endeavouring to capitalize upon his defeat and the crisis that followed it. An extraordinary blaze of nationalist fervour consumed Prussia, exciting its leaders to seek another alliance with England, while Austria cautiously edged her way towards joining this coalition.

It has been argued by leading military historians that here, Napoleon fought a defensive campaign of such genius as to rival his previous masterpieces of aggression at Austerlitz, Jena-Auerstadt, Friedland and Wagram. Certainly he managed to inspire his troops with his desire to crush his enemies and destroy the last vestiges of feudalism, which he wished to see replaced by a pan-European meritocracy. His strategic aims were hampered by the repeated victories of Wellington in the Peninsula, a war which looked likely to threaten southern France, drove the French back towards their homeland, and which deprived him of troops he so urgently required.

The campaigns of 1813 were hardly easy for Napoleon. The French armies were operating on hostile territory, rendering it difficult to establish and maintain adequate supplies, and to extract information about their enemies. As Fézensac declares in

Souvenirs Militaires de 1804 à 1814: 'His orders had to be executed whatever the means of command. This habit of undertaking everything with insufficient means, this determination not to recognize any impossibilities, this boundless assurance of success, which in the beginning were the causes of our triumphs, in the end became fatal to us.' Napoleon proceeded to combine within himself the roles of Commander-in-chief and Chief-of-Staff, working for twenty hours a day at the two tasks, a feat many think to be impossible. That last word, however, did not exist in Napoleon's vocabulary. 'The change from a defensive to an offensive attitude is one of the most delicate of operations,' he had stated, and now he reversed those attitudes. Moreover, his newly recruited young soldiers were as eager to fight for their Emperor as had been their fathers. The legal and social reforms, the Imperial encouragement of science, art and industry, all following the sweeping reforms of the Revolution, had created a better society within France. As a result, her soldiers were prepared to follow Napoleon anywhere.

A series of brilliant victories by Napoleon, most notably at Bautzen which left open Berlin to his forces, caused the Tsar to seek an armistice, to which Napoleon acceded. Many historians have seen this as a terrible error, since he had by his victories reduced the allies to an appalling position. It has been held that one more battle, holding the centre and turning the right flank, could have won him the war. Perhaps this was so: but Napoleon was in no position to do that. By this time, 90,000 of his men were suffering from disease. His losses in battle exceeded his enemies' by more than 25,000. His lines of communication were continually disrupted by Cossacks and allied partisans; on 30 May 1813, for instance, a French artillery convoy had been captured near Halberstadt. Moreover, his cavalry, was presently too weak to bring about a decisive action, he only had ammunition for one day of battle, and, owing to the speed of his march, his supply columns could not provide him with enough to attempt the *coup de grâce* he desired.

England promptly exploited Napoleon's temporary weakness, giving Russia and Prussia £2 million to continue the war, and offering Austria £500,000 should she declare it. Sweden, too, was won over to the Allied cause. Austria then offered France a treaty under which Prussia was to recover all possessions lost since 1805; and Napoleon's creations of the Grand Duchy of Warsaw and the Confederation of the Rhine were to be abolished. This, obviously, would have destroyed the Continental System Napoleon had devised for Europe. The French Emperor therefore refused these terms, the armistice ended, and France, with 442,000 men, found herself assailed by a coalition of England, Prussia, Russia, Austria and Sweden, whose forces comprised 184,000 Russians, 162,000 Prussians, 127,000 Austrians, 39,000 Swedes and 9,000 'Anglo–Germans', a total in the field of 521,000 soldiers, backed by 143,000 reserves and another 112,000 in defending the fortresses of Prussia and Bohemia.

At the Battle of Leipzig, known as the 'Battle of the Nations', on 18 October 1813, which lasted until the following day, Napoleon was decisively defeated by overwhelming weight of numbers. Typically, he retreated and then, despite the disastrous defeat, undertook a series of skilful campaigns to protect eastern France despite his disastrous defeat at Leipzig. There is a chance that these might even have succeeded had not Wellesley smashed through the last French forces confronting him in the Peninsula and, on 10 April 1814, taken Toulouse in southern France. Faced with invasion by Russia, Prussia, Austria, Sweden and England, Napoleon had no alternative but to abdicate. On 11 April 1814 he went into exile on the island of Elba, a few miles off Italy's west coast.

Subsequent quarrels among the Allies gave Napoleon another opportunity. He escaped from Elba in February 1815 and landed in the south of France. Near Grenoble, he single-handedly confronted a regiment of French soldiers who had been detailed to capture him. Striding towards the soldiers' bayonets, he threw open his grey overcoat, bared his breast and asked the troops to 'fire upon your Emperor!' It says much for his charisma that they flung down their muskets and joined him. Next day, he won over another regiment and began to march on Paris, prepared now to retake Europe. 'Before Grenoble,' Napoleon mused, 'I was only an adventurer. After Grenoble, I was a Prince.'

The Allies, profoundly shocked by their adversary's return to power, moved as swiftly as they could to counter this threat as Napoleon, beginning his rule of the 'Hundred Days', as it became known, rallied France once more. The eventual result was the battle of Waterloo against Wellington (who had been raised from Marquess to Duke after his victory in the Peninsula) of England and Marshal Gebhard von Blücher of Prussia, which Napoleon lost for reasons which are described in the subsequent chapter on Wellington. The French Emperor was now exiled to the lonely island of St Helena, in the South Atlantic, where he died in 1821.

There have since been allegations that the British slowly poisoned Napoleon by the steady introduction of tiny doses of arsenic into his food, and this contention receives some support from forensic evidence based upon a scientific analysis of the former Emperor's hair. Certainly the British were happy when 'Boney' died; but it is difficult to see any reason why they might have been worried by his continuing existence on St Helena, an island too remote for sensible escape, its sole approaches guarded by the most powerful navy in the world. Perhaps, though, since Napoleon in exile worked to rebuild the myths and legends surrounding him which he himself had garnered and garnished, his British captors saw in the ex-Emperor a threat similar to that in the twentieth century posed by the exiled Trotsky to Stalin, who had his rival assassinated in consequence. It is difficult here to discern the precise truth, which in any case can never now be proved, one way or the other.

The military and administrative genius of Napoleon has never been in dispute. His vision of a United States of Europe led by the French is still promoted, albeit in political and economic, rather than military, terms to this very day. Paradoxically, those of his policies which were designed to curb the growing power of England in fact led to the precise opposite. Nevertheless, he remained, even in defeat, venerated by his countrymen, and the Napoleonic myth he established was to fuel two more revolutions in France, in 1830 and 1848, the latter of which led to his nephew, Charles Louis Napoleon Bonaparte, being made first President of France, and then in 1852, being proclaimed the Emperor Napoleon III, a venture which ended in the fiasco of the Franco–Prussian War of 1870.

The average citizen of France and her subject or conquered territories was in fact much better off than he or she had been under the previous, more repressive, regimes of the French monarchs. Napoleon was rarely a brutal tyrant, save in his brutal suppression of the black slaves' revolt in Haiti; his troops were also guilty of atrocities in Spain against the guerrillas and anyone thought to support them. Even so, the memory of Napoleon remained to inspire not only the French people, but also generations of military strategists. As he himself had said – words which he might himself have heeded during his abortive invasion of Russia, which ultimately brought about his downfall – '*Truth alone wounds.*'

15

Horatio, Viscount Nelson (1758–1805)

Nelson was arguably the greatest naval commander the world has ever seen: a pedant, however, might argue that whatever his many virtues, he has no place in a book about military (i.e. land) commanders. However, it is essential to include him, however briefly, since without him, Britain's Continental victories in the Napoleonic Wars, the rise to pre-eminence of her navy, and her eventual triumph over France and her allies would not have been possible.

Horatio Nelson was dastardly and audacious both in love and in war. He also applied his brain, both in terms of intellect and of intuition, to master the skills of seamanship, gunnery, and everything else that went with the naval warfare of his time. His personal courage astonished even the boldest. His practical skills terrified his enemies. He inspired his sailors by a similar sort of charisma which distinguished Napoleon, and in common with the French Emperor, he promoted his subordinates according to merit and made his captains feel part of a team, dedicated to a shining ideal. Unlike Napoleon, however, who wanted his juniors (which, in his case, was everybody in France and French-held territories) to obey his instructions and copy his own plans of battle, Nelson demanded individual initiative.

Certainly, and again in common with Napoleon, Nelson had his faults. He could be vain, pugnacious, over-ambitious, egotistical, and, on occasion, was given to making major mistakes, though the latter was something which, once realized, he always made every effort to rectify. The poet Lord Byron, later to perish as a warrior in Greece, had written: 'A man has two faces: one to show the World; and the other to show a woman when he loves her.' Perhaps Nelson had three (or even more) faces, given this account by Wellington, then General Sir Arthur Wellesley, concerning a conversation of 1805: '[He talked all about himself ... and really, in a style so vain and silly as to surprise and almost disgust me.' When Wellesley/Wellington (typically) finally made his own identity known, the manner of Nelson altered dramatically. 'A more sudden and complete metamorphosis I never saw,' the general commented, '... I don't know that I ever had a conversation that interested me more.... [I] should have had the same impression of a light and trivial character that other people have had, but luckily I saw enough to be satisfied that he was really a very superior man....'

Wellington recognized that Nelson's virtues far outweighed his vices. Those virtues included a mastery of both strategy and tactics at sea based upon seamanship, speed, a single-minded desire to destroy any enemy fleet he confronted, and an intuitive ingenuity which enabled him to adopt unplanned tactical innovations in the midst of battle, thus utterly confounding his opponents.

Nelson's rise in the Royal Navy was swift, for he rose to the position of post-captain before his twenty-first birthday in 1779, having seen service in the Arctic and the West Indies. In 1793, he was finally promoted full captain and given command of HMS *Agamemnon* for Mediterranean operations, one of which, the occupation of Corsica in 1774, cost him the use of his right eye. Appointed to the rank of commodore in 1796, Nelson played a vital and distinguished part in the victory of Admiral Sir John Jervis over the French off Cape St Vincent on 14 February 1797. In his *Nelson the Sailor*, Captain Grenfell called his brilliantly brave contribution: 'a piece of individual initiative ... unsurpassed in naval history ... an act of supreme valour'.

Rightly promoted rear-admiral and knighted, in July 1797 Sir Horatio Nelson lost his right arm in an abortive endeavour to capture Tenerife. Nothing daunted, he resolved to make the Mediterranean secure for British interests by ruining Napoleon's attempt to take Egypt and, he hoped, Syria, and thus cut British trade routes. Sailing from Toulon, Napoleon's fleet initially managed to evade Nelson, landing a French army safely in Egypt, but Nelson pursued it to Aboukir Bay, a few miles north-east of the harbour at Alexandria, and opened battle there on 1 August 1798.

Risking the fire of the shore batteries, Nelson positioned his thirteen ships to block the French fleet from reaching the safety of the harbour at Alexandria, and sank or captured eleven out of the opposing thirteen French warships. The defeat at Aboukir Bay (also known as the Battle of the Nile) was a disaster for Napoleon, who was forced as a result to abandon his Middle Eastern campaign; moreover, Britain now reasserted her naval command over the Mediterranean.

Nelson was perhaps compensated for the head wound he had received in the battle by his elevation to the peerage as Baron Nelson of the Nile. The King of Naples created him Duke of Brontë in return for his assistance (Naples, then a separate kingdom, had allied herself with Austria against France), and it was here that he indulged in his celebrated affair with the beautiful Emma, Lady Hamilton, wife of the British Ambassador to the Neapolitan Court, the tolerant Sir William Hamilton, Emma's senior by some thirty years. Nelson was recalled to active service in 1801 and promoted to vice-admiral. His behaviour at the first Battle of Copenhagen on 1 April 1801, an action aimed at neutralizing the Danish fleet, has passed into legend. When his superior, Admiral Sir Hyde Parker, ordered him to break off the action, due to stiff Danish resistance, Nelson placed his telescope against his blind eye, professed that he could not see the signals from the flagship, and went on to win yet another devastating victory. His initiative, his disobedience, and his resounding triumph earned him a viscountcy. The phrase 'to turn a blind eye' entered the English language, its immortality assured.

Nelson's greatest challenge came in 1805. Promoted to command in the Mediterranean in 1803, he had become bored by a task which was little more than the simple organization of an efficient blockade of southern French ports. Napoleon planned to invade England, transporting his armies in flat-bottomed barges across the English Channel from Boulogne. The terrain of South-East England – that is, the area which allows the shortest crossing from France – makes for poor defensive ground in which to fight an invader. The British therefore relied for their main defence upon the Royal Navy holding the Channel, and to this end positioned a strong force – the Channel Fleet, under Admiral the Hon. William Cornwallis – to the west of the Channel's Western Approaches, off Ushant, to deter any French fleet. Napoleon knew that if only this defence could be broken, his troops could invade England in relative safety.

Both sides now engaged in an extraordinary series of manoeuvres. For once, the Admiralty was right, and Nelson wrong. The former was convinced that the French threat lay in a heavy attack by the combined fleets of France, Spain and Holland to achieve naval supremacy in the English Channel, thus enabling Napoleon's crossing by sea and subsequent invasion. By contrast, Nelson was convinced that the primary thrust of French naval and military operations lay in the Mediterranean, and misguidedly moved there.

There followed a series of confused messages, which show that neither side seemed to be precisely sure of what it was doing, let alone to have any estimation of its adversary's intentions. Eventually, Nelson pursued the Franco–Spanish fleet, under Admiral Pierre de Villeneuve, to the West Indies. This was precisely what Napoleon had desired, for he now hoped that Villeneuve could outsail Nelson, make for Brest, and there form an allied fleet fit enough to storm, by sheer weight of numbers, the British fleet in the western Channel under Cornwallis.

Unfortunately for Napoleon, Villeneuve, who would have made an eminently capable chief of staff, was not up to the job of commanding the French fleet in action at crucial moments. He had no confidence at all in Napoleon's plan to invade England, and was terrified of engaging Nelson in the pitched battle the latter so desired. Villeneuve therefore retired, back across the Atlantic, to Cadiz. Nelson missed him in the West Indies, and failed to catch him on the way back eastwards. That was Villeneuve's only luck, however. His French and allied Spanish commanders and sailors appeared to be engaged in a series of perpetual quarrels. To his dismay, the Emperor ordered him to break out: 'Our intention is that wherever you meet the enemy in inferior force you will attack them,' Napoleon wrote, 'without hesitation and obtain a decision against them. It will not escape you that the success of these operations depends essentially on the promptness of your leaving Cadiz.'

Obeying his orders, Villeneuve reluctantly put to sea, which was just what Nelson wanted.

As a commander, Nelson always wanted to destroy any enemy fleet he encountered. He intended to do just that now, even though he had twenty-seven ships to the Franco–Spanish fleet's thirty-three. Had Nelson but known it, he was at an additional disadvantage, for Villeneuve had predicted his enemy's tactics with remarkable accuracy. 'The British Fleet will not be formed in a line of battle parallel with the Combined Fleet.... [Nelson] will seek to break our line, envelop our rear, and overpower with groups of his ships as many of ours as he can isolate and cut off.' This was Nelson's plan exactly – and neither Villeneuve nor his captains had the tactics or the ability to counter it. Eventually, and with much difficulty owing to almost windless conditions, the Combined Fleet formed a series of inefficient battle lines off Cape Trafalgar on 19 October 1805.

By contrast, Nelson spoke with the utmost confidence to his admirals, commodores and captains. His plan posessed a characteristic simplicity, obeying some of the established rules of naval engagements of the day, but breaking others. He had discerned the flaw in the theory that a line of ships, firing in broadside (in the day before rotating gun turrets, a ship's main armament could only be brought to bear on an enemy abeam, or a few points ahead or astern of abeam), could deter an enemy, since the cannons of the day were so inaccurate that their real danger lay only in the last hundred yards or so of an attack, as the opposing ships closed. Dividing his fleet into two, he aimed to drive at the enemy's fleet in columns, rather than sailing alongside it, as was traditional. His plan was to have the capable Admiral Collingwood, commanding the right-hand column, take the Franco–Spanish fleet in the rear whilst he, dividing his own column, split the enemy's forward centre with a left hook and a right hook. Nelson wanted, indeed, demanded, close engagement. The Royal Navy's gunners had been trained, during long, tedious years of the blockade, to fire twice as rapidly and twice as accurately as their opponents. This ability effectively gave any English warship the firepower of two enemy ships of the same number of guns. Moreover, Nelson ordered the two columns of the English fleet to attack in random groupings which would completely confuse the Franco–Spanish fleet. It was on this occasion that his captains acclaimed 'the Nelson touch'.

The British sailors were rallied by Nelson's signal: 'England expects that every man will do his duty.' They knew that their commander, wounded often and with only one eye and one arm, was always the first in battle. Nelson wanted 'an electric shock' to promote 'a pell-mell battle. Breaking all the established rules of the naval engagements of his day, he sent in frigates.

A pell-mell battle certainly developed once Collingwood assaulted the rear of the enemy. Although fire from several enemy ships reduced Collingwood's flagship, HMS *Royal Sovereign* to a battered dismasted hulk, the same fate befell the giant Spanish flagship, the *Santa Ana*, which surrendered. Collingwood, his own ship taken under tow by HMS *Euryalus*, thereafter sent in ship after ship to assail the enemy with a continuous concentration of firepower. Nelson then attacked the rear of the enemy's vanguard, his flagship, HMS *Victory*, placed at the head of his left column. Again there was a pell-mell battle, one which was decided by the superiority of English gunnery and seamanship. The line of the Franco–Spanish fleet was broken in two, and the bravery of the French and Spanish seamen could not repair that breach. Once the English gunners had the enemy ships in range, the outcome of the battle was a foregone conclusion, as Nelson had forecast.

Unfortunately for Britain, Nelson insisted on parading in his full-dress uniform, wearing all his orders, on the top-deck of his ship so as to inspire his men. Such a glittering and important target could not long escape, and he was hit by a musket ball as he walked with Captain Hardy on the quarterdeck. This ball, fired by an unknown sniper perched in one of the masts of the French ship *Rédoutable*, penetrated his chest and lodged in his spine at around 1.30 pm. 'They have done for me at last, Hardy ... my backbone is shot through!' Nelson gasped. He was carried below, and died around 4.30 pm; by then, however, he knew that a counter-attack launched by France's Dumanoir had failed, and that the Battle of Trafalgar was won.

'Trafalgar was really the decisive battle of the Napoleonic War,' H.W. Wilson wrote in *The Cambridge Modern History*. It is easy to see why this should be so. The victory gave Great Britain naval supremacy which would last for a century, enabling her to impose a *Pax Britannica* equal in effectiveness to the fabled *Pax Romana*. Trade was good for Great Britain, and peace was good for trade; it followed, therefore, that there should be peace throughout the world. The seal was set on this by Wellington's defeat of Napoleon at Waterloo in June 1815. Had it not been for Nelson's victory at Trafalgar, Wellington's Peninsular campaign, which had its true culmination in Belgium, at Waterloo, could not have taken place.

At Trafalgar, Villeneuve lost 18 out of 33 ships, and 14,000 men. The British, by contrast, suffered 1,500 casualties and did not lose a single ship, though a number were severely damaged. Many may forget the precise details of Nelson's astonishing victories, but no one, whatever their country of origin, who walks in London will ever forget Trafalgar Square and the glorious sight of Nelson's Column.

16

Arthur Wellesley, Duke of Wellington (1769–1852)

Military historians still argue as to who was the greatest British general of all time: Marlborough or Wellington. The education of the latter at Eton was not graced by any particular distinction, though he is alleged to have said later that 'The battle of Waterloo was won on the playing fields of Eton.' (Whether by this comment he referred to strategy, tactics or brutality is not known.)

In any event, the British system whereby officers were able to buy their commissions enabled Arthur Wellesley to become a lieutenant-colonel at the age of twenty-five by 1794. Commanding the 33rd Foot against the Dutch and French Revolutionary Armies in the disastrous Walcheren campaign of 1794, he observed: '[This taught] what one ought not to do, and that is always something.'

He next proceeded to make his mark in India, winning victories over Tippoo Sahib, whose forces were allied to the French, at Seringapatam in 1799, and over an alliance of maharajas at Assaye in 1803. Knighted and promoted major-general, and having, by his experience, honed his skills in command and in the use of topography, he was sent on the expedition to Copenhagen and won a victory against the Danes at Kiöge in August 1807. In

1808, he was promoted lieutenant-general and sent to Portugal in command of a British force to support that country against French invasion, winning tactically sound victories against the French at Roliça and Vimeiro in August. The negotiation of a disgraceful armistice by incompetent advisers, which Wellington signed, and which allowed the French to withdraw rather than surrender, led to the equally disgraceful convention of Cintra, under which it was agreed to transport the beaten French troops back from Portugal to their homeland in British ships. Wellesley was replaced and sent home, where he was acquitted by a court martial. Napoleon promptly took advantage of English stupidity by a renewed attempt to conquer the Iberian Peninsula, as General Wellesley had forecast.

Wellesley's replacement was Lieutenant-General Sir Harry Burrard, who in turn, and still in 1808, was superseded by Lieutenant-General Sir John Moore. Moore, with pitifully few resources, and heavily outnumbered, made an excellent job of harassing the French, cutting their lines of supply and communication, and raised a corps of swift-marching, lightly armed skirmishers – the light infantry – for the purpose, which more than proved its worth. He learned in December, however, while campaigning in Spain, that both Marshal Nicolas Soult and Napoleon himself were seeking to destroy his force. Vastly outnumbered, Moore, learning that Napoleon had already occupied Madrid and cut off the British line of retreat to Portugal, organized a daring fighting retreat through the mountains of north-western Spain, to the port of Corunna. There, turning on the harrying French forces, he defeated Marshal Soult on 16 January 1809, but was himself unfortunately killed in the battle. Corunna saved the British expeditionary force, which there embarked safely for England. Moore had also fanned the flame of Spanish resistance, and diverted Napoleon from menacing southern Spain. 'We'd not have won, I think, without him,' Wellesley subsequently commented, for in 1809 he was again sent to command the British troops in Portugal.

Wellington's command (he was created Viscount Wellington in 1809) of the Peninsula Campaign must assuredly rank among the finest feats of generalship. He demanded obedience rather than individual initiative from his troops: in return, he was minutely attentive to matters of food, health and supplies. In common with Napoleon, he united within himself the positions of both commander-in-chief and chief of staff, though he was dealing with a much smaller army. Unlike Napoleon, however, Wellington usually preferred common sense and reason to intuition and imagination. This habit of mind in Wellington led Napoleon to regard him as being no more than a cautious and sensible defensive general. For once, Napoleon was badly wrong.

Wellington was a brilliant tactician. He capitalized upon the stolid steadiness of the English soldier, realizing that French troops tended to lack those qualities, whatever their courage and daring. He discerned that the musket was a useless weapon at a distance but could be deadly at close quarters. (John Moore's creation, the light infantry, were armed with the far more accurate, though slower to load, Baker rifle.) He therefore positioned his infantry in two lines, enabling each rank to fire a volley while the other reloaded. Knowing that his resources were slender, Wellington was sparing of the lives of his troops, and in return they applauded him. His army, he said, was composed of the 'scum of the earth'; many forget, however, that he added: '... and it really is wonderful that we should have made them the fine fellows they are....' Of his subordinate generals: 'When I reflect upon the characters and attainments of some of the general officers of this army ... I tremble; and as Lord Chesterfield said of the generals of his day, "I only hope that when the enemy reads the list of their names, he trembles as I do." '

He cut the leave of his officers to forty-eight hours behind the lines since in his view, this was as long as any reasonable man could wish to spend in bed with any woman. Eventually the troops and his enemies came to respect, and the former even to revere, 'the Iron Duke', who declined the officers' pastimes of drink and the gaming tables in favour of discreet womanizing and military victories.

As a tactician, and in common with Napoleon, Wellington exploited the topography of an area, frequently using the cover of natural features in order to surprise and confuse the enemy. At Busaco, Salamanca, and even Waterloo, his opponents mistook his centre for its right. His custom was to choose a good position and then encourage the enemy to attack. Superior positioning and excellent British musketry at short range would then bedevil the oncoming enemy troops; Wellington would then take advantage of their confusion by ordering a bayonet charge. However, since in the Peninsula he was usually outnumbered by figures varying from two to five to one, the war there proceeded slowly.

In 1809, Wellington defeated Soult again at Oporto in Portugal, then proceeded to invade Spain, co-operating with the Spanish rebels. Unfortunately for him, these were of poor quality, and although he won the victory at Talavera on 28 July, he had to retreat back to Portugal. There he reorganized the Portuguese army under the capable Major-General William Beresford (who was seconded to that army, in which he held the rank of marshal), training its divisions to become 'fighting cocks'. For his endeavours, Wellington was made a viscount.

In 1810, the French, under Marshals Michel Ney and André Masséna, assaulted Portugal once again. Having proved himself as an attacking general, Wellington now displayed a genius for the defensive. He ordered his troops to build three lines of trenches and defensive fortifications at Torres Vedras, across the neck of the peninsula which has Lisbon situated at its south-eastern end. The narrowness of this peninsula negated French numerical advantage, while the defences at Torres Vedras protected the Portuguese capital from attack by land. At Busaco in 1810, the Anglo-Portuguese armies made a sortie from their fortifications and, skilfully positioned in line on the top of a steep ridge, forced back the intruding French columns. Wellington then scorched the earth before and behind him and retreated to the lines of Torres Vedras. There, supplied by the Royal Navy, he was able to leave the French to forage for food as best they could, continually harassed by the Spanish guerrillas with whom Wellington was building cautious alliances. On this matter, Wellington could not lose. If the French somehow managed to take the first line of the Torres Vedras defences, he would order a retreat to the second, and if the second were taken, he would retire to the third. If the worst came to the worst, he could simply sail away with his army, courtesy of the Royal Navy, now supreme at sea, thanks to Nelson, and return again at some moment inconvenient for the French.

The French had no answer to Wellington's defensive strategy

other than reinforce their armies, which were dying of starvation and disease. Wellington now showed himself to be superb on the offensive. Pushing north-eastwards from his fortifications in 1811, in May he won a tough battle at Fuentes de Oñoro, just across the border in Spain, effectively destroying the French threat to Portugal and driving them from that country. He now set about ending the French threat to Spain and in 1812, made lightning strikes, unparalleled in audacity, on 'the keys to Spain', the border fortresses of Ciudad Rodrigo and Badajoz, which he took, consolidating his gains by an awesome victory at Salamanca on 22 July 1812. On 12 August his army entered Madrid. That year, too, he was made an earl, then a marquess.

Having forced the French effectively to abandon southern Spain, Wellington retired to winter quarters in Portugal. He attacked again in 1813, and won a splendid victory at the battle of Vitoria in June. Now wielding the baton of a field marshal, Wellington chased the French troops into the Pyrenees, then broke through to invade France in 1814, taking the south by his defeat of Soult at the battle of Orthez and at Toulouse on 10 April. What happened next is well told by Elizabeth Longford:

> An hour after Wellington's entry into Toulouse while he was dressing for a dinner he was to give in the Prefecture, Colonel Frederick Ponsonby galloped in from the royalist town of Bordeaux.
>
> 'I have extraordinary news for you.'
>
> 'Ay, I thought so,' [said Wellington] 'I knew we should have peace; I've long expected it.'
>
> 'No; Napoleon has abdicated.'
>
> 'How abdicated? Aye, 'tis time indeed.'
>
> Suddenly the penny dropped.
>
> 'You don't say so, upon my honour! Hurrah!' The Commander-in-Chief, still in his shirt sleeves, spun round on his heel snapping his fingers like a schoolboy.

Wellington was elevated to a dukedom and hailed throughout Europe as 'the conqueror of the conqueror'. In August 1814 he became British Ambassador at Paris, and in February 1815 he represented Great Britain at the Congress of Vienna, intended by the Austrian Foreign Minister, Prince Metternich, to be 'the Concert of Europe'. This intended concert, attended by representatives of the four victorious powers, Britain, Austria, Prussia and Russia, and by those of France and the Papacy, sat from September 1814 to June 1815. However, it became somewhat out of tune when Napoleon escaped from his exile in Elba in February 1815 and proceeded to regroup his forces, hoping and believing that by mastery of the interior of France, he could divide and defeat the Allied Forces. Tsar Alexander I declared to the newly created Duke: 'It is for you to save the world again.' In consequence, Wellington assumed command of the Allied forces at Brussels in April. The two most outstanding commanders of the time were now, finally, to be drawn into pitched battle.

The place chosen was Waterloo, north of Charleroi and on the road to Brussels. Napoleon's strategy was to divide and separately defeat Wellington's Anglo–Dutch army and the Prussian army of Blücher, enabling him to take Brussels, upon which he was marching, and arouse Belgium in his cause. It seemed as though Napoleon might succeed when, on 16 June 1815, he sped through the separate armies of Wellington and Blücher, defeating though not destroying the Prussians at Ligny, while Ney forced Wellington to retreat at the indecisive engagement of Quatre Bras.

'War is mainly a catalogue of blunders,' Sir Winston Churchill wrote; and now both Wellington and Napoleon made grievous errors. The latter intended to continue with his 1813–14 strategy of relying upon interior lines of supply and communication, and his first great error lay in the appointment of his subordinate generals. Marshal Louis Berthier had been an able chief of staff and Napoleon's closest collaborator, but when he was accidentally killed on 1 June, Napoleon chose Marshal Soult to replace him. Soult could capably command an army in the field, but he had no experience of staff work, and his inefficiency would adversely affect the campaign. In later years Napoleon declared that Soult did not do his job well. To command the cavalry on his right wing, he chose Marshal Emmanuel Grouchy rather than Marshal Joachim Murat, regretting that mistake in later years, since Grouchy had never even commanded a corps; in exile on St Helena, Napoleon informed the historian Emmanuel, comte de

Las Cases, that he would have won had he only appointed Murat. He expressed a similar regret over his choice of Ney to command the left wing. 'It was a great mistake to employ Ney', Napoleon later admitted. However, the greatest mistake of all was not to use the skills of Marshal Davout, who against all the odds had won such a devastating victory over the Prussians at Auerstadt in 1806. Instead, Napoleon made him Governor of Paris. 'But sire,' Davout protested, 'if you are the victor, Paris will be yours, and if you are beaten, neither I nor anyone else can do anything about it.' Napoleon unwisely ignored this objection. As the *Memoirs* of General the marquis de Caulaincourt, Napoleon's Foreign Minister, declare: 'He had a wholly incalculable antipathy for any thoughts or ideas about what he disliked.'

Meanwhile, Wellington was making his own blunder. He had in his Anglo–Dutch army a force somewhat inferior in size to that with which he had fought the Peninsular War: roughly 49,000 infantry, 12,500 cavalry and 7,000 artillery with 246 guns. By contrast, Napoleon had the same number of infantry, 16,000 cavalry and 7,250 artillery, also with 246 guns, outnumbering Wellington's forces by nearly 4,000 men. Wellington was relying on being reinforced by the 89,000 Prussians, led by Marshal Blücher, a capable general, but these were in retreat from Ligny, pursued by Grouchy. Moreover, Blücher was renowned for bravery and determination rather than brains. As a result Wellington placed 17,000 men with 30 guns under Prince Frederick of the Netherlands to guard the Mons–Brussels road, a wholly unnecessary action, condemning one-quarter of his force to pointless inaction, troops which would be sorely missed at Waterloo.

The fascination of Waterloo lies not only in the action, but also in the skills of the two opposing generals. The essence of generalship is not found only in calculation, essential though this is. It is vitally a matter of will and idea; as Wellington later said, Waterloo was 'a damned near thing – the nearest run thing you ever saw in your life'. It is clear from the account by General the Earl of Uxbridge, commanding the British cavalry and horse artillery, that on the eve of the battle that was to determine the fate of Europe, Wellington had decided on no plan in particular other than to use his comprehension of topography to place his troops in advantageous defensive positions. Uxbridge, his second-in-command, visited him on 17 June to ask after his plans, and had the following conversation:

'Who will attack the first tomorrow, I or Bonaparte?' Wellington demanded.

'Bonaparte.'

'Well,' the Iron Duke replied, 'Bonaparte has not given me any idea of his projects: and as my plans will depend upon his, how can you expect me to tell you what mine are?' Napoleon, as always, wanted to seize the initiative; Wellington wanted to counter-punch.

Wellington drew up his lines on a narrow front south of the village of Mont St Jean, his troops mainly positioned on a low ridge running roughly north-eastwards from the Château of Hougoumont to his right, past the farmhouse of La Haye Sainte in his centre for another mile and a quarter, concentrating his men in the centre of this short front on a battlefield of which the maximum width was only four miles. Napoleon's aim, given that he was a master of concentration, was simply to smash this centre.

At 11.00 am on 18 June 1815, Napoleon began the battle, just as Wellington had predicted, though his opening artillery bombardment did little damage to the carefully placed Allied troops. Napoleon now essayed a diversionary attack on his enemy's left at Hougoumont, led by his brother Jerome. It was intended not to be a full-scale assault, but to draw troops from the English centre. However, in the event it had the effect of drawing in more French troops: the garrison held out and Jerome had to pour in two further divisions to no further avail. These soldiers could have been used better elsewhere on the field. In a tactical blunder, the French tried successive attacks by waves of infantry, trying to determine the outcome by musketry rather than destroying the buildings with artillery. At one point there was an especially daring assault in which the French broke into the courtyard, as is described by Elizabeth Longford:

> Pandemonium broke out. The defenders slashed and hewed at the invaders in desperate hand-to-hand duels. But the real thing was to prevent any more of the enemy from entering the yard. Five powerful Coldstreamers ... threw themselves

bodily against the huge door and slowly, slowly, by main force pushed it back against the pressure outside. This done, they turned their attention to the invaders ...

'The success of the battle of Waterloo depended on the closing of the gates of Hougoumont.' So said Wellington afterwards.

As repeated and futile attacks upon Hougoumont failed and ate up French forces, Napoleon resolved upon a central assault. His intention was to use his artillery to force the enemy to remain in their lines, a formation which minimized losses in such bombardments. In the next move, the advancing cavalry would compel the opposing infantry to form into squares, then the securest formation with which to meet attacking horsemen. Squares, however, are vulnerable to the fire of artillery and, because each side presents only a quarter of its available firepower, to advancing infantry. Napoleon's intention was by this means to throw the Allied forces into total confusion and then break through with infantry charging with the bayonet, while his cavalry cut down any enemy troops in retreat.

Wellington anticipated these tactics and kept the bulk of his men lying down *behind* the ridge, where they were relatively immune to the French artillery bombardment. When the enemy's infantry finally came within range, the British arose on command and discharged volleys of fire into them. The French assault was stopped dead. A counter-charge by the British cavalry routed this wave of attack, though La Haye Sainte was coming under overwhelming attack from the French on Wellington's left. Unfortunately for the British commander, the initially successful cavalry charge of Somerset and Ponsonby ignored Uxbridge's orders to regroup and retire and were driven back in disorder and with heavy losses by a French counter-attack, in which Ponsonby was killed. This misuse of the heavy cavalry, destroyed when, their horses blown from the charge, they were caught by enemy lancers, left Wellington without effective horsemen.

By 3.00 pm, both Napoleon and Wellington were anxious. Wellington had lost 2,500 cavalry in that disastrous charge and Blücher appeared to be advancing at the pace of a tortoise. Napoleon, meanwhile, was desperate to win the victory before the

Prussians could arrive. Marshal Ney consequently doubled the assaults on La Haye Sainte, in the hope of capturing the farmhouse and using it as a pivot for further French assaults. Ney was encouraged by the sight of massed wagons leaving the field and mistook what was in fact the wounded being borne away for a general retreat. On his own initiative, he threw in his cavalry, not on Wellington's left at La Haye Sainte, as Napoleon had ordered, but at the centre. This attack, sorrowfully inept, was launched without either infantry or artillery support. Wellington's forces remained in place, desperately holding the ridge until Blücher should arrive. Instead of perceiving his error, however, Ney kept making futile cavalry charges against unbroken British squares. While French troops were slaughtered by heavy and accurate musketry, Wellington was always visible and at the centre of the action, riding from position to position, constantly encouraging his troops. One staff officer stated: 'While he was there, nothing could go wrong.'

'Hard pounding, this, gentlemen,' the Duke said to his officers, 'hard pounding; try who can pound the hardest', and 'Stand fast. We must not be beat – what will they say in England?' At another moment, a member of his staff pointed out that there was a distinct view of Napoleon and that the guns of a nearby battery were in range and aimed in that direction. It was a tempting target, but 'No! no! I'll not allow it,' the Iron Duke exclaimed. 'It is not the business of commanders to be firing upon each other.'

Between 4.15 and 4.30, a massive French cavalry attack was launched on the centre between La Haye Sainte and Hougoumont. With cries of '*Vive l'Empereur!*', the French horsemen assaulted the front line of the English artillery. There then occurred an astonishing example of military ineptitude. Ney had not thought of providing extra horses to drag the guns away, nor were there any tools to spike the touch-holes of these guns, thus making them unserviceable, not even nails and hammers, which could have done the job adequately. English grapeshot wrought havoc among the French cavalry, and it can be argued that for want of a few nails, this part of the battle was lost. Given the capture or spiking of the British guns, infantry support for his cavalry attacks, and the taking of La Haye sainte *before* this assault, Ney might have turned the day. As it stood, there was a stalemate. Napoleon, rallying his own troops by a display to rival that of Wellington, ordered Ney to take La Haye Sainte at no matter what cost. The latter succeeded through a successful combination of cavalry and infantry, which combination might have proved a decisive factor had it been used imaginatively earlier.

By 6.30 pm, matters were looking increasingly grim for Wellington. His centre was weak, and Napoleon was now assaulting it with artillery fire at relatively close range. 'Night or Blücher,' the Duke kept muttering, 'night or Blücher.' Ney urged an attack on the centre, and for once in this battle he was right, since it is probable that the enemy forces could have been taken by storm at that juncture. Napoleon demurred, for he was holding back reserves to combat a possible Prussian attack upon his left flank. Finally, at 7.00 pm, Napoleon sent in his crack troops, the Imperial Guard. It was half an hour too late, for the British had regrouped to meet this assault. The Allied troops were indeed pushed back slowly until Wellington himself gave the order to Maitland's Guards Brigade, which had been lying concealed, relatively safe from French fire. 'Now, Maitland, now's your time!' These troops stood up on command and fired upon the French, with so devastating an effect that the Imperial Guard suddenly stopped. At that moment, Sir John Colborne's 52nd Light Infantry advanced on the French columns, fired a devastating volley into their flank, and followed through with a bayonet charge. For the first and last time, the Imperial Guard of the Emperor Napoleon Bonaparte broke and fled.

This rout was compounded by the final arrival of Blücher's main force, whose troops cut down the fleeing French survivors. At 9.00 pm, at Mont St Jean, now occupied by the Prussians, Blücher and Wellington rode forward to greet one another, meeting on the Brussels road which Napoleon had intended to take.

'*Mein liebe Kamerad!*' the old Prussian general shouted joyfully. He leaned forward from his horse to kiss Wellington. '*Quelle affaire!*' 'That was about all the French he knew,' Wellington said later.

It is hardly surprising that at the climactic moment of this great battle, Wellington had stood in his stirrups and waved his hat three times. The effect of this victory was devastating. The casualty figures of 15,000 for Wellington's Army, 25,000 for that of Napoleon and 7,000 for Blücher are only a very small part of the overall picture. 'I never saw [the French] behave ill except at the end of the battle of Waterloo. Whole battalions ran away and left their arms piled,' Wellington later wrote.

Napoleon abdicated, surrendered to the Allies and was sent into exile at St Helena under British guardianship. The Bourbon monarch Louis XVIII was restored to the throne of France. Wellington and the astute Foreign Minister, Robert, Viscount Castlereagh, represented Great Britain once more at the renewed Congress of Vienna, helping to remake the map of Europe. 'I have never fought such a battle, and I trust I shall never fight such another,' said the victor of Waterloo. 'In all my life I have not experienced such anxiety, for I must confess I have never before been so close to defeat.' The peace that was made – the Second Treaty of Paris, signed in November 1815 – confirmed by the Congress of Vienna resulted in there being no major European conflict of long duration for the next ninety-nine years; the division and apportionment of territories largely established the states of Europe until the First World War.

The defeat of Napoleon at Leipzig in 1813 had put an end to French hegemony over Europe and aroused the forces of nationalism therein. The defeat of Napoleon at Waterloo was a specific triumph for Britain. Trafalgar had given her domination over the seas; Waterloo gave her domination of world markets. Given her lead in the Industrial Revolution, Great Britain would become both the workshop of the World and its banker. By Treaty, she also took the vital strategic points – vital both in military and commercial terms – of Ceylon, Mauritius, the Cape of Good Hope and Malta. It is a paradox that the very power Napoleon had sworn to destroy redoubled its might, and then trebled it, as a result of his actions. Britain proceeded to establish and defend the most stable and prosperous peace that the western world had known since the Roman Empire of the second century.

It is possible that there are some who do not respect the memory of the Duke of Wellington but, to borrow a phrase from Chesterton, 'these should be removed at once, if possible by persuasion.' One conceited young man who hoped to insult him at a party with the line: 'Good afternoon, sir, Mr. Smith I believe,' was answered with a brisk: 'If you believe that, then you will believe anything.' A publisher who threatened to blackmail him by publishing indiscreet and untruthful memoirs of Harriette Wilson, was told: 'Publish and be damned.'

The Iron Duke, by then a Cabinet Minister, became increasingly unpopular during the 1820s, because his entrenched conservatism made him resolutely opposed both to Catholic emancipation and Parliamentary reform. The Tory Government of the day endeavoured a weak compromise with the liberal Lord Goderich in charge; when faced with problems, however, the man just kept bursting into tears. Finally, in 1830, Wellington reluctantly agreed to become Prime Minister, in which post he put the interests of his country before his own opinions. Convinced that revolution might break out in England, as it did in France in 1830, he persuaded his peers in the House of Lords, still at that time the dominant parliamentary body, to pass the Bills for Catholic Emancipation and Parliamentary Reform.

'You must be very pleased that the measure is carried, sir,' a colleague remarked, on the assembly of the new parliament, known as the First Reform Parliament, after the Great Reform Act of 1832.

'No, sir,' Wellington growled. 'I never saw so many shocking bad hats in my life.' He promptly resigned the premiership. In later years, he became a national icon, and all Britain – and much of Europe – mourned his passing in 1852. Fittingly, perhaps, his death came in the wake of the Great Exhibition of 1851, an attempt to show the world the technological achievements of the first half of the nineteenth century, and the peak of English supremacy which he had fought so hard to establish. Yet probably the finest clue to his character, and to the reason why his officers and men were so loyal to him, is given to us by David Howarth in *A Near Run Thing*:

> In his quarters at Waterloo, the table had been laid for the whole of the staff. He sat down at it alone, and people noticed that whenever the door was opened he glanced at it eagerly, as if he hoped to see some of his friends who had eaten breakfast there and now were missing. When he had eaten, he lay down to sleep on a pallet on the floor, because an officer was dying in his bed.

17

Time to Meet the World's Worst: Lord Fitzroy Somerset, Lord Raglan (1788–1855)

'The Crimean War is one of the bad jokes of history,' Philip Guedalla wrote in *The Two Marshals* (1943). There is an awful truth to the statement. The war need never have happened had there been intelligent diplomacy, though its causes lay with a legitimate British fear of Russian expansionism. In 1853 Tsar Nicholas I had informed Sir George Seymour, the British envoy in St Petersburg: 'We have on our hands a sick man – a very sick man,' by which he meant the decaying Ottoman Empire of the Turks. The Tsar then proclaimed himself to be Protector of the Holy Places, sacred to Christians, in Jerusalem, then under Ottoman rule.

This aroused the ire of the Sultan of Turkey since there were Holy Places in Jerusalem sacred to Muslims and he regarded himself as being their Protector; it provoked, too, the anger of Napoleon III of France, nephew of the late and more illustrious Napoleon I, who, eager to restore French international prestige, announced that he was the Roman Catholic Protector of the Holy

Places in Jerusalem. The British Government was at that time an uneasy coalition headed by Lord Aberdeen, of whom it was said: 'He drew down war by suffering himself to have an undue horror of it.' In 1853 Lord Stratford de Redcliffe, the British Ambassador at the Court of the Sultan in Constantinople, who was violently anti-Russian, vastly exceeded his brief by advising the Sultan to refuse Russia's demand for a protectorate over the Greek Church, and informing him that Great Britain would back him in event of a war between Russia and Turkey. Given this assurance, the Sultan refused to compromise with any Russian demand (the Tsar, in any case, was known to have proposals for the eventual division of Turkish territory.) The Russians responded by occupying the Ottoman Turkish provinces of Moldavia and Wallachia in the Balkans. Turkey declared war on 23 September, to which the Russians responded by sinking a Turkish flotilla at Sinope on the Black Sea on 30 November. In order to maintain their international prestige and to resolve their own differences with Russia to their advantage, Great Britain and France declared war on Russia in March 1854. All sides now wondered what on earth to do next.

It is not known who it was who came up with the bright idea of launching a punitive Anglo-French and Turkish expedition to capture the fortress of Sevastopol in the Crimea, a peninsula in the southern Ukraine bounded to the south and west by the Black Sea, and to the east by the Sea of Azoz. Just such an expedition was dispatched, however. General Lord Fitzroy Somerset was created Lord Raglan and appointed to command the British forces in the Crimea. Aged sixty-six, he had lost an arm at Waterloo and found it difcult to ride a horse. During the Peninsular War he had been one of Wellington's aides-de-camp, and had been present at all the major engagements. There, as was said of the courtiers who surrounded Louis XVIII, he had 'forgotten nothing and learnt nothing'. In 1852, he had been appointed Master-General of the Ordnance, the department responsible for military supplies, and which Wellington had acidly criticized. With the exception of the Queen's cousin, the Duke of Cambridge, who commanded a division, all the other senior commanders were aged between sixty and seventy; Lieutenant-General Sir John Burgoyne, the Chief Engineer, was the oldest at seventy-two. They thought that war in the Crimea would be the same as in the victorious Peninsular campaign. It does not seem to have occurred to Raglan that in the Peninsula, Wellington was operating on relatively easy terrain, among Spanish and Portuguese allies, and with supply ships just a few days' sail from England – all of which was rather different from an operation in country hostile in terms of both climate and inhabitants, a long voyage distant from England, and difficult to supply by sea. Raglan, however, shrugged away the difficulties, declared that the war would be won easily in time for Christmas, and made no plans for the eventuality that this might not quite be the case.

On 14 September 1854, the Allies landed in the Crimea and, their troops fresh and enthusiastic, repelled a Russian assault on the River Alma six days later. Raglan did not capitalize on the Russian retreat, however, not least because some of his inept deputy commanders such as the abominable Major-General the Earl of Cardigan, commanding the cavalry's Light Brigade, spent five days out of seven on private yachts in which they had sailed to the Black Sea (Cardigan had once had one of his officers arrested for the heinous crime of drinking Moselle rather than champagne at dinner in the mess). Raglan's lack of drive gave badly needed time to the Russian engineer, General Edward Todleben, who promptly reinforced the fortress of Sevastopol, employing his ingenious and effective conception of 'flying entrenchment'.

As Cardigan and other commanders drank more, worked less, and remained more or less remote from their men, Raglan idled complacently and inefficiently. There was a further factor to add to the misery of troops already suffering from bad weather, poor equipment, and indifferent or incompetent commanders: the Commissariat, a civil service department entrusted with the duty of supplying them. Geoffrey Regan puts the matter well in his *Someone Had Blundered*:

> Men are the raw material of any army: a general who forgets this is committing a crime not only against humanity but also against his own professional code. The logistics of battle, involving the movement of large numbers of men, stores, munitions, guns and animals in relation to the enemy, are designed eventually to place the soldier in the most effective

position – well-armed, well-equipped, well-fed and, if necessary, well-mounted – to strike against the enemy. It is the task of the commander to ensure that his men are protected as far as possible from exposure to inclement weather, from deprivation of food and drink, from needless exposure to disease and from situations of morale-sapping boredom. If he fails in this respect, or if he feels that such ideals are not necessary for the common soldier, then he is contributing to his own downfall. Failures of this kind were so common during the Crimean War that it is impossible to do justice to the problem, yet the particular failure of the Commissariat can serve as an example of administrative ineptitude rare even in British military history.

The principal culprits here are William Filder, of whom Colonel William McMurdo of the Land Transport Corps said, 'I never in the whole course of my existence met so disagreeable a coxcomb and so utterly impracticable an official as this little viper'; and Sir Charles Trevelyan, Secretary to the Treasury, who appointed him. Incredible though Filder's ineptitude was, and astonishing as was the nonchalant negligence of Raglan, much blame must be shouldered by Trevelyan. For example, the (justly) much maligned Filder did actually send a requisition to London for 2,000 tons of hay on 13 September 1854. This was fulfilled eight months later, by which time most of the horses were dead.

Raglan blithely ignored every problem. The quarrels between his useless subordinates, Cardigan and his senior, Major-General the Earl of Lucan, commanding the cavalry division, made up of the Light and Heavy Brigades, which often led to one refusing to reinforce the other's troops at critical moments out of personal jealousy and dislike, do not seem to have perturbed him. Nor did the grim fact that 16,422 of his soldiers perished from cholera, typhoid, dysentery or exposure. On 25 October 1854, the Russians endeavoured to drive away the foreign invaders by attacking the British base at Balaclava. This battle witnessed incredible bravery from the soldiers and, once more, incredible incompetence on the part of their commanders. It is impossible not to applaud the spirit of the troops, as J.B. Priestley did in his *Victoria's Heyday* (1974):

Two things saved this small, odd, rather absurd British Army, challenging so far from home a gigantic empire, from imminent defeat and then total disaster. First, the Russians, with more men in the field and immense potential reserves, were even bigger muddlers than their invaders, and seemed to move in a vague dream of battle. Secondly, and not for the first or last time, the British owed almost everything to the courage, obstinacy and superb discipline of the regular infantryman.

Florence Nightingale, who mercifully arrived with a contingent of nurses on 5 November 1854, wrote to her sister about those same British infantry in 1856:

> Give them opportunity promptly and securely to send money home and they will use it. Give them schools and lectures and they will come to use them. Give them books and games and amusements and they will leave off drinking. Give them work and they will do it.'

As Winston Churchill declared in another context, these were indeed the 'bravest of the brave, led by the vilest of the vile'.

> Hail, ye indomitable heroes, hail!
> Despite of all your generals ye prevail.

This dismal doggerel from 'The Crimean Heroes' by Walter Savage Landor (1856) rather obscures the frightful reality. Let us take the Charge of the Light Brigade, an attempt during the Battle of Balaclava to prevent the retreating Russians from dragging away some British-made guns captured from the Turks during the engagement. The order sent to Lord Lucan by the Quartermaster-General in the Crimea, Major-General Sir Richard Airey, on Raglan's behalf was unclear: 'Lord Raglan wishes the cavalry to advance rapidly to the front – follow the enemy and try to prevent the enemy carrying away the guns.' Which guns? From his vantage point behind the scenes of battle and atop a hill, Raglan could see that the body of Russians retiring with the captured guns were vulnerable, but from his position in the valley, Lucan could not; he had, moreover, neglected to keep himself informed of what was happening in the battle. His mind was further confused by Captain Louis Nolan, ADC to Airey. 'A braver soldier than Captain Nolan the army did not possess,' wrote W.H. Russell, the celebrated war correspondent of *The Times*. Whatever Nolan's courage, Russell's admiration was not shared by one of the Light Brigade officers, Lieutenant E.A. Cook, who wrote to his father: 'Our order to charge was brought by a half madman Capt. Nolan, the order was very difficult to understand rightly.' When Lucan was told by Nolan that he had been ordered to attack immediately, he understandably asked where he should attack? And to which guns was Raglan referring? Nolan, having been with the staff officers on the hill, and knowing where the captured guns were being dragged away, pointed wildly at some guns in the distance, well away from the site Raglan intended, yelling: 'There is your enemy! There are your guns!' The Light Brigade, with Cardigan at its head, promptly did its duty, charged the main Russian artillery position, and was slaughtered by the enemy fire, though it took the guns and killed the gunners. As the French General Pierre Bosquet commented as he watched the Light Brigade charge to its destruction: '*C'est magnifique, mais ce n'est pas la guerre.*'

It was in fact the Heavy Brigade and the Highland (infantry) Brigade which rescued the British from their sorry plight at Balaclava. The former, under Brigadier-General James Scarlett, charged uphill and took a vastly larger body of Russian cavalry in one flank, routing them. The 93rd Highlanders from the Highland Brigade, under its commander, Major-General Sir Colin Campbell, had no time to form a square when the enemy horse charged, and so drew up in a line, two deep. As Cecil Woodham-Smith puts it in *The Reason Why*:

> To the Russian Cavalry as they came on, the hillock appeared unoccupied, when suddenly, as if out of the earth, there sprang up a line two deep of Highlanders in red coats – the line immortalized in British history as 'the thin red line'. Every man in that line expected to be killed and, determined to sell his life as dearly as possible, faced the enemy with stern steadiness.

The Russian charge was deterred by the Highlanders' steadfast and (for its time) dazzlingly rapid and accurate rifle fire, which was followed by the wicked application of the British bayonet to the retreating disorder. Certainly these two displays of ferocious courage saved the Allied base at Balaclava, although Russian casualties were fewer. But the Russians now retreated to Sevastopol and, as was their custom, left the next stage of the war to General Winter.

Raglan reacted with the ineptitude that was his hallmark. His liaison with his French allies was minimal, so he probably missed the astute remark of the Swiss military historian, Henri Jomini, to the French C-in-C, General Certain Canrobert, in 1854: 'The Russian army is a wall which, however far it may retreat, you will always find it in front of you.' It would have made some sense to billet the men in the port of Balaclava, thus securing shelter, food and supplies from the sea. Raglan, however, decided upon a winter siege of Sevastopol; his troops camped in open country.

Raglan and the Commissariat, and the general administrative chaos (which, to be fair, afflicted the Russians as well), killed more British soldiers in the Crimean War than the Russians. As Lieutenant Cook wrote to his father:

> ... and those two fools who command us Lucan and C. [Cardigan] have been kind enough to place us such a distance from our supplies, the roads being very deep, that they can't feed the wretched little wreck of a brigade, the consequence is that they are dying 8 and 10 a day, now it requires no mathematician to see that this can't last, besides the horses are so weak that I don't think any one of them could trot a mile.

Filder of the Commissariat was a stickler for rules and regulations, which mattered much more to him than the winning of a war or the saving of the lives of his countrymen. Raglan was too spineless and complacent to challenge him. Regulations did not specifically authorize the baking of bread or the issue of fresh vegetables and lime juice (essential to combat scurvy and other diseases), therefore these things could not be done. When the medical officer of a ship docked in Balaclava urgently requested stoves on account of the extreme cold from which his sick men were dying, he was curtly informed that this was impossible without the proper requisition forms being completed and sent along the proper channels, and the clerks were inflexible. Of course, by the time the forms were filled in and processed and the stoves finally arrived, all the men concerned were dead, as the medical officer had originally warned.

One officer went to Balaclava to obtain some vegetables for his regiment and was told that regulations stipulated no issue less than two tons. Major Foley de St Georges, as Christopher Hibbert relates in *The Destruction of Lord Raglan*, needed a few nails, but was informed that these were only sold by the ton: the gallant major paid for them himself. Horses died at the rate of three a day. In 1855 the official inquiry into the Commissariat Department and the general organization of the troops in the Crimea, headed by Sir John McNeill and Colonel Alexander Tulloch, reported that 'this excessive mortality is not to be attributed to anything peculiarly unfavourable in the climate, but to overwork, exposure to wet and cold, improper food, insufficient clothing during part of the winter, and insufficient shelter from inclement weather....'

'An Army marches on its stomach,' Napoleon had said. At the camp before Sevastopol, the men frequently received half rations, and on Christmas Day 1854, the regiment of Colonel Bell received no rations at all. Moreover, the diet of salt beef and biscuits upset the digestive systems of the men and caused further sickness. Incredibly enough, Filder had at his disposal 8,000 head of cattle to provide fresh meat, but claimed that the meat could not be shipped to Balaclava. Colonel Tulloch acidly made the point that British sea transport was available and the port was open.

It is astonishing to realize that whilst a contemporary inmate of a Scottish prison received 25.16 ounces of food daily, which included meat, milk, fish, bread and vegetables, the British infantryman was given a paltry 23.52 ounces of salt beef and biscuits. On 4 November, the supply ship *Harbinger* arrived bearing 150 tons of vegetables. Unfortunately, some documents were not in order, according to the Commissariat, and so the food rotted and was thrown overboard, the soldiers meanwhile having to subsist on a ration of two potatoes and one onion a month. Raglan, when in Moldavia, had (for once) sensibly commanded that 2 ounces of rice be issued to each man, but he forgot to renew the order. Filder had stores of rice but its issue was against regulations. Filder also neglected to inform Raglan of the supply situation and Raglan neglected an inspection of the matter. Filder also had copious supplies of potatoes, peas and Scotch barley, but these rotted and were not issued to the troops, owing – of course – to regulations. Christopher Hibbert paints an unlovely picture of the harbour at Balaclava in his *The Destruction of Lord Raglan*:

> For days, for weeks on end, ships lay outside Balaclava waiting to come in and unload. And when they did so their crews, although well used to Eastern harbours, were appalled. Since the storm the ghastly pale-green waters were like a stagnant cesspool into which all imaginable refuse had been thrown. Dead men with white and swollen heads, dead camels, dead horses, dead mules, dead oxen, dead cats, dead dogs, the filth of an army with its hospitals, floated amidst the wreckage of spars, boxes, bales of hay, biscuits, smashed cases of medicines and surgical instruments, the decomposed offal and butchered carcasses of sheep thrown overboard by ship's cooks.

The *Esk* arrived in Balaclava harbour on 10 December 1854 carrying 20,000 pounds of lime juice, essential to combat the problem of scurvy and other diseases among the troops. This sat there until the first week in February. Filder did not see fit to inform Raglan of the cargo's arrival – for that was not required by the regulations – and Raglan did not see fit to make inquiries. Although the French had established bakeries and were giving their troops fresh bread, it never occurred to the British high command that they could do this too. When in January 1855 the French fraternally offered supplies, Filder frigidly replied: 'We are not now, nor have been at any time in want of them.' To compound a folly that amounts almost to an evil, he then insisted that green, unroasted coffee beans should be sent to the soldiers. The commanding officer of the 1st Regiment observed disgustedly:

> A ration of green raw coffee berry was served out, a mockery in the midst of all this misery. Nothing to roast coffee, nothing to grind it, no fire, no sugar; and unless it was meant

that we eat it as horses do barley, I don't see what use the men could make of it, except that they have just done, pitched it into the mud!

Meanwhile Filder failed to inform Raglan that he had 2,705 pounds of tea.

Meanwhile, too, men were dropping dead from the extreme cold. All the wood around the camp went swiftly to make fires and the soldiers were reduced to scavenging far from camp to dig up wet roots in the snow, returning from their foraging with icicles four inches long upon their moustaches. Ink froze, rendering it impossible to issue written orders. Filder held to his position that the issue of fuel to troops in the field was against regulations. Raglan did not manage to countermand him until 29 December 1854, by which time many more soldiers had died in their misery.

There was nothing like a sufficient number of horses to transport the supplies, and since there was also nothing like enough hay to feed the horses, most of such animals as there were died. Men had to do the work, often marching with full pack for twelve hours a day in atrocious weather conditions.

The British troops were devoid of knapsacks, spare kit, blankets and greatcoats. There were in fact 12,000 greatcoats in store by the end of November 1854, but only 3,000 were distributed because regulations stated that a soldier could only have a greatcoat once every three years. By the end of January 1855, there were 25,000 rugs in store but only 800 were distributed. There were boots aplenty, but they proved to be for the left foot only, or else were too small or so shoddily made that after one day in the snow, the soles came away.

There was a large supply of nosebags for the horses aboard the *Jason* in Balaclava harbour, but these were not distributed, with the inevitable result that half of every feed was wasted. Matters of health were probably even worse for human beings. In the hospital at Scutari, the floors were swimming in sewage. By November 1854, the death rate there was 50 per cent. That month Florence Nightingale arrived with thirty-eight English nurses, and at once insisted upon clean floors, fresh bed linen and nourishing food, only to be opposed in her every sensible proposal by the Commissariat, and to receive virtually no encouragement whatsoever from Raglan. Her iron will and determination enabled her to succeed in getting much of what she wanted eventually – and within six months the death rate had been reduced to 2.2 per cent.

Not for nothing did one Robert Portal declare in a letter to his mother of October 1854: 'Not since we landed has Raglan shown one particle of military knowledge.... I wish they would reinforce us with a new Commander-in-Chief, and put this one into petticoats and send him home.' In spite of Raglan, however, matters improved slightly for the men when Alexis Soyer, the renowned chef of the Reform Club in London, arrived in March 1855, and began to perform such delicious miracles with army rations that the men cheered him wherever he went. According to Cecil Woodham-Smith, one problem remained, however:

> Like Miss Nightingale, he strongly objected to the way the meat was divided; since weight was the only criterion one man might get all bone; why should not the meat be boned, and each man receive a boneless portion, with the bones being used for broth? The answer from Dr Cumming was that it would need a new Regulation of Service to bone the meat.'

With the coming of spring in 1855, and having wasted the winter, Raglan, already ill, staged a few more inconsequential and futile attacks against the Sevastopol defences. He died on 28 June, wholly out of touch to the end, as Christopher Hibbert ably demonstrates:

> Science and mechanics, which were beginning already to change the whole life of Europe, meant nothing to him. Nor did painting, nor music; nor did books. In fact in the great mass of his personal correspondence only once does he mention having read one. It was *The Count of Monte Cristo*. 'So far as I have got in it,' he confessed, 'I find it tiresome – very poisonous.'

This wretched war in the Crimea finally came to an end when, on 9 September, the French used effective artillery fire and stormed Sevastopol. The Tsar (by now Alexander II, Nicholas I having died in 1855) suggested an armistice, to which all the parties involved thankfully agreed. Napoleon III held the Congress at Paris in February and March 1856, once more making his city the centre of diplomatic affairs. The terms of peace were not onerous, and especially not for any of the countries which had participated in this pointless slaughter. For Great Britain, some lasting good emerged from the Crimean War. Nursing care was greatly improved and the brisk Florence Nightingale replaced the popular notion of a nurse as defined by the drunken Mrs Gamp in Charles Dickens's *Martin Chuzzlewit*. The dispatches in *The Times* of its war correspondent William Russell gave impetus to a growing public demand for army reform, though this was not to come about until Edward Cardwell became Secretary of State for War in Gladstone's first ministry of 1868–74.

It is perhaps fitting that Lord Fitzroy James Henry Somerset, first Baron Raglan, field marshal, had died of dysentery in front of Sevastopol on 28 June 1855, after yet another British assault on the city had failed abjectly.

His troops did not mourn his passing. For every 1,000 Allied soldiers who took part in the campaign, 35 were killed in action or died of wounds; 190 died from disease.

18

The Civil War
in the United States of America:
Ulysses S. Grant (1822–1885)
versus Robert E. Lee (1807–1870)

The American Civil War of 1862–5 was the first war involving mass movements of men in which the technological advances of the Industrial Revolution were put to full use. This does something to explain the extraordinarily high rate of casualties. When the war started, even the best commanders, whatever their virtues, still based their notions of strategy and tactics for the most part on those of sixty years before, when muzzle-loading muskets were the norm. Now there was the muzzle-loading percussion rifle, in which the main charge was ignited by a self-contained cap, with an effective range of 400 yards to the 100 yards maximum of the smoothbore flintlock muskets they replaced. The absence of priming meant that a percussion rifle could be reloaded four times as swiftly, while the cap ensured far more reliable ignition, especially in damp conditions. This weapon gave the advantage to the defence and also to the use of mobility in attack, while the speed at which it could be reloaded made it very effective in breaking up the bayonet charges. Besides improvements in weapons and ammunition, there were the railways, which allowed swift transportation of troops; and the telegraph, which enabled swift transmission of information. Elsewhere, massive technological advances improved everything from the manufacture of artillery and shells to the production of foodstuffs and medicines.

The war came about initially owing to the quarrel between the more industrialized Northern states and the largely agricultural Southern states over slavery. The use of black slaves, primarily in the production of raw cotton, it was thought in the South, was essential to the economy and continued prosperity of those states. The factories of the North could do without this repulsive institution, though it could nevertheless be argued that the lot of the black labourer was actually better on a Southern cotton farm than in a Northern factory, where the conditions for the black worker amounted to another form of slavery. However, the South declined to emulate the Northern mode (there was, in any case, a good deal of rivalry between North and South). It can be argued that if only the South had had the sense to abolish slavery as a political institution, then it would have had its former slaves back on the farms on a contract basis, for where else could those workers have found paid labour? Unfortunately, common sense, even at its most cynical, did not prevail, though racism did. The South withdrew from the Union, its eleven states (Alabama, Arkansas, Florida, Georgia, Louisiana, Mississippi, North and South Carolina, Tennessee, Texas and Virginia) declaring themselves the Confederate States of America. A provisional government was set up in Alabama in February 1861, with Jefferson Davis elected as President. Now the issue of slavery became virtually irrelevant. The resulting conflict took the form of a crusade on both sides.

For the Confederacy it was essential to establish the right of American states to secede from the Union; for the Union it was essential that the Confederacy failed in this. The Confederacy had to resist invasion; the Union had to conquer the South. The Confederacy hoped to exhaust the Union, bring in European aid, and negotiate an armistice from a position of strength. In studying the American Civil War, one astonishing question immediately comes to the fore: given the fact that the Confederacy had a population of 9 million, of whom 3.5 million were (largely non-combatant) black slaves, and little industry, against the industrial might of the Union with a population of 22.5 million, its young men aged between 15 and 40 outnumbering the South's by 4,010,000 to 1,140,000, how was it that the war lasted as long as it did?

The answer does not lie in arguing for the superiority of the individual Confederate soldier, although there were contrasts. The Confederate soldier was a semi-guerrilla, expected to employ his individual initiative, a countryman used to the terrain; yet the Union's (mainly) city dwellers, drilled to operate in a more regular manner, were equally brave, enduring and disciplined in combat. The answer does not lie in the quality of general officers, for of the senior commanders on both sides, many had been trained at the US Military Academy at West Point. Three extraordinary men came close to forcing an armistice which would have created an independent Confederacy by military means.

The first was the Southern Chief of Ordnance, General Josiah Gorgas, who accomplished miracles in creating a munitions industry, organizing supply lines, and running the Union blockade to trade despite the overwhelming naval superiority of his opponents. Without him it would have been impossible to keep the Confederate Army in the field.

The second man was that remarkable Southern gentleman, General Robert E. Lee, who, paradoxically enough, had initially been offered command of the *Union* forces by President Abraham Lincoln. He had declined the offer, however, and joined the South, being made commander of the Army of Northern Virginia. 'His Virginia was to him the world,' said his Northern adversary, General William T. Sherman. '... He stood at the front porch battling with the flames whilst the kitchen and the house were burning, sure in the end to consume the whole.'

'He was a foe without hate,' said Benjamin H. Hill,

a friend without treachery, a soldier without cruelty, and a victim without murmuring. He was a public officer without vices, a private citizen without wrong, a neighbour without hypocrisy, and a man without guilt. He was Caesar without his ambition, Frederick without his tyranny, Napoleon without his selfishness and Washington without his reward.

Lee saw the obvious fact that the line between the opposing sides stretched across a 3,000-mile front that was only connected loosely. Mountain ranges divided Virginia itself into eastern and western spheres of operations. If Union forces were to take the Mississippi River in the deep south, then all Confederate States south of this great waterway would be cut off from Virginia. Richmond, Virginia, the Confederacy's capital and the centre of Southern industrial production, was a mere 100 miles from the Union capital at Washington, DC. Consequently Lee rejected the strategy of conservation and defence in favour of taking the initiative and the offensive. War broke out in April, and once military operations began in June Lee marched on Washington, forcing the enemy to concentrate so as to meet the attack – he then intended winning the war with one decisive and devastating victory.

'Lee is the only man I know whom I would follow blindfold,' said Thomas J. 'Stonewall' Jackson, Lee's brilliant and audacious commander of cavalry. 'Such an executive officer the sun never shone on,' Lee said of Jackson in return; 'I have but to show him my design, and I know that if it can be done it will be done.' Few generals have inspired their troops as Jackson did. At the first Battle of Bull Run on 21 July 1861, Brigadier-General Bernard Bee roared to his troops: 'There is Jackson, standing like a stone wall. Let us determine to die here, and we will conquer!' When the Federal Union Army threatened Richmond, Jackson's force was outnumbered 4–1, yet he held off Fremont, by advancing from the west with a cunningly disguised feint of merely 8,000 men and by the superlative use of mobility, defeated Banks, by assaulting from the north. He then moved forward to force the Union to retreat across the River Potomac, the Confederate Army thus threatening Washington itself.

Abraham Lincoln now had his forces on the defensive. This was, perhaps, just as well since Lee defeated General Pope at the second Battle of Bull Run on 29–30 August 1862 and advanced, hoping to win the decisive victory he had originally intended. On 17 September 1862, Lee faced General George McLellan at Antietam

Creek, Maryland, for the bloodiest one-day battle of this bitter civil war. Tactically, it was the outnumbered Lee who won. The Union lost 17,000 men and the Confederacy 12,000. The Federal Army would not be able to attempt another offensive against Richmond for a considerable time.

Strategically, however, Antietam was a victory for the Union. Lee had to retreat in good order and evacuate Northern territory, having won what amounted to little more than a victory, given the dearth of men in the South. The battle had not been as decisive as he had hoped. On 1 January 1863 Lincoln seized this opportunity to announce his Emancipation Proclamation, his intention to free the slaves, though it would not come into effect for two years. This was a political master-stroke. The French Emperor, Napoleon III, had suggested to Britain that two European Great Powers should press for an armistice, but the latter, which had abolished her own slave trade in 1808, and emancipated her remaining slaves in 1833, did not want to be perceived as supporting slavery, while her merchants, bankers and industrialists were supporters of the Union. Indeed, the cotton manufacturers of Manchester believed that labour costs might be cheaper *without* the institution of slavery. The American conflict was consequently left to the Americans; the Confederacy's hopes of European intervention perished.

Lee remained undeterred and convinced of ultimate victory. In December 1862, he defeated a Union army under Burnside, and in May 1863, he faced another under General Joseph 'Fighting Joe' Hooker at Chancellorsville in Virginia. Hooker's plan of battle was sound in theory, especially since he had 143,000 men to Lee's 60,000. The plan called for a feint at Lee's headquarters at Fredericksburg by 40,000 men; an outflanking westward march past Lee's left flank by 70,000 men, with cavalry to be positioned in the south so as to cut off the anticipated retreat; whilst his force to the east remained strongly entrenched in their defensive positions. Unfortunately for Hooker, Lee's excellent commander of reconnaissance, Colonel J.E.B. 'Jeb' Stuart, had scouted the Federal troop movements and positions with such accuracy and intelligence that Lee was able to anticipate his opponent's every move. He promptly ordered an immediate counter-attack on Hooker's right which checked the Union general for the night.

On the following day, Lee held the Federal forces at bay behind the entrenchments and barbed wire of which he had become a master. The power of the rifle gave the advantage to the defenders, even though they consisted of only 17,000 men. Meanwhile 'Stonewall' Jackson and 26,000 men crept through 'the Wilderness', tangled undergrowth previously considered impenetrable, and stormed Hooker's right flank on 2 May, driving them back in confusion. Lee added to the disorder of the enemy by ordering swift strikes of concentrated force on whichever part of the enemy line he considered to be weak. Hooker was forced into a sad retreat, his casualties 16,792 to the Confederacy's 12,754. Sadly for Lee and the South, one of the dead was 'Stonewall' Jackson, shot by mistake by a sentry from his own side as he returned from a brief mission of reconnaissance.

This was a severe blow to the Confederacy; but the disorganized retreat of Hooker's men allowed Lee to attempt a second campaign in the North. Leading an army now increased to 75,000 men, Lee tried for a decisive strike at Gettysburg, Pennsylvania, on 1 July 1863. Chancellorsville had been a tactical masterpiece by Lee, but Gettysburg was not.

The Union's General Meade, who had replaced Hooker, took position on high ground, and Lee's assaults on these defensive positions lacked co-ordination. 'Jeb' Stuart, given his own initiative by Lee, abandoned the task of guarding the Confederates' flanks in favour of reconnaissance of the Federal positions, a task at which he had always excelled; this meant, however, that his force was not present at Gettysburg when it was crucially required. On 3 July, after repeated assaults upon the Union positions had failed to do little other than dent them, Lee gambled on a concentrated assault on Cemetery Ridge, but the Confederate General Longstreet, whose troops had fought well earlier, declined to engage in what he regarded as being a suicidal operation. Nevertheless, the celebrated 'Pickett's Charge' ensued but, desperately gallant thought it was, it was turned back by the skilled defences and steely infantrymen of General Hancock. Battle was over by the next day. Lee had lost one-third of his soldiers and was forced to retreat to Virginia. Henceforth, he was condemned to fighting a series of wearisome defensive battles.

On 4 July 1863, the Union's General Ulysses S. Grant took

Vicksburg, a vital fortress on the Mississippi, and with it 31,000 Confederate prisoners, despite having been, in earlier life, a failure in all his endeavours, an alcoholic and a manic depressive. The victories at Gettysburg and Vicksburg made the defeat of the Confederacy only a matter of time – but how long would it take? And could the outstanding generalship of Lee, fighting on his home terrain, conceivably bring about some form of stalemate, leading to an armistice?

President Lincoln made Grant Commander-in-Chief on 3 March 1864. Opinions concerning Grant vary so much that it is hard to form an accurate estimation of him, both as a man and as a general. 'I knew him,' said Sherman, 'as a cadet at West Point, as a lieutenant of the Fourth Infantry, as a citizen of St. Louis, and as a growing general all through the bloody Civil War. Yet to me he is a mystery and I believe he is a mystery to himself.'

'Grant was five feet eight inches and slightly stooped. He had cold blue eyes and a big jaw hidden behind a scrubby, messy light brown beard which went well with his scrubby, messy uniform,' said Herbert Agar.

'How is it,' Mulrat Halstead indignantly demanded of Lincoln, 'that Grant, who was behind at Fort Henry, drunk at Donelson, surprised at Shiloh, and driven back from Oxford, Miss., is still in command?'

'You just tell me the brand of whiskey Grant drinks,' said President Abraham Lincoln. 'I would like to send a barrel of it to my generals.' Later the President added: 'When Grant once gets possession of a place, he holds on to it as if he had inherited it.'

'He is a scientific Goth,' John Tyler complained, 'resembling Alaric, destroying the country as he goes and delivering the people over to starvation. Nor does he bury his dead, but leaves them to rot on the battlefield.'

Grant's colleague, his enemy, and the man himself all left their own comments:

'Grant stood by me when I was crazy,' said General Sherman, 'and I stood by him when he was drunk, and now we stand by each other.'

'We all thought Richmond, protected as it was by our splendid fortifications and defended by our army of veterans, could not be taken,' said General Robert E. Lee. 'Yet Grant turned his face to our capital, and never turned it away until we had surrendered. Now, I have carefully searched the military records of both ancient and modern history, and have never found Grant's superior as a general. I doubt if his superior can be found in all history.' This was high praise indeed; but Grant's own view was very different:

'The truth is that I am more of a farmer than a soldier. I take little or no interest in military affairs,' he declared to Germany's Prince Otto von Bismarck, 'and although I entered the army thirty-five years ago and have been in two wars ... I never went into the army without regret and never retired without pleasure.'

Grant had to operate in a war of rapidly evolving technology, including the use of novel weapons such as breech-loading rifles, machine-guns, barbed wire protecting trenches, grenades, mortar bombs, booby traps, rockets, and even land mines and flamethrowers. For all that, he still had to defeat his enemy and occupy the South. He therefore decided on a pincer movement as the means by which to destroy the Confederacy. His victory at Vicksburg, followed by Sherman's capture of Chattanooga in Tennessee, in November 1863, had given him control of the Mississippi River, thus splitting the Confederate forces and taking all Tennessee. Although Lee continued to stage skilful and exceptionally brave rearguard operations, Grant concentrated his superior manpower on repeated assaults towards Richmond, which kept Lee largely pinned down and unable to manoeuvre.

General Sherman was essential to Grant's strategy. It was his job to drive right through the western theatre of operations as Grant held the eastern. The objective was to capture the key city of the deep south, Atlanta, Georgia, and then take the coast to block all possibility of supplies to the South by sea. The Confederacy, provided that this strategy worked, would then be squeezed and starved into surrender. Attrition was part of the plan; for neither Grant nor Sherman were good tacticians. The Union could afford to lose, for instance, 5,000 men to gain an objective: the Confederates could not afford to lose 5,000 men in order to hold it. 'War ... is hell,' as Sherman said.

'Unsated still in his demoniac vengeance he sweeps over the country like a simoon [a sand-bearing, suffocating wind] of destruction,' the *Macon Telegraph* observed of Sherman. At times his strong frontal assaults were completely unsuccessful, most notably at Kenesaw Mountain, where the commander of the Army of Tennessee, the cautious General Joseph Johnston, reluctant to give open battle (like Quintus Fabius Maximus against Hannibal) repulsed Sherman's attack and left him with 3,000 casualties. Sherman's response was to make war not only upon enemy soldiers but also upon the civilian population, using terror as a strategic weapon. His 100,000 troops looted, burned, plundered and pillaged their way through the South, even though they had yet to break through the enemy line covering Atlanta. It was now that the Confederacy made a fatal blunder, dismissing Johnston and appointing in his place the impetuous Hood. Hood appears to have thought that morale alone can overcome a vast superiority in both men and munitions; and pitched battles were precisely what Sherman wanted. 'Famine follows Sherman,' it was said as his army swept away that of Hood and took Atlanta on 1 September 1864, then razed everything to the ground as it marched south-eastwards to Savannah, Georgia, thus gaining control of the Southern coast.

Liddell Hart noted the paradoxes in Sherman's character when he wrote, in *Sherman: Soldier, Realist, American* (1959), of 'the dispassionateness of an impulsive man, the restfulness of a restless man, the patience of an impatient man, the sympathy of a relentless man'. Ulysses S. Grant was warmly appreciative, writing: 'You have accomplished the most gigantic undertaking given to any general in this war, and with a skill and ability that will be acknowledged in history as unsurpassed if not unequalled.' That may have been true, but the legacy of hatred aroused in the South by Sherman's merciless crackdown on civilians would not be buried for many a generation.

Nevertheless, the steadfastness of Grant on the eastern front and Sherman's capture of Atlanta on the western gave Abraham Lincoln the political victory he so sorely required in the presidential election of 1864. Re-elected, Lincoln could now give total support to Grant, who was further bolstered by the successes of his subordinate, the brilliant General Philip H. Sheridan: the latter's operations in the Shenandoah Valley in 1864–5 had left Washington free from all possibility of future attack.

On 9 April 1865, after Grant had taken Richmond, Virginia, through hard siege warfare and overwhelming numbers, Robert E.

Lee surrendered at Appomattox, some seventy miles east of the Confederate capital. The American Civil War was finally over, and the American states were once more united, at an estimated cost of $20 billion. Karl Marx pointed out that this huge increase in the American National Debt vastly increased the power of bankers, industrialists, and mining and railway speculators. This is perfectly true: but if wealth is to be measured in terms of goods and services produced, then the resulting performance by the now United States of America from 1865 to 1925 is without parallel in human history. The Old South and its Confederate ideal decayed and died miserably: but the United States expanded to the Pacific, subsequently defeated the Spanish in Cuba in 1898 to take a formidable position in the Atlantic, and by 1914 was arguably the most powerful country in the world.

There were many military lessons to be learned from the American Civil War. The industrialized North had demonstrated the essential power of railways and the telegraph. The use of mines, barbed wire and trenches, the breech-loading cartridge rifle, even magazine rifles, the evolving machine-gun, and the power of artillery had shown that the strength had passed to defence, rendering charges by horsed cavalry or by infantry with the bayonet all but obsolete. It is deeply unfortunate that the generals of the First World War did not learn from these lessons.

On 14 April 1865, in his hour of triumph, President Lincoln was shot, dying the next day. And what of the generals? Sherman became General-in-Chief of the United States Army from 1869–83. In 1884 he was urged to run for President. 'I will not accept if nominated, and will not serve if elected,' he replied, by telegram.

Robert E. Lee, a superb strategist and tactician, died of a heart attack on 12 October 1870. Possibly the best words spoken about him are those of Gamaliel Bradford:

Here was a man who failed grandly, a man who said that 'human virtue should be equal to human calamity', and showed that it could be equal to it, and so, without pretense, without display, without self-consciousness, left an example that future Americans may study with profit as long as there is an America.

As for Ulysses S. Grant, a good strategist but, at best, no more than a competent tactician, he was elected President twice (1869–73, 1873–7), yet after his terms had ended – periods, noted, it must be said, for horrendous financial corruption in the Administration – he was eventually declared bankrupt. This did not stop him from completing his war memoirs even though he was dying of cancer, the success of which posthumously published work preserved his family from the poorhouse. His praises were also sung by the American poet Walt Whitman, who had served for a time as an army nurse in the Civil War:

How those old Greeks, indeed, would have seized on him! A mere plain man – no art, no poetry – only practical sense, ability to do, or try his best to do, what devolv'd upon him. A common trader, money-maker, tanner, farmer of Illinois – general for the republic, in its terrific struggle with itself, in the war of attempted secession – President following, (a task of peace, more difficult than the war itself) – nothing heroic, as the authorities put it – and yet the greatest hero. The gods, the destinies, seem to have concentrated upon him.

Certainly, many people believed that Grant, acting under Lincoln, had united the states for an all-American pursuit of a glorious and ultimately imperial destiny.

19

Helmuth, Count von Moltke (1800–1891)

There have rarely been such swift and intelligent expansions from weakness to strength as that achieved by Prussia during the mid-nineteenth century. By the time Wilhelm I came to the Prussian throne on 2 January 1861, Prussia was the junior partner in the German Confederation, dominated by Austria, which consisted of thirty-eight states. Prussian economic strength derived from the *Zollverein*, a customs union forming a free trade zone, under Prussian auspices, across northern Germany. King Wilhelm I now wished to increase not only his nation's economic power, but also her military might. In his first speech from the throne he proclaimed: 'The Prussian Army will, in the future, also be the Prussian Nation in Arms.' Clearly the new king saw himself as the rightful successor to Frederick the Great.

To this end, he made or endorsed three eminently sensible appointments: in 1862, Count Otto von Bismark was made Minister-President; Count Albrecht von Roon was confirmed as Minister for War, which he had been for three years; and Count Helmuth von Moltke was confirmed as Chief of the Prussian General Staff, a post he had occupied most capably since 1857.

The resulting collaboration produced a sensational combination of political, economic, diplomatic and military strategy and tactics which led to the creation of the German Empire, also known as the Second Reich (the Holy Roman Empire was retrospectively titled the First Reich), and thus of the modern German state.

General Roon prepared for forthcoming wars with ruthless efficiency, especially in the establishment of munitions factories and in encouraging the expansion of railway systems, which, because of the *Zollverein*, were in any case centred upon the Prussian capital, Berlin. General Moltke reorganized the Prussian Army by encouraging a staff system based upon the elite graduates of the Prussian War Academy. It was the job of these staff officers to analyse any military situation and thence to advise commanders in the field. Moltke also researched all data concerning the American Civil War, in order to understand how best to deploy rail and telegraph assets. Bismarck employed diplomacy, his eventual object being to unify Germany under Prussian leadership and make the Fatherland the most powerful country in Europe.

Opportunity arose in 1864. The year before, Christian IX had acceded to the Danish throne on the death of Frederick VII and claimed sovereignty, as Duke, over the southern duchies of Schleswig and Holstein. The former was partly German, the latter almost wholly so; neither accepted Christian's claim to the throne as it had passed through the female line, a process denied in the duchies under Salic Law, under which they operated. Saxony and Hanover challenged that claim and marched troops into Holstein, asserting that the rightful ruler was the Duke of Augustenburg. Bismarck, perceiving that Russia had still not recovered fully from the effects of the Crimean War and that France was involved in a doomed endeavour to set up the Archduke Maximilian of Austria as the head of a Catholic Empire in Mexico, backed the German states. Posing as a peacemaker, he formed an alliance with Austria, and sent Prussia's large army of conscripts into Denmark, where the armies of Moltke supported by the munitions of Roon won a swift victory. 'Pointed bullets are better than pointed speeches,' Bismarck had said; and under the Treaty of Vienna of 1864, the two duchies were ceded to the German states, with Christian IX retaining the Danish throne. In 1865, under the Convention of Gastein, Schleswig came under Prussian administration, and

Holstein under Austrian. Bismarck now plotted how to provoke Austria into a war it could not win. Moltke planned for a victory he hoped to be inevitable. The latter had studied *On War* by Major-General Karl von Clausewitz (published posthumously, 1832–7), probably the most influential work of this nature ever to appear in the industrial West. As late as 1951, a U.S. Military pamphlet informed the officers: 'Clausewitz's influence is not dead. The philosophy of *On War* is the philosophy of Bismarck's Blood and Iron and the philosophy of *Mein Kampf.*'

Clausewitz's philosophy can be summarized as follows:

1. 'War is only a continuation of State policy by other means.'
2. 'Destruction of the enemy's military forces is in reality the object of all combats.'
3. 'The combat is the single activity in war.'
4. 'A war should be waged ... with the whole weight of the national power.'
5. 'The chief qualities are the talents of the Commander; the military virtue of the army; its national feeling....'
6. 'The defensive form of war is in itself stronger than the offensive ... the attack is the positive intention, the defence the negative ... only great and general battles can produce great results.'
7. 'War is divided into preparation and action.... War belongs not to the province of Arts and Sciences, but to the province of social life.' (Point 7, of course, had been demonstrated in the American Civil War by General Sherman.)

Clausewitz had based his statements upon a close analysis of the campaigns of Napoleon. Moltke endeavoured to adapt the principles of *On War* to his own time and circumstances. He identified the mistakes which, despite the rapid victory, he had made in the Danish campaign, and as a result made adjustments to the basic deployment of the Prussian artillery. In addition, given the vastly improved weaponry of the day, as armies changed over to breech-loading cartridge rifles, and realized that frontal assaults by massed infantry and cavalry, had now become counter-productive. In the future he would look for flanking assaults and encirclement, defending at the centre whilst attacking at right and left, and varying these assaults so as to confuse the enemy regarding his intentions. Whereas Napoleon looked for a vulnerable spot and concentrated his forces upon it before battle was joined, Moltke marched his armies from a bewildering variety of different directions, giving him the initiative suddenly to concentrate them on a weak point *during* a battle.

In 1866, with the Prussian Army ready after Moltke's reforms, Bismarck deliberately provoked a war with Austria over that country's conduct in Holstein, claiming anti-Prussian agitation in the duchy as the reason. Italy had recently been unified as a single kingdom in 1861, but still laid claim to the province of Venetia, held by the Austrians. Bismarck promised Venetia to the Italians providing they entered the war on the Prussian side. This alliance forced the Austrians to divert troops to their southern flank, to meet the threat from Italy. To neutralize France, Bismarck offered Napoleon III a free hand in Belgium. Russia was persuaded to stay neutral. The decisive battle took place on 2 July 1866 at Sadowa, also known as Königgrätz.

Speed in mobilization was one of the keys to Moltke's offensive. His use of German railways which ran north-south to the vital junction of the lines at Königgrätz in Bohemia (now Hradec Králové in the Czech Republic) took Austria by surprise, especially since most of her railway system ran east-west. Moltke was able to field two armies, nominally under the command of King Wilhelm, with a total of 250,000 men; Austria had 20,000 fewer. In just six weeks, Prussia smashed the power of Austria, whose troops were outnumbered and outclassed at Sadowa. The Austrians lost roughly 45,000 men killed, wounded or captured, but 150,000 retreated in good order since the Prussian armies became too confused to achieve a successful pursuit. This did not dismay Bismarck, who had no wish to humiliate Austria, for political reasons, and who gladly granted the Austrian request for an armistice. The words of one of Britain's greatest military experts, B.H. Liddell Hart, in his book *Strategy: The Indirect Approach*, summarize Bismarck's policy at the time:

> The object in war is a better state of peace. Hence it is essential to conduct war with constant regard to the peace you desire.

Victory in the true sense implies that the state of peace and of one's people, is better after the war than before. Victory in this sense is only possible if a quick result can be gained or if a long effort can be economically proportioned to the national resources. The end must be adjusted to the means.

Bismarck, who became Chancellor of Prussia in 1867, ensured this in the peace he made with Austria. There would now be a North German Confederation based upon the economic *Zollverein* and dominated by Prussia. The Austrian sphere of influence in southern Germany would be limited to Bavaria, Württemberg and Baden, all of which states would be expected to stay neutral in the event of a future European conflict. Such a conflict came about in 1870, when Prussia challenged France for supremacy in Continental Europe.

It was a relatively easy matter for Bismarck to draw France into war. The throne of Prussia had been occupied by a member of the Hohenzollern dynasty since 1701. In 1870, a group of Spanish politicians proposed a Hohenzollern princeling as a candidate for the throne of Spain, a notion to which France, already fearful of Prussian power, violently objected. On 13 July 1870 the French Ambassador to Prussia, Benedetti, had an interview with Wilhelm I at the spa town of Ems, in order to seek assurances that Prussia would never support a Hohenzollern candidate for the Spanish throne. The King refused this last request, though he had already agreed to persuade his kinsman to withdraw his candidature, and a dispatch reporting the discussion was sent to Bismarck in Berlin. The latter doctored the text of this, the 'Ems Telegram', and released it to the press, arguably the first time that 'black' propaganda – disinformation – had been used to real effect as a military weapon. Although the exchanges between the Kaiser and the French Ambassador had been courteous, to the readers of both French and German popular newspapers it appeared from the altered text of the telegram that insults had been exchanged on both sides. In Paris and Berlin feelings ran high, and there was a demand for war; and war was declared by France on 19 July.

Britain opted for neutrality: she had not forgotten the failed bluster of the Prime Minister, Lord Palmerston, over the Danish War of 1864, when he had threatened to intervene on the Danish side: 'If the British Army lands in Schleswig-Holstein,' Bismarck had said, 'I shall send the police to arrest them.' In any event, the present Prime Minister, William Ewart Gladstone, was wholly opposed to any British involvement in a European war. Furthermore, Bismarck had continued to cultivate good relations with Russia in order to neutralize her as a potential ally of France. Any ideas of intervention in the French cause were halted in their stride by Bismarck's astute move in having a letter published in *The Times* disclosing Napoleon III's plan, put forward in 1866, to annex Belgium and Luxemburg, a plan which the Prussian Chancellor had originally encouraged.

The Germans had cause for anger at the French. France had invaded German lands on fourteen occasions between 1675 and 1813, an average of once every ten years. The vainglorious Napoleon III, was by now a sick man, unable to take swift decisions. An Emperor composed more of style than substance, and encouraged by his beautiful but not over-intelligent wife Eugénie, he was convinced that he could unite his increasingly disaffected nation by beating the Germans in the cause of '*la Gloire*'. This was despite the fact that Austria and Denmark had declared their neutrality, as had Italy, to whom Bismarck had promised Rome, then occupied by a French garrison at the behest of the Vatican, a move promoted by the ardently pro-Catholic Eugénie. Moreover, Bismarck had ensured that Italy duly received Venetia from Austria at the conclusion of the Austro–Prussian War, 1866.

In studying the Franco–Prussian War of 1870, it is initially hard to determine whether the Prussians won the war or the French lost it. Certainly Moltke was able to deploy 500,000 well-trained and well-equipped troops of Prussian and other German soldiers allied within less than three weeks, owing to his highly efficient staff system. When Bismarck asked Moltke, 'the Great Silent One', about the probable outcome, the latter replied that the odds were 80 per cent in Prussia's favour.

For their part, the French were utterly unprepared. They seemed to think that *élan* and morale would be enough to overcome *matériel*. The Germans put 380,000 men on the front line, holding back the reserves, against the French forces of 224,000. The answer of the French emperor Napoleon III was a grandiose and audacious plan to cross the Rhine and threaten Berlin by means of a swift strike. Obviously precise preparation and exact timing were crucial to the matter yet gross inefficiency reigned. There were no tents, railway time-tables and in many cases no transport, guns, ammunition, ambulances or even supplies for fortresses. By contrast, the Prussian military machine worked like a Swiss clock.

There were two major French armies, one commanded by Marshal Achille Bazaine, and the other by Marshal Edmé, comte de Macmahon. Moltke proceeded to divide them. Having bottled up Bazaine at the siege of Metz, he looked for advantageous opportunities by which he could destroy MacMahon. After a complex series of movements during which Moltke outguessed the French at every turn, he trapped MacMahon's forces in the fortress of Sedan, and brought them to battle there on 1 September 1870. The French were positioned with a strong centre, a reasonably firm right, and a weaker left.

The Prussions proceeded to surround this formation. A strong centre faced all three French formations. The weak French left was taken in the rear by two solid German blocks, one moving in column and the other in line. The French centre had to face two angled groupings at its rear, attacking there from both right and left. The French right was threatened at its rear by a strong grouping deployed as an 'L' formation.

'We are in a chamber pot and we are going to be shat upon,' the French General Auguste Ducrot had said on the eve of battle, prior to being relieved of his command by the inept – and aptly named – General Félix, baron de Wimpffen. Wimpffen proceeded to countermand all Ducrot's orders, to the delight of the Prussians. Moltke echoed Ducrot, if less earthily: 'We have them in a mousetrap.' 'Our superiority was so overwhelming that we suffered no loss at all,' said Prince Kraft zu Hohenlohe-Ingelfingen in his *Letters on Artillery* (1888). 'The batteries fired as if at practice.' In fact, the allied Prussians and Germans did lose some 460 officers and 8,500 men killed and wounded: the French lost 3,000 killed, 14,000 wounded, and 21,000 prisoners. When, two days later, Napoleon III, who had witnessed the crushing of his army at Sedan, surrendered himself and the Army of Châlons, the Prussians captured another 83,000 men, 419 field guns, 139 garrison guns, 1,072 carriages and 6,000 well-conditioned horses.

On 4 September the Paris mob invaded the Assembly and declared, without opposition, the Third Republic. It was the end of the Second French Empire and of the Bonaparte dynasty. Napoleon III, imprisoned in Germany until March 1871, joined his Empress in exile in England's green and pleasant suburb of Chislehurst in Kent, where he died in 1873. Eugénie, whose enthusiasm for war with Prussia had done so much to bring about the disaster, died, still exiled, in Madrid in 1920, aged ninety-four.

The victory at Sedan meant that Metz capitulated and Paris, having heroically endured a four-month siege, finally surrendered on 29 January 1871. Paintings of Moltke, who went on to refine the use of railway timetables so that German troops could be rapidly deployed by the issue of a single order, were subsequently displayed in every Prussian schoolroom. The outcome of the battle of Sedan was cataclysmic, not just for France but, in the end, for Europe and for Germany.

On 18 January 1871, even before the surrender of Paris (by then regarded, and rightly, as a foregone conclusion), King Wilhelm I of Prussia was proclaimed Kaiser – Emperor – of Germany in the Hall of Mirrors at the Palace of Versailles. Bavaria, Württemberg and Baden had chosen to become part of this new empire, and Austria, nervous of Prussian power, dared not interfere. Berlin now replaced Paris as the diplomatic centre of Europe, as was demonstrated in 1878 with the Congress of Berlin, over which Bismarck presided, a convening of the Great Powers in order to avert a potential major war between Russia and Turkey, in which Great Britain had threatened to become involved on the Turkish side. War did not take place, Bismarck ably positioned himself as an 'honest broker' (an expression he gave to the world), Great Britain's Prime Minister, Benjamin Disraeli, returned to England rightly proclaiming 'peace ... with honour'; an uneasy but general European peace was preserved for the next thirty-six years; and the German Empire was confirmed as the leading power on the Continent.

There were, too, military lessons to be learned from Moltke's victories. Just as infantry had earlier replaced cavalry as the main force on the battlefield, artillery now replaced infantry as the decisive factor. Artillery, by now breech-loading, quick-firing, capable of hurling explosive shells over great ranges, and the use of railways for transport, supply and resupply to the front lines, increased the advantages of a defensive position. Finally, the benefits of a trained staff system, akin to modern business management principles, had been demonstrated to devastating effect.

The German Empire proceeded to surpass Great Britain in terms of industrial productivity, especially in coal and steel. Bismarck strove ardently to preserve a peace which would increase German power, and negotiated alliances between Germany, Austria–Hungary and Russia in 1881, between the two former and Italy in 1882, and with the Russian Empire in 1887. It was unfortunate for the Second Reich that when Kaiser Wilhelm II succeeded his father as Emperor in 1890, he 'dropped the pilot' by dismissing Bismarck, and repudiated the 1887 Reinsurance Treaty with Russia. This would ultimately lead to the bloodiest war that history had so far seen, and, in 1919, to the Germans having to sign the humiliating Treaty of Versailles within that palace's Hall of Mirrors.

20

The First World War (1914–1918)

The First World War was a cataclysm which changed the old order irrevocably. It was also the theatre in which were played out scenes of astounding military incompetence. It is possible, however, that the politicians were even more incompetent in allowing the war to start. Its outbreak was the result of a ghastly chain of events involving both accidents and failures of diplomacy, exacerbated by inflexibility, which made war almost inevitable. The tragedy was that none of the Great Powers really wanted a Great War.

On 28 June 1914, the Archduke Franz Ferdinand, heir to the throne of the Austro–Hungarian Empire, went with his wife to Sarajevo in Bosnia to inspect some troops. Bosnia, in which there were large numbers of Serbs who had been agitating for union with Serbia for some years, had been annexed by the Austro–Hungarian Empire in 1908. This made Austria–Hungary the enemy of the independent state of Serbia, which since 1903 had sought the 'liberation' of Serbs still within the Austro–Hungarian Empire. A secret Serbian nationalist society, the 'Black Hand', laid plans for assassinating the Archduke, using young Bosnians which it had trained as terrorists. After a series of bungles Franz Ferdinand and his wife were shot and killed by a

young Serbian student, Gavrilo Princip, a member of a secret
Bosnian liberation movement – the weapons used in the
assassination were supplied by the Black Hand. Thus bullets
which killed the Archduke and his wife precipitated the First
World War.

Austria–Hungary, determined to prove that she was still a Great
Power, now had a golden opportunity to destroy her rival Serbia,
although the Serbian government in fact had no part in the
assassination, and was indeed opposed to the Black Hand.
Austria's belligerent demands were supported by the sabre-rattling
Kaiser Wilhelm II of Germany. Certainly the Kaiser's attitude was
not part of any sinister capitalist conspiracy: German financiers,
merchants and industrialists saw all too clearly that the German
economy would very soon be the strongest in Europe, and that
almost the only thing which could prevent this would be a
European war of long duration and uncertain outcome. German
capitalists indulged the bombast of the Kaiser in the belief that this
would be merely a move in a localized Balkan conflict. Although
the Serbs met some of the Austro–Hungarian demands, and
remained conciliatory, the latter sent an ultimatum on 23 July, and
when, as was intended, its terms were refused, declared war on
Serbia on the 28th.

War is of course the best way to unite a discontented populace.
In Russia, the weak Tsar Nicholas II, who was highly unpopular
with his subjects, was also traditionally the protector of the Serbs,
as of other Slav peoples. Russia, too, like Austria–Hungary, had
ambitions in the Balkans. On 29 July 1914, the Russian Empire
declared a general mobilization, not only to deter Austria–
Hungary, but also to prevent action by her far more powerful ally,
the German Empire. Germany, choosing to regard this as a threat
to her, now sent ultimatums to Russia, demanding that a stop be
put to mobilization, and to Russia's ally, France, demanding that
the French give a guarantee of their neutrality. When neither
country complied, Germany declared war on Russia on 1 August
and France on 3 August.

This brought into effect the German plan prepared by the late
Field Marshal Alfred, Count von Schlieffen, Chief of the German
General Staff from 1891 to 1906, designed to counter the
Franco–Russian alliance of 1891. Schlieffen had thought that to

obviate the possibility of war on two fronts, and given the fact that it should take the Russian Empire several weeks to mobilize, the German Empire should attempt only a holding operation against Russia, but make a lightning, pre-emptive strike against the French Third Republic, sweeping through Belgium so as to take Paris and knock out France within six weeks, enabling all resources thence to be concentrated upon Russia. On 4 August, France having refused Germany's ultimatum, over 1 million German troops poured into neutral Belgium.

Great Britain could allow neither the violation of Belgian neutrality, which she had guaranteed, nor German domination of Europe. On the same day on which Germany invaded Belgium, Britain therefore declared war on Germany and Austria–Hungary. All sides thought that this war would be over by Christmas, and would be followed by a negotiated peace after a grand affair of great marches and sweeping victories. For reasons which still remain to be fully explored, and which are outside the scope of this work, the peoples of the Great Powers involved initially rejoiced at the coming of war, crying out for their enemies' blood. There would soon be enough to sicken the stomach of anyone.

1914

The success of the Schlieffen Plan in knocking out France within six weeks depended on the dying words of its planner: 'Only make the right wing strong.' Colonel-General Helmuth von Moltke, Chief of the German General Staff (in which post he succeeded Schlieffen), nephew of the legendary 'Great Silent One', whose ideas he copied slavishly despite the elapse of time, sixty-eight years old, committed to German Staff rigidity, and generally ignorant of the practicalities of war, was hardly the man for the job. Indecisive at all times, despite his mastery of railway timetables, he tinkered initially with the Schlieffen Plan by weakening the right wing, which alone could make it successful, taking divisions to reinforce German defences in Lorraine against an anticipated French attack there. Such an attack did indeed occur – but the reinforcements were not needed.

The French had appointed General Joseph Joffre as

Commander-in-Chief of their Armies of the North and of the North-East, a man who had never commanded an army in action, and who knew nothing of General Staff work. He neither wrote nor read memoranda. Although he was cool and courageous in a crisis, he had no ideas other than the General Staff theories that wars must be won by means of an offensive based upon 'mass plus velocity'; and that the metaphysical concept of morale could overcome the actuality of bullets and shells. Consequently, Joffre ordered an all-out assault on Alsace–Lorraine, to begin on 14 August, convinced, as were the officers of the French General Staff, that intuition is much more important than intelligence. Joffre had clearly not studied the lessons of the American Civil War, which had proved that the advantage in battle had shifted to the defenders of any securely held position. Encouraging the French armies to recapture Alsace and Lorraine, border provinces seized by the Germans in the Franco–Prussian War of 1870–1, Joffre appeared blithely ignorant of barbed wire, concealment as a tactic, machine-guns, the need for heavy artillery – which the Germans possessed in far greater abundance than did the French – reconnaissance by aircraft in order to direct troops and artillery, and the plain fact that the Germans wanted the French to charge into this eastern trap, since their principal strike was in the west. For the Germans, this battle was like a turkey shoot since it was easy to spot the brightly coloured red-and-blue uniforms of the advancing French. The lances and sabres of the French cavalry and the bayonets of the infantry never came close to the enemy lines, and they were mown down mercilessly by machine-gun and aratillery fire. The flower of the French Army perished in Lorraine: casualty estimates vary from 100,000 to 500,000.

The German armies of the right wing, meanwhile, advancing through Belgium, had taken the crucial fortress of Liège on 16 August, and on 23–4 August drove back from Mons the heavily outnumbered British Expeditionary Force under Field Marshal Sir John French, after initial stubborn and brave resistance against overwhelming odds. Nevertheless, Moltke, nervous in a way which would never have occurred to his uncle, kept demanding frantically: 'Where are the prisoners? Where are the captured guns?' To add to his anxieties, the Russians had advanced much more swiftly than anyone could have anticipated and were now threatening East Prussia. Moltke responded by further weakening his right wing, poised to strike into northern France, transferring divisions to the Eastern Front and appointing as commander there General Paul von Hindenburg, with the able General Erich Ludendorff, victor of Liège, as Chief of Staff.

The Russian armies under Generals Rennenkampf and Samsonov, who detested each other so bitterly that, like Lucan and Cardigan in the Crimea, they would not assist one another in a crisis, proved to be shamefully ill equipped. Some divisions possessed only one rifle for every three men; or rifles aplenty but no ammunition; or copious supplies of ammunition but no rifles. There were compasses without maps, or else maps without compasses. Most divisions had radio transmitters, but their operators found codes so inextricably complex that messages were transmitted in plain Russian, to the delight of German Intelligence. Russian generals tended to owe their rank and advancement entirely to accident of birth. Although Hindenburg – who had been brought out of retirement at the age of sixty-seven – took the credit, it was the generalship of Ludendorff which smashed the Russian invasion at the Masurian Lakes and Tannenberg on 27–30 August 1914, clearing German soil of Russian troops for the remainder of this war and taking 30,000 wounded and 95,000 unwounded Russian prisoners.

By 24 August, the German offensive was sweeping through northern France. However, the transfer of troops by Moltke to reinforce Alsace–Lorraine and the East Prussian front had drastically weakened the right wing, which Schlieffen had regarded as being essential to the success of his plan. Matters were not assisted by the fact that Moltke's headquarters was 200 miles behind the battle front. Failing to take advantage of French and British confusion in retreat, Moltke then allowed Colonel-General Alexander von Kluck, commanding the extreme right wing, to act upon his own initiative. Kluck thought that he no longer had the strength to encircle Paris as planned and instead wheeled around south-eastwards in front of the city to attack the exposed flank of the retreating French armies. The French and English then counter-attacked in a last, desperate, attempt to save Paris and on 5 September, the Battle of the River Marne commenced, Joffre having obtained the co-operation of Sir John French.

'To sum up Joffre,' Alistair Horne writes in *The Price of Glory* (1962), 'it might be said that the war was very nearly lost with him, but that it would almost certainly have been lost without him.'

A series of desperate assaults on the German lines and columns commenced, throwing Moltke into further anxiety and confusion. Perturbed by the stubborn resistance, Moltke sent a staff officer, Colonel Hentsch, to the front, granting him complete authority. Heutsch, dismayed by the confusion and casualties, and by the continuing Allied attacks, ordered a temporary retreat from the River Marne to the River Aisne in order to regroup. This was the final German error of the year, and it made the Battle of the Marne, which ended on 11 September, one of the most decisive in world history. The German advance was halted; Paris was saved; and the French and British Armies now had time in which to recover their equilibrium.

There followed a race by each side to outflank the other, which in the west ended in a dead heat at the sea. Both sides then dug trenches, which stretched from the English Channel to Switzerland. Attempts by either side to break this stalemate were stopped in their tracks by machine-gun and artillery fire. The Schlieffen Plan had failed, partly through the dithering of Moltke, and partly through a concatenation of circumstances which no one had foreseen.

On the Eastern Front, the failure of the Schlieffen Plan was also glaringly apparent. Although Germany herself no longer had anything to fear from Russia, the same was not true of Austria–Hungary, whose armies were defeated by the Russians in Galicia. German troops were now faced with the task of propping up their ally, so that the war on two fronts which they had dreaded became a reality. Even the most unrealistic of optimists now realized that the war would not be over by Christmas. The general who probably understood most clearly the nature of what was to come was Ludendorff. 'A general,' he wrote in *My War Memories 1914–1918* (1929), 'has much to bear and needs strong nerves.' (Moltke, made a scapegoat for the failure to capture Paris and the defeat on the Marne, suffered a nervous breakdown and on 14 September was replaced by General Erich von Falkenhayn.)

The civilian is too inclined to think that war is only like the working out of an arithmetical problem with given numbers.

It is anything but that. On both sides it is a case of wrestling with powerful, interwoven physical and psychological forces, a struggle which inferiority in numbers makes all the more difficult. It means working with men of varying force of character and with their own views. The only quality that is known and constant is the *will* of the *leader*. (Author's italics.)

This emphasis would dominate the generalship of the next four years.

1915

Any account of 1915 is bound to make depressing reading. Equally bewildering are the unavailing heroism of the soldiers in the trenches and the monumental imbecility of most of their commanders. The French under Joffre clung like limpets to the dogma that the war could only be won by massive offensives on the Western Front. As A.J.P. Taylor wrote in his vitriolic yet astute *The First World War* (1963):

> In this curious way, the French, who had little faith in Joffre, kept him as Commander-in-Chief because they thought that this would please the Allies; and the Allies, who had no great faith in Joffre, conformed to his wishes because they thought that this would please the French.

The British Commander-in-Chief, French, had distinguished himself as a cavalry commander during the Boer War at the turn of the century, lifting the siege of Kimberley in 1900, although he all but destroyed the Cavalry Division in the process. Unfortunately, he thought that the tactics of cavalry deployment could be applied to trench warfare, and there were hideous losses as a result. It ought to have been obvious to any thinking person that in attempting to break through a line of well-fortified trenches, it is vital to make use of intelligence reports (and aerial reconnaissance, if available) to ascertain the enemy's weakest point, and then to strike there with speed and surprise. This did not occur to French, however. In common with his subordinate, Lieutenant-General Sir Douglas Haig, commanding the BEF's I Corps, he believed in the metaphysical doctrine of 'breaking the *will* of the enemy' by attacking at the strongest point.

Normal Franco–British strategy now consisted of assaulting the strongest German point after an artillery bombardment of at least twenty-four hours; the latter, however, alerted the Germans to the fact that an attack was imminent, and churned the ground between the trenches to mud, thus rendering a successful infantry advance against barbed wire and machine-gun and artillery fire virtually impossible. For their part, the Germans insisted that every trench lost must be retaken, which led to bloody and futile battles where the prize was a few hundred yards of mud. Allied attacks in Champagne (twice), at Soissons, Neuve Chapelle, Festubert, in Artois, and at Loos accomplished nothing but pointless slaughter. Loos, a battle upon which Haig, who had charge of that sector of the Western Front, insisted, is a poignant example. After the failure of the main attack on 25 September, Haig was adamant that the assault should be renewed on the following day, sending in another 10,000 men. In his *The Donkeys* (1961), Alan Clark quotes a German account of the battle:

> Ten columns of extended line could clearly be distinguished, each one estimated at more than a thousand men, and offering such a target as had never been seen before, or even thought possible. Never had the machine gunners such straightforward work to do nor done it so effectively.... As the entire field of fire was covered with infantry the effect was devastating and they could be seen falling literally in hundreds.

It is quite incredible to realize that out of the 10,000 British soldiers of XI Corps committed that day, 385 officers and 7,861 men became casualties; more incredibly, the Germans suffered no casualties at all. Even more incredibly, there are still some people who argue that Haig was a good commander. Most incredible of all, in December 1915 the British Government, possibly owing to the personal influence Haig exercised upon King George V, chose to replace the obviously inept French with Haig. What is not incredible is that Alan Clark entitled his book on the British commanders of 1914 and 1915 *Donkeys*.

A German offensive at Ypres, in Belgian Flanders, in April 1915 had introduced soldiers to a new horror, poison gas; but although the attack was initially successful, the wind changed, blowing the gas back on to the German troops, and the assault had to be halted. Despite the obvious facts that the strategy of the Western Front was as limited and unimaginative as it was murderous, soldiers continued to die in their thousands and generals continued to stare at the trench lines and order more offensives with the determined obstinacy of half-wits.

The Central Powers enjoyed a greater degree of success in 1915. Serbia was all but crushed, and an offensive was launched against Russia, under the nominal command of Hindenburg and the actual command of Ludendorff. This well-planned offensive conquered what is now Poland, and only Russia's vast expanses of territory and huge resources of manpower saved her in that year. Never popular with the masses, Tsar Nicholas II, who had appointed himself Commander-in-Chief, took the blame for the catastrophe, and revolution inched nearer.

The theatre of war expanded. As the result of some clever German machinations, Turkey had entered on the side of the Central Powers in December 1914, and had launched a disastrous winter campaign against Russia in the Caucasus Mountains. By 23 January 1915, frost, famine and bullets of the Russians had reduced this Turkish Army of 66,000 combatants to 12,400 half-starved and freezing men.

In May 1915, Italy entered the war. Because she had no coal, she had been condemned to adopt a jackal diplomacy. She had engaged in the Triple Alliance with Germany and Austria-Hungary in May 1882. On the outbreak of the war, she had broken the treaty to remain neutral; and having first offered to ally herself with the Central Powers, she now allowed herself to be bribed by Great Britain and France, entering the war on the Allied side given the promise of future gains – a promise largely broken later. Italian action began with a series of futile and costly assaults on the mountainous terrain of her border with Austria–Hungary.

In Britain, the First Lord of the Admiralty, Winston Churchill, proposed what seemed to be a war-winning idea. The plan, which was accepted on 15 January 1915, called for an Anglo–French naval expedition to force, 'by ships alone', the passage of the Dardanelles Straits, the strategic waterway, some 150 miles from Constantinople, which forms part of the channel between the Mediterranean and the Black Sea; the ultimate objective was the taking of the Turkish capital. If successful, Turkey would be knocked out of the war, and the stalemate on the Western Front would be broken since, at least initially, Germany would be bound to try to support her ally Turkey. The operation began with naval bombardments of Turkish positions on 19 and 26 February, and the Anglo–French fleet attempted the passage of the straits on 18 March. The Allies retired later that day, by which time a third of the capital ships involved, among other vessels, had been sunk or crippled by mines or fire from Turkish shore batteries. The attempt, though strategically imaginative, failed because it was inadequately planned, badly co-ordinated, lacked persistence, and had abandoned surprise in favour of preliminary bombardments. The naval assault was therefore dropped in favour of landing an Allied force on the Gallipoli Peninsula, one side of which forms the north shore of the Dardanelles, to take the Turkish forts there and thus dominate the straits and clear the way to Constantinople. The initial landings were made on 25 April, but although enormous gallantry was displayed on both sides, the main Turkish positions were never taken, and despite further landings in August, which came close to success, the operation settled down into bloody trench warfare. On 1 January 1916, the last Allied troops left the peninsula after a brilliant evacuation in which not a single man was lost. Churchill, made a scapegoat for the Dardanelles fiasco, resigned and went to the Western Front in command of an infantry battalion. General Sir Ian Hamilton, the commander at Gallipoli until replaced in October, was blamed, not altogether unfairly, for the poor leadership that had bedevilled the campaign, and never held command again. To some extent, however, the campaign failed because senior Allied commanders, believing the war could only be won on the Western Front, resented the diversion of troops, equipment and supplies to the Eastern Mediterranean. Allied casualties at Gallipoli amounted to 214,000 men, almost one-half of them from disease; Turkish losses were some 20,000 fewer.

In October, an Anglo–French force was sent to Salonika, in neutral Greece, in order to support the Serbs against the Bulgarians, who had joined the war on the side of the Central Powers that month. There were many who regarded the Salonika venture as a sideshow, resenting the fact that the troops and equipment sent there might have been better employed on the Western Front. The expeditionary force grew to number 600,000 troops and suffered an illness rate of 80 per cent, mainly from malaria, and achieved little. Serbia was overrun by Austro–Hungarian, Bulgarian and German forces in 1916.

Elsewhere, British and Empire forces began a campaign from Egypt that would eventually conquer Palestine and Syria. Another campaign in Mesopotamia (Iraq) secured the Persian Gulf oil supplies vital for the British war effort, and would in the end conquer the country and take Baghdad. These two campaigns, supported by British-backed Arab insurrections in what is now Saudi Arabia, destroyed the decaying Ottoman Empire. However, with the Salonika expedition, they cost the British Empire 174,000 men killed, dead of disease or wounded.

But 1915 did not only demonstrate the ineptitude of Europe's generals and of its governing classes. For it was not men alone who died in that year, but also their values. Everything incompatible with war was sacrificed: freedom, moderation, justice, tolerance, humanitarianism and reason. As soldiers died to no effect, civilians raged against anyone who failed to display a total, unquestioning commitment to the war effort. Their passions were fed by the slick patriotism and monstrous lies of their overtly propagandist newspapers, and all intelligent debate about ending the war was silenced by a torrent of hatred.

1916

'Attrition' was the word which dominated the thinking of the various generals in 1916. This concept can be defined as one side killing more of the enemy's troops than the enemy kills of its troops; given equally matched opponents, the side that has more men will eventually win. It is hardly an intelligent strategy, since it wastes a nation's manpower, and especially its youth.

Falkenhayn, Chief of the German General Staff, and thus

effectively commander-in-chief, nevertheless adopted the strategy of attrition in endeavouring to 'bleed France white'. He reasoned that the Russians could be contained by a relatively small force; that a major battle could knock France out of the war and thereby deprive the British Army of a base for operations on the Western Front. He chose to attack at Verdun, a fortified city on both banks of the River Meuse where the French front line projected as a salient (a bulge in the line which can therefore be assaulted from three sides) to the north and east. In fact, Verdun had no strategic importance to the French whatsoever, other than as a symbol of prestige. It would have made sense for the French to retire and regroup in order to remove the salient and straighten their line, but Joffre would not hear of it. The Germans attacked on 21 February 1916; when the battle finally ended on 16 December, their 1,400 artillery pieces had fired some 2 million shells on an 8-mile front. The French defended with magnificent courage and unshakeable resolve; and a hideous battle which gave new meaning to the concept of hell, and from which neither side gained any strategic advantage, dragged on until December, by which time French counter-attacks had recovered much of the territory taken by the Germans. Verdun was almost totally destroyed, but remained in French hands, at a cost of about 337,000 casualties to the Germans and 377,000 to the French. In the end, both armies had been 'bled white', from which neither was fully to recovery by the war's end.

On 31 May, the Grand Fleet of the Royal Navy under Admiral Sir John Jellicoe and his subordinate, Vice-Admiral Sir David Beatty, commanding the Battle-Cruiser Squadron, intercepted the German Grand fleet at the Battle of Jutland, in the North Sea off the west coast of Denmark. In an indecisive engagement, the Germans sank more British ships than they lost themselves but, finding themselves outnumbered as British reinforcements steamed towards the action, sailed back to port and safety. The German Imperial High Seas Fleet was no longer to be a significant factor in the war, having assaulted its gaoler and having been forced to retire to port; thereafter German surface vessels remained close inshore. Jutland was therefore a strategic victory for Great Britain, which now endeavoured to use a naval blockade to starve Germany into submission.

On 4 June, the Russian General Alexei Brusilov launched an unexpected onslaught, primarily against the Austro–Hungarians, between the Pripet Marshes and the Carpathian Mountains. The Russians had been reeling from a previous battle, north of the Pripet Marshes, where they had lost 150,000 men compared to the Germans' 50,000. By shunning preliminary bombardments and similar dogmas embraced by other commanders, Brusilov ensured the most spectacular advance of the war so far, in a month clearing a corridor 200 miles wide and up to 60 deep, capturing 500,000 prisoners and crippling Austria–Hungary's military strength on the Eastern Front. Had this success been exploited, it might have had a decisive outcome, but the advance petered out in mid-August when supplies of munitions began to fail, and because Brusilov's Russian colleagues were so jealous of his success that – incredibly enough – they deliberately delayed sending essential reinforcements. The Germans counter-attacked and by 17 August the Russians were virtually back where they started, closer still to revolution, having suffered more than 1 million casualties.

From February, as the pressure upon Verdun grew, the French had repeatedly begged the British to launch a major attack on another part of the line, the aim being to draw German troops and *matériel* away from the desperate fighting at Verdun. Eventually, Haig had agreed, aiming to attack in September in order fully to prepare his almost wholly untried infantry. The latter consisted mainly of volunteer battalions raised from 1914 in answer to the call from the Secretary of State for War, Field Marshal Lord Kitchener, for 1 million volunteers. French pressure forced Haig to bring the attack forward, and on 1 July, on an eighteen-mile front on the Somme, he launched his vast army of volunteers against the German defences, with the French also attacking on Haig's right, south of the British sector. After a seven-day artillery bombardment, which did little damage to German dugouts or barbed wire, the British attack went in, and was almost everywhere repulsed with terrible casualties. 'The first day on the Somme' is probably the blackest day in British military history, for in what was to become the grave of Kitchener's 'New Armies' some 57,000 men became casualties, nearly 20,000 of them killed. This – to put it mildly – perturbing figure did not deter Haig from continuing the battle until 18 November. British and Empire casualties amounted to just under 420,000 men, and French just over 204,000; estimates of German losses vary between 450,000 and 680,000. The Allies gained seven miles of mud in five months.

Such was the dismal tale of 1916. There is not much to add. Italian attacks continued to fail at high cost, although the Austro–Hungarians were equally unable to drive the Italians back. Romania, encouraged by Brusilov's successes, joined the Allies but collapsed within four months; by January 1917, most of the country was occupied by German or Austro–Hungarian forces. Even the governments of the belligerent powers began to sicken of the slaughter, and both the Allies and the Central Powers examined the possibility of making peace. This proved to be infinitely more difficult than making war, however, since none of the sides involved could agree upon a settlement that would not render manifestly pointless the past two and more years of war and sacrifice.

The people of Europe, now as weary of blood as earlier they had been enthusiastic for it, prayed fervently that new men would bring about a new situation. In December, David Lloyd George replaced H.H. Asquith as Prime Minister of Great Britain, and since he had always publicly urged a more vigorous prosecution of the war, he could not possibly advocate a more determined approach to the making of peace. Lloyd George did not, however, see eye to eye with Haig, whom he believed wasted lives for no tangible benefit. France put Joffre out to grass, replacing him with the handsome and dashing General Robert Nivelle, a man who claimed that he alone had 'the secret of victory'. Germany posted Falkenhayn to Romania, whose armies he defeated, and replaced him as Chief of the General Staff with Hindenburg, with Ludendorff as Chief Quartermaster-General. From this position, Ludendorff came to wield enormous power in Germany; Hindenburg, although nominally his superior, in fact deferred to him. Ludendorff now became a semi-dictator, influencing almost every aspect of German political, economic and military policy. Among other things, he played upon nascent anti-Semitism in Germany, slandering the Jews as slackers and war profiteers, thus breeding the germs of a future and even more poisonous myth.

There was, it seemed, nothing that anybody could do to stop this dreadful war. Certainly 1917 brought about a new situation, but it in no way resembled what anyone had envisaged in 1916.

1917

It was in 1917 that the world balance of power altered fundamentally, for this most terrible year gave birth to the Soviet Union, and saw the mobilization for total war of the United States of America, and that country's first steps on the road to becoming a superpower.

On 8 March, a revolution in Russia forced Tsar Nicholas II to abdicate on the 15th: later, he and his family were slaughtered. His rule was replaced by a provisional government under Alexander Kerensky, pledged to liberal reforms and to a continuation of the war. In that, however, one disaster followed another, and Russian soldiers began to desert in droves, often shooting their officers and simply returning home. The Germans took advantage of the confusion to send to Petrograd (until then, St Petersburg) a sealed train containing one Vladimir Ilyich Ulyanov, better known as Lenin, a Marxist revolutionary who had been living in precarious exile in Switzerland. Lenin, a leading member of the Bolsheviks, the militant wing of the Russian Social Democrats, was committed not only to a socialist revolution in Russia, but also to withdrawal from a war he regarded as being the inevitable cataclysm of capitalism. After an initial failure in July, on 7 November Lenin and his closest adherent, Leo Trotsky (whose surname had originally been Bronstein) seized power and set up a communist dictatorship. Four months later, the new regime signed the Treaty of Brest–Litovsk with the Central Powers, which took Russia out of the war, albeit for the loss of considerable territory. The Allies now faced the prospect of German divisions, released from the Eastern Front, joining their compatriots in France and Flanders.

Ludendorff now decided that Great Britain could be starved into submission by *unrestricted* submarine warfare, a policy under which any ship trading with Britian would be sunk, and which would also break the British blockade now beginning to bite upon German civilians. The campaign very nearly succeeded. One out of four British merchant ships was sunk, neutral countries declined to trade with Great Britain, and at one stage the latter indeed appeared to be only some ten weeks away from national starvation. Amazingly enough, as late as January the British

Admiralty had rejected the notion of reintroducing convoys as a means of protecting the merchantmen; and had it not been for the insistence of the Prime Minister, Lloyd George, who intervened personally to demand the adoption of the convoy system, it is probable that Great Britain would have been forced to withdraw from the war, and Germany's U-boats would have ruled the waves. Fortunately, the convoys, with their naval escorts armed with new weapons like the depth charge, dropped the the loss rate from 1 in 4 to 1 in 120. Great Britain retained her supremacy at sea, and her naval blockade of Germany tightened.

There was a further backlash upon Germany. Propaganda, in some hands, at least, was now becoming an effective weapon of the war. It was the aim of German propaganda to keep America neutral: it was the aim of British propaganda to bring America into the war on the Allied side. German propaganda was embarrassingly inept, at one stage even claiming that alleged German atrocities had been caused by 'the bloodthirsty behaviour of the Belgians'. British propaganda was more subtle and skilful, and had been aided by incidents, which it fully exploited, in which American ships, or ships bearing American nationals, had been threatened or attacked by German vessels. The most notorious of these incidents had occurred on 7 May 1915, when the British liner *Lusitania*, out of New York, had been torpedoed and sunk without warning off the south coast of Ireland. Some 1,153 passengers died, among them 128 Americans. The British were further assisted by that strange poet, mystic and mountaineer, Aleister Crowley, who managed to infiltrate German propaganda headquarters in New York and become editor of their organ, *The Fatherland*, which he proceeded to fill with deliberately counter-productive propaganda. When, on 6 April 1917, President Woodrow Wilson, who had won the 1916 election with the slogan, 'He kept us out of the war,' declared war on Germany and her allies, the Americans roared their approval as they marched to support him.

Given the Russian collapse and the enormous military, economic and industrial resources of the United States, it is surely obvious that Allied strategy should have been to husband their manpower and merely defend their lines until America could make her presence felt. This, however, was not obvious to General

Nivelle, who wanted to prove that he indeed possessed the secret of victory; nor to Italy's General Luigi Cadorna, who wanted to demonstrate his country's military prestige; nor to Britain's brave Sir Douglas Haig (by now a field marshal) who wanted to win the war before the Americans could arrive.

Whilst the Allies were preparing new offensives for the summer, the Germans withdrew to a more defensible line of especially prepared, enormously strong, fortifications, the Siegfried Line, or the Hindenburg Line, as the Allies called it. This left Nivelle unmoved. On 16 April, the French attacked for the second time on the Aisne (the first offensive, by the French and British after the Battle of the Marne in September 1914, had ended in stalemate), guided by a plan which had been outdated and rendered useless by the German withdrawal. The fact that the Germans had captured French plans did not assist Nivelle's 'We have the formula' offensive; the Germans had the 'formula' too. In just four days, the French suffered 187,000 casualties to the Germans' 163,000, though they persisted with their attacks into May.

This finally broke the offensive spirit of the French Army. The troops mutinied. In some cases, soldiers began to desert; in most, however, the troops simply held their positions as doughtily as ever, but would not attack. Nivelle was dismissed on 15 May and the new Commander-in-Chief, General Philippe Pétain, a defensive specialist whose tenacity at Verdun had earned him considerable praise, had to struggle to restore order. In time, and despite courts martial and some executions, he managed to restore morale, but the French Army in that war was not to be what it had been before Verdun.

A week earlier, on 9 April, Haig had attacked on a fifteen-mile front at Arras, north of the old British sector on the Somme, in order to support the Nivelle offensive and to draw German troops away from the area of the French attack. At the northern end of Haig's front of attack, the Canadian Corps stormed the dominating Vimy Ridge, taking and holding all their objectives and driving the Germans back in disarray, for the cost of 11,000 casualties. Vimy was one of the most outstanding actions of the entire war on the Western Front; the capture and continued occupation of one of the key positions on that front was to pay huge dividends to the defence of Arras and Amiens during the

German onslaught of March 1918. South of the Canadian sector, around Arras itself, British and Australian divisions also made gains and took considerable numbers of German prisoners, even in places capturing the first Hindenburg Line positions, as well as key villages fortified as part of that defensive line, but they were not able to exploit the advances of the first five days, and stalemate resumed. Haig might well have called off the offensive then, but he was committed to supporting the developing fiasco of the Nivelle offensive, and so maintained the attack until 5 May. British and Empire casualties in the Battle of Arras numbered some 150,000 men; German about 100,000; a further example of waste.

It has been argued for Haig that he now came to the rescue of the French. If so, this purported rescue is without parallel in the annals of military history; indeed, it is hard to find a man more guilty of the mass slaughter of his own troops. Although he had been largely responsible for the massacre of his own soldiers by machine-gun fire at Loos in 1915, Haig nevertheless dismissed the machine-gun as a weapon of no relevance, arguing that an allotment of two per battalion was sufficient, and resisting the endeavours of Lloyd George to increase the number to sixty-four, though this was finally done against Haig's wishes. He thought that the charge with rifle and bayonet would break through the German lines, despite repeated experiences demonstrating that it would not.

But how *was* the stalemate of attritional trench warfare to be broken? How was mobility to be restored? The problem was clearly understood by the then Lieutenant-Colonel J.F.C. Fuller, who served as a senior officer with the newly formed Tank Corps from 1916 and who was one of the principal advocates of armoured warfare. Fuller discerned that though the soldier could not carry bullet-proof armour, he could be carried in a bullet-proof vehicle, crossing acres of mud on caterpillar tracks instead of wheels.

Haig had used such tanks, as he had forty-nine of them in all, in an attack on the Somme on 15 September 1916 but although these met with some success, initially they were too few and too unreliable to produce the huge advances that had been hoped for them. Their effect on the Germans, however, was electrifying and considerable gains were made on that day. Even so, as late as the

1920s, Haig would still be declaring that the tank was a much over-rated weapon, just as he had of the machine-gun. Devoid of adequate tank support or intelligent tactics, the infantry continued to suffer. Some soldiers even shot themselves in the foot or injured themselves in other ways rather than risk life and limb under so stubborn and unimaginative a commander.

Matters grew worse when Haig's summer offensive, the Third Battle of Ypres in Flanders, commonly known as Passchendaele, opened on 18 July. In reviewing this, perhaps the most nightmarish battle the British and Empire troops fought, it is instructive to consider a collage of quotations about Haig:

'He was devoid of the gift of intelligible and coherent expression,' said David Lloyd Geroge, adding: 'Brilliant to the top of his army boots.'

'His war diary is a self-revealing document,' Lord Beaverbrook wrote in his *Men of Power* (1956); 'frank, truthful, egotistical, self-confident and malicious. His spear knew no brother.'

'Haig,' Major-General E.K.G. Smith states in *British Generalship in the Twentieth Century* (1970), 'failed perhaps to see that a dead man cannot advance, and that to replace him is only to provide another corpse.'

'In World War I,' William Manchester wrote in *American Caesar* (1979), 'Douglas Haig butchered the flower of British youth in the Somme and Flanders without winning a single victory.'

'A plan,' Liddell Hart wrote of Third Ypres, 'that was founded on faith rather than reason; both plan and faith were to be sunk in the mud of Flanders.'

Passchendaele was to have been the first stage of Haig's plan for a series of offensives in Flanders that would clear the Germans out of Belgium, freeing the Belgian ports and thus shortening the BEF's lines of supply, while at the same time leaving the German line in the north, driven back to Germany's border, weak and dangerously exposed. The prelude to the battle was another outstanding success: on 7 June, General Sir Herbert Plumer's Second Army took the vital Messines Ridge, consolidating its gains over the next four days, by which time it had suffered 25,000 casualties to the Germans' 23,000. 'Yet,' writes Peter Simkins in his *World War 1 1914–1918: The Western Front* (1991), 'as at

Arras, the British failed to follow up the victory.... Once again the Germans were allowed a respite, while the British threw away a fine chance of exploitation.' The Third Battle of Ypres proper began on 31 July, and ended, after repeated costly attacks almost every single one of which stalled in atrocious weather conditions and seas of mud, on 9 November, when Canadian troops finally took the few acres of cratered and rubble-strewn mud, coloured with brick dust, which constituted all that remained of the village of Passchendaele. This was the furthest point of the British advance in this sector; getting there had cost each side some 250,000 casualties. Almost worse, however, the advance had left a dangerous salient, five miles in depth, projecting from the British line, which would cost Haig dearly some months later during the Ludendorff Offensive of March 1918.

At Passchendaele, Haig blithely ignored the advice of meteorological experts that he could only operate within two weeks of fine weather. A memorandum from Tanks Corps HQ to General HQ pointed out that Haig's proposed artillery bombardment would destroy the intricate drainage system of the area, low-lying and notorious for its wet weather, rendering the ground an impassable swamp. Lesser failures included the fact that wire-cutters issued to British troops proved virtually useless. Haig neglected facts in favour of his fantasy, a massed assault, or series of massed assaults, by which the British would slice through the German lines in Flanders and take the Belgian ports. As Liddell Hart stated, however, the offensive was doomed before it even began. Haig can conceivably be defended for his handling of the first week of his failed mass assault, but certainly not for its stubborn continuation, long after it had become clear that the appalling weather and conditions, more even than the German defence, made any success savagely costly. This tactically impossible battle, fought in a swamp that became a vast bog in which the wounded drowned, and which all too often smothered the effects of bursting high-explosive shells, making artillery bombardments sometimes virtually pointless, finally petered out without any notable gain, and at a terrible cost to the lives or health or sanity of the troops who had fought there.

In desperation, Haig finally allowed Colonel Fuller, Chief of Staff to the Tank Corps, to launch the style of offensive he had constantly advocated and planned for: an assault by *massed* formations of tanks. The resulting victory at Cambrai on 20 November made the greatest British advance on the Western Front since 1914 and took 10,000 prisoners; however, incompetent infantry generalship failed to exploit the breakthrough, and successive German counter-attacks eventually recaptured all ground taken.

These were not the only disasters for the Allies. On 4 October, Austro–Hungarian and German forces assailed the Italian armies at Caporetto, a small town on the River Isonzo, some ten miles inside Austria, which marked the limit of Italian advances during eleven offensives over the previous two and more years. By 4 November, the Italians had been driven back to the River Piave with losses of 293,000 captured; 40,000 men killed or wounded; and another 400,000 deserted. General von Bulow's German Fourteenth Army had caused the Italian front line to collapse with gas shells, and had then exploited every weak point by concentration of force upon it. By the end of the first week of November, however, the front had been stabilized on the Piave by a stiffening of British and French troops, though these could be ill-spared from the Western Front, whence they had been detached with their sterling commander, Plumer, who was virtually unique in the attention he paid to the welfare of his men.

But by the end of 1917, unless American power and resources could be deployed in time, a victory for the Central Powers looked likely.

Meanwhile, the matter of Haig's generalship is best summarized by the story of a British lieutenant-colonel who had won the Victoria Cross on the Somme and who was sent to inspect the front line at Passchendaele. This gallant officer burst into tears at what he saw.

'Oh, my God,' he sobbed, 'did we send men to die in that?'

1918

On 21 March, eighteen days after the signing of Germany's peace treaty with Communist Russia at Brest–Litovsk, Ludendorff flung the entire resources of Germany at the Allies in a final bid for victory. 'The English soldiers fight like lions,' Ludendorff had said, only to be answered by his adjutant Hoffman: 'True. But don't we know they are lions led by donkeys?'

The Germans, attacking without preliminary bombardment and using new tactics including storm troops – who bypassed defended positions, leaving them to be mopped up by following troops, thus maintaining the momentum of the advance – proceeded to smash their way through the unprepared Anglo–French forces.

The British Fifth Army on the Somme was destroyed within the first ten days of Ludendorff's offensive and the British suffered more casualties than they would during 1944–5.

If nothing can so far be said for Haig in terms of attack, he did at least rally his troops in defence, notably by his Order of the Day of 11 April, issued as the Germans commenced the Fourth Battle of Ypres, the second thrust of what came to be called the Ludendorff offensive: 'There is no other course open to us but to fight it out. Every position must be held to the last man: there must be no retirement. With our backs to the wall and believing in the justice of our cause each one of us must fight on to the end.'

Although words do not stop bullets, the British line swayed but held. Much territory was given up, however, including the tactically important Messines Ridge, as British forces in the north and French in the south and east of the front retired before successive German attacks. The Germans launched two more massive assaults, on 27 May and 9 June, one just west of Rheims and another further to the west, between Montdidier and Noyon. Early in July, a fifth attack was launched to the east of Rheims, near Châlons sur Marne, in the area of eastern France which Ludendorff believed to be vulnerable.

A further offensive, launched on 27 May, led to a second battle of the Marne as the Germans once again came within sight of Paris. By 2 August, both sides had lost roughly 1,000,000 men but Ludendorff's gamble had ended, though it had come perilously close to success. The Germans could not make up their losses, but Allied resistance was stiffened by the large numbers of American soldiers who were finally beginning to take their place in the defensive line.

General Pétain, who had restored order to the French Army after the mutinies of 1917 by promising no more bloody offensives, had stayed calm in his defensive role. In the crisis, as the Germans broke through in March and pushed forward in April, the Allies had at last realized the need for a single unified command.

General Ferdinand Foch, who had commanded the French Ninth Army at the first battle of the Marne, and French operations during the 1916 battle of the Somme, had therefore been appointed Supreme Commander to co-ordinate the British Expeditionary Force under Haig, the French Army under Pétain (to whom Foch had been Chief of Staff until his new appointment) and the associated American Expeditionary Force under General John 'Black Jack' Pershing, as well as various other troops on the Western Front, such as the Portuguese. The inexperienced Americans proved to be extraordinarily brave and suffered high casualties in consequence.

Foch had been renowned as the expounder of the offensive. During the first battle of the Marne in 1914, he had sent a signal to Joffre: 'Hard pressed on my right. My centre is yielding. Impossible to manoeuvre. Situation excellent. I am attacking.' '*L'audace!*' was his motto; '*et toujours l'audace et encore l'audace!*' His audacious generalship in the opening years of the war had in fact resulted in small gains and high losses; yet, as he wrote in *Principles of War* (1919): 'The unknown is the governing condition of war.'

In 1918, and probably for the first time in his life, Foch saw the virtue of well-organized retirements, leading the German invaders into a series of salients as his armies regrouped, thus rendering the enemy vulnerable to counter-attacks from right, left and centre. From August, the Allies launched a series of attacks, driving the Germans back before them. Before long, war of mobility was therefore restored. Foch called himself the 'conductor of an opera who beats time well.' Wherever the Allies counter-attacked, there were the tanks, often spearheading the advance and having a shock effect out of all proportion to their actual achievements, for the apparent remorselessness of their advance tended to demoralize the exhausted German troops. On 8 August the great Battle of Amiens began, termed by Ludendorff 'the black day of the German Army' and 'the worst experience I had to go through'. Assisted by mass tank formations, the Allies forced retreat upon the Germans. The British and Empire forces fought eight victorious battles in succession, storming the Hindenburg Line on 27 September. To the south and east, the French and Americans also drove the Germans back before them. Meanwhile, the Royal Navy's work had finally come to fruition. The blockade had reduced German civilians almost to the level of starvation, and things were little better for the troops; in Germany itself, there were riots in protest at food shortages. The Imperial High Seas Fleet, bottled up in Kiel, was driven to mutiny, and more mutinies among army and naval units based in other major cities followed. On 9 August, Ludendorff, desperate and close to nervous breakdown, advised Kaiser Wilhelm II to seek am armistice. He himself then fled to neutral Sweden, disguising himself with a false beard and tinted glasses.

It is ironic that Ludendorff, arguably the best commander of the war, and who, in his great offensive of March 1918, had captured more ground – ten times more – than had the Allies during all their 1917 offensive operations, should have been the first senior German commander to recognize that the war was over. On the night of 7–8 November 1918, a German delegation cross the Allied lines under a white flag to negotiate an armistice with Foch. Wearied of the old order, of autocracy and militarism that had brought her to bankruptcy and near-starvation, and left at least 1.8 million of her young men dead and a further 4.2 million wounded, Germany began to drift towards revolution. Trade unionism, socialism, even communism, all emerged as new threats amidst the clamour of approaching defeat. In cities and ports, in barracks, on warships, at naval bases, from town halls, the Red Flag began to appear, something unthinkable in the Germany of 1914. On 9 November, the Kaiser abdicated, fleeing to neutral Holland, where he was to live in exile until his death in 1941 (by which time, ironically, Holland was occupied by the troops of a new and altogether more sinister Germany). On the 11th, representatives of the German and Allied forces signed an armistice, and at 11 o'clock that morning all fighting ceased. There followed the Paris Peace Conference of January 1919 to January 1920, as a result of which, on 28 June 1919, the Treaty of Versailles was signed, the terms dictated to Germany by the victorious Allies. So severe were those terms, however, that the Germans signed only under protest, while the US Congress refused to ratify the treaty.

Whereas the Treaty of Vienna in 1815, marking the end of the Napoleonic Wars, had prevented a major pan-European war for ninety-nine years, the Treaty of Versailles provoked one in twenty. The empires of Germany, Austria–Hungary, Turkey and Russia ceased to exist; new borders were drawn, new countries created. Germany descended into economic and social chaos, her armed forces limited to a bare minimum of men and equipment necessary for defence, and forbidden tanks, heavy warships, military aircraft; ordered to pay massive and punitive reparations; her industry restricted; some of her territory lost to her former enemies; forced to confront the notion of 'war guilt' for her part in starting and prosecuting the conflict. Not many years later, out of the rubble of hyper-inflation and shattered national pride, there arose new politicians, to build a new order founded upon the myth that the German Army in the Great War had not been defeated, but had been stabbed in the back by subversive forces – communists and Jews in particular – within Germany herself.

Of the victors, France was left crippled by the cost, both human and economic, of the war, while her fear of a German resurgence, born in 1870 and confirmed between 1914 and 1918, led her to seek to weaken, restrict and humiliate her former enemy. Great Britain, too, once the banker to the world, was crippled by the cost, while a deep war-weariness after 1918 caused her, in the 1930s, to promote the cause of appeasement until it was almost too late. Japan, which had played a minor part on the Allied side, emerged as a major power. The United States of America became the world's most powerful nation, but shortly after the Peace Conference chose to shelve her international responsibilities, refusing to join the League of Nations that had been set up under the Versailles Treaty, a treaty which she had not in any case ratified. Meanwhile, Western European culture and civilization as they had hitherto been known had been ruined. The last words on the Treaty of Versailles belong to Foch, by then a Marshal of France: 'This is not a peace treaty, it is an armistice for twenty years.'

21

The Second World War (1939–1945)

It was once said of Adolf Hitler that he was the greatest general of all time – by his sycophantic Minister of Propaganda, Josef Goebbels. He has also been criticized by military experts as a clueless amateur who relied on intuition rather than intelligence. Two facts are certain. The first is that within a short time he won for Germany an empire stretching from the Arctic to North Africa, from the Bay of Biscay in the west to the Caspian Sea and the suburbs of Moscow in the east. The second is that he lost this empire, this Third Reich 'which would endure for a thousand years', in an equally short space of time, and in doing so reduced his own country, and others, to rubble, killing between 40 and 52 million people in the process.

As Winston Churchill had discerned, Hitler had made his aims for German world domination all too clear in his boring, unpleasant and wretchedly written autobiography, *Mein Kampf* ('My struggle', written while Hitler was in prison during 1923–4). Having become, first, Chancellor in 1933, then President, and finally Führer (leader or chief) of the German nation in 1934, he wanted to avenge the humiliation of the Versailles Treaty.

Moulding his country into a war machine, like the Prussia of old, he sought to dominate Western Europe and to conquer Eastern Europe up to the Ural Mountains, achieving *Lebensraum* (living space) for the German people. Within this Third Reich, he would exterminate the Jews, the gypsies, the congenitally diseased or deformed, the mentally handicapped and all dissidents, then breed from the remaining 'racially pure' 'Aryan' stock the Superman for the future not just of Germany, but of the world. Destiny called. At the time, a surprising number of people thought Hitler's objectives laudable; others believed that they would result in George Orwell's nightmare vision expressed in *Nineteen Eighty Four*: 'A boot stamping on a human face – for ever.' (This matter can be studied in greater detail in my book *Hitler: Black Magician*, 1995).

From 1933, in a history beyond the scope of this work, Adolf Hitler, once a shabby beggar on the streets of Vienna, and a corporal during the First World War, in which he was gassed, and won the Iron Cross First Class, proceeded to subvert and subjugate every German institution. In time, he restored employment by adopting a war economy, and drafted every man, woman and child into units dedicated only to war or its support. However, his initial victories were diplomatic, and in these he was ably abetted, as A.J.P. Taylor demonstrated, by the appeasement policies of Great Britain and France between 1936 and 1939. In March 1936, Hitler ordered the military reoccupation of the Rhineland in flagrant defiance of the Versailles Treaty, under which the area had been permanently demilitarized – British occupying troops had been withdrawn in 1926, and French in 1930. In March 1938, and acting with the consent of Benito Mussolini, the Fascist dictator of Italy who two years earlier had defied him, moving divisions up to the border between Austria and Italy in order to threaten any German move, Hitler annexed Austria. At the Munich Conference in September the same year, in order to avoid another European war, Great Britain and France allowed Hitler, who was supported at the conference by its fourth member, Italy, to take the heavily industrialized border region of the Sudetenland and its fortifications from Czechoslovakia, which latter country had only come into existence as a result of the Treaty of Versailles. In March 1939, Hitler tore up the Munich

Agreement by seizing the Czech provinces of Bohemia and Moravia. Now he sought to take Poland, as Eastern Europe fell under German economic domination. Great Britain's blinkered, stubborn and inept Prime Minister, Neville Chamberlain, made a half-hearted attempt to form an alliance with Russia under its leader, Josef Stalin. The attempt failed. On 29 August Hitler promptly concluded a Nazi–Soviet Pact (also known as the Molotov–Ribbentrop Pact, after the Soviet and German Foreign Ministers who negotiated it, Vyacheslav Molotov and Joachim von Ribbentrop) between Germany and the USSR, essentially a mutual non-aggression treaty, but containing secret clauses amounting to an agreement to partition Poland, and to parcel out Lithuania, Latvia, Estonia, Finland and Bessarabia between the two countries. Hitler did not believe, despite guarantees which Britain and France had given to Poland,·that there would be any Allied intervention in the event of a Nazi invasion, which took place on 1 September 1939, Soviet Russia invading eastern Poland soon after. In this, however, Hitler was wrong. Great Britain and France declared war on 3 September. 'If we lose this war, then God help us,' commented Reichsmarschall Hermann Göring, the commander of the Luftwaffe, the German air force.

Hitler was possessed of a formidable military machine. His plans, and those of his commanders, were also based to a considerable extent upon the thinking of two of the greatest British military historians and strategists, Captain Basil Liddell Hart and Major-General J.F.C. Fuller (who had retired from the army in 1933). The British High Command, foolishly, had rejected most of their theories, many of which were eagerly adopted by the German High Command, and studied by the resurgent German Army's leaders. Fuller, in particular, the architect of the tank victory at Cambrai in 1917, advocated the use of massed formations of tanks combined with air support, and with paratroopers and collaborators causing disruption behind enemy lines, in order to spread terror and confusion, in a concept that came to be known as *Blitzkrieg* (lightning war). 'A prophet is not without honour, save in his own country' – Fuller was invited to the Führer's fiftieth birthday celebrations.

While the Germans and the Russians carved up Poland, the Allies resorted to *Sitzkrieg* (sitting war), and remained behind the

allegedly impregnable Maginot Line on France's eastern border
even though they could have destroyed the negligibly small
German force guarding its country's western frontier, they did not.
Fuller had called the Maginot Line 'the tombstone of France';
General Charles de Gaulle, who had been wounded and captured
at Verdun, was of the same opinion. A.J.P. Taylor entitled one of
his essays, on the French Commander-in-Chief, 'General Gamelin:
Or How To Lose'. When in April 1941, having conquered Poland,
Hitler turned his attention westwards, the boast of Göring was
fulfilled ('guns before butter') as the German armies turned the
Maginot Line with thrusts through Belgium and, at the eastern
end, around Sedan. Pushed back to the English Channel, the
British Expeditionary Force was evacuated at Dunkirk, aban-
doning most of its equipment, as France collapsed and
surrendered. In the end, nearly 200,000 British troops, and
140,000 French, were got away to Britain.

The conquests of Hitler up to this time were without historical
parallel. He had overrun Poland in twenty-seven days, Denmark in
one, Norway in twenty-three, Holland in five, Belgium in eighteen,
Northern France in thirty-nine; he would go on to take Yugoslavia
in twelve days, Greece in twenty-one and Crete in eleven, all
before the end of June 1941, meanwhile using German political
and economic muscle to make satellites of Hungary and Bulgaria.

In the wake of the disastrous defeat of May–June 1940, Great
Britain was offered peace proposals by Hitler. There is every
reason to suppose that these were genuine, since they were based
upon all he had expounded in *Mein Kampf*. Germany would be
allowed a free hand in the control of Continental Europe; Great
Britain, which would would not interfere in Europe, would in
return keep both her empire and her naval supremacy; the United
States would be given a free hand on the North American
continent, though Britain would retain its relationship with
Canada in return for not interfering in Europe and Asia; and
Japan, which in September 1940 had signed the Tripartite pact
with Germany and Italy, by which the three countries agreed to
support each other if any of them were attacked, would dominate
the Pacific Ocean and what is today called the Pacific Rim. Alan
Clark is of the opinion that Great Britain should have accepted
these peace proposals since these would have preserved the empire

and her position as a Great Power. This might have been a reasonable proposition had Britain been dealing with Kaiser Wilhelm II, but not with Adolf Hitler, as the ensuing collage of the Führer's remarks illustrates:

> Whoever sees in National Socialism [Nazism] nothing but a political movement doesn't know much about it.... We are often abused for being the enemies of the mind and spirit. Well, that is what we are, but in a far deeper sense than bourgeois science, in its idiotic pride, could ever imagine.... The idea of treating wars as anything other than the harshest means of settling questions of very existence is ridiculous. Every war costs blood, and the smell of blood arouses in man all the instincts which have lain within us since the beginning of the world: deeds of violence, the intoxication of murder.... Everything else is empty babble.... [National Socialism] is even more than a religion. It is the will to create mankind anew.

Winston Churchill, who became Prime Minister on 10 May 1940, when Chamberlain resigned, whatever his faults, discerned that Hitler intended to alter the nature of humankind without either humanity or kindness. For Churchill, therefore, this was not just another British war to prevent a nation from dominating the continent of Europe; it was a *Kulturkampf* – a struggle between two cultures for civilization. All who see fascism as the principal threat to human evolution have reason to be grateful to Churchill, who publicly stated:

> Even though large tracts of Europe and many old and famous states have fallen or may fall into the grip of the Gestapo and all the odious apparatus of Nazi rule, we shall not flag or fail. We shall go on to the end. We shall fight in France, we shall fight on the seas and oceans, we shall fight with growing confidence and growing strength in the air; we shall defend our island, whatever the cost may be. We shall fight on the beaches, we shall fight on the landing grounds, we shall fight in the fields and in the streets, we shall fight in the hills; we shall never surrender.

Under Churchill, Britain defied Hitler and his peace proposals. Whatever the cost of the defeat in France, she still had forces in the Mediterranean and the Middle and Far East; she had the resources in men and *matériel* provided by the Dominions and the Empire; her navy was still dominant; and her air force and most of her army had got back to Britain from France. Hitler therefore proposed Operation Sea Lion, the inention being to invade England from the south, take London, restore the Nazi sympathizer, the Duke of Windsor, who had reigned briefly as King Edward VIII in 1936, before abdicating in order to marry an American divorcee, and install a collaborationist government similar to the one now governing defeated France. Great Britain still enjoyed naval supremacy, however, which precluded a mass transportation of German troops, although most military experts agree that once the Wehrmacht (German Army) had landed, it would have taken London and forced a pitiable armistice. Technology had reached a point at which superiority in the air could negate naval supremacy. If Göring's Luftwaffe could destroy the Royal Air Force, then after that it would be easy to destroy the Royal Navy and the Wehrmacht would be able to land in full force.

The magnificent courage and skill of the Royal Air Force saved the British Isles. As Wellington might have said, however, it was a damn near thing. At the beginning of July 1940, Air Vice-Marshal Hugh Dowding, commanding RAF Fighter Command's 11 Group, which covered the south and south-east of England, had just 640 fighter aircraft to deploy against the 2,800 fighters, fighter-bombers and bombers of the Luftwaffe. The British had two technological advantages. One was radar, which enabled an enemy approach to be detected and RAF fighters 'vectored' on to the raiders, thus allowing the RAF's resources to be tactically deployed with speed and precision, with the additional benefit of conserving fuel. The other was the Supermarine Spitfire, a fighter which, while of roughly the same performance as the German Messerschmitt Bf109, was more manoeuvrable. The other notable British fighter, the Hawker Hurricane, though slower than the Spitfire, was both sturdier and had a better gun platform; some two-thirds of the German aircraft shot down in the Battle of Britain were downed by Hurricanes. These advantages enabled the

British to shoot down two German aircraft for every one lost, but Dowding was in despair: aircraft losses could be made good (albeit slowly at first) but pilots could not be replaced quickly. He saw that if this war of attrition continued at the pace at which the battle was fought between July and early September, eventually there would be so few British aircraft and pilots that the Germans would have achieved total air supremacy.

Fortunately for Great Britain, the defiance and resolve of the Royal Air Force caused such heavy losses among the Luftwaffe, that Göring, the man Hitler called 'Iron Hermann', lost his nerve. The Germans had in fact been succeeding with the tactic of bombing British airfields and catching RAF fighters either during take-off or landing, or as they returned, short of fuel and ammunition, after combat; by mid-September, however, the Luftwaffe's severe losses, and especially those suffered in two actions on 15 September, persuaded Göring to halt the bombing offensive against the airfields at a critical moment for Britain, and instead to switch to a strategy of battering the country into submission by the indiscriminate bombing of larger cities, especially London. The invasion of the British Isles was postponed. Britain still fought on. Churchill's tribute to the Royal Air Force in the Battle of Britain is well known: 'Never in the field of human conflict has so much been owed by so many to so few.' It is, however, worth remembering his words at the time of the Fall of France: 'Mr Hitler has promised to wring England's neck like a chicken. Some chicken! Some neck!'

Hitler condemned Churchill's words as mere empty bluster, not least because it was at the time impossible for Britain to land an army in Europe. The Führer therefore turned his attention to his ultimate objective, which was to colonize Russia up to the Ural Mountains. On 22 June 1941, Operation Barbarossa commenced without a declaration of war as Hitler casually tore up the Nazi–Soviet Pact; cynically, his directive for the operation dated from December 1940. Soon the two most disgusting tyrannies that the world has ever known would be locked together in the bloodiest campaign in history on a front that stretched from the Baltic to the Black Sea.

The initial German successes were again quite extraordinary and credit must be given to the extraordinary commander of the

Second Panzer (i.e. armoured) Army divisions, Lieutenant-General Heinz Guderian, who had proved himself in the Blitzkrieg in France in 1940, where his Panzers had broken through at Sedan and made a lightning advance to the Channel coast. Hitler's strategy was as direct as ABC. Army Group A would strike north to take Leningrad and so command the Baltic Sea; Army Group B would take Moscow, thus breaking the Soviet political will to resist; and Army Group C would take the great granary of the Ukraine.

Army Group A encircled Leningrad at the beginning of September, but the city refused to surrender despite appalling privations. Army Group C, under the capable Field Marshal Gerd von Rundstedt and with its astonishingly efficient panzer divisions commanded by Guderian, won a sensational victory at Kiev from August to October 1941, using the tactics similar to those of Hannibal at Cannae, encircling the Russian defenders with a pincer movement and taking 650,000 prisoners. 'Russia is now virtually defeated,' the Führer announced. However, Kiev was a tactical rather than a strategic victory. The advance towards Moscow by Army Group B had been temporarily halted in order to send reinforcements to Army Group C, so as to win the battle of Kiev. Army Group B did indeed reach the suburbs of Moscow, and it is arguable that in full strength it might have achieved its objective and taken the city but the incredible bravery of the Soviet troops and civilians, the workers who dashed out of factories to fight in the streets with hammers, forced the Germans to withdraw. It was beginning to become clear that in his invasion of Russia, Hitler had made a series of errors, which may be summarized as follows:

1. The campaign against Yugoslavia, successful though it was, had delayed the start of Operation Barbarossa by twenty-eight days.

2. The delay meant that the German campaign fell victim to adverse weather conditions. The rains came early in the autumn of 1941, churning the ground to mud and rendering any advance difficult. The first snow fell in early October. By the beginning of November, temperatures had fallen to below zero. Lubricating oil froze and jammed the German guns. German synthetic fuel separated into its two component parts. Hitler, normally most

attentive to the needs of his troops, had been convinced by some occult nonsense and his own megalomania that he could control the weather. The soldiers of the Wehrmacht, dressed in light summer uniforms, lacking warm headgear, winter boots, protective clothing, or goggles to prevent snow blindness, died in their thousands from frostbite and expired of exposure while performing their natural bodily functions. In December the temperature dropped to minus 40 degrees centigrade and Stalin, aided by General Winter, ordered an all-out attack on the German Army Groups A, B, and C, on a front running from the Baltic to the Black Sea. Hitler had gambled on winning before the onset of winter, and also on that winter being mild. What no one could have foretold was that the winter of 1941–42 in Russia would prove to be the earliest and coldest in 250 years.

3. The Russians had already pursued a policy of 'scorched earth' as they had fallen back (and as they had done against Napoleon), harassing the German supply lines and ensuring that there was nothing left in the way of food or other supplies in any area through which they had retreated.

4. When, in 1941, Stalin had appointed himself as Commissar of Defence and a Marshal, he had the sense also to appoint Marshal Georgi K. Zhukov as his deputy in the post of Chief of Staff. The interaction between the two is described well in *Command*, edited by James Lucas (1988):

> The relationship was not an easy one. Stalin was a dictator who had murdered millions in the past and was to murder millions more in the future. He crushed any opposition with torture and the firing squad. Zhukov was a blunt, outspoken peasant with a reputation for ruthlessness, vindictiveness and viciousness. On one occasion Stalin shouted that a proposal Zhukov had made was rubbish. Zhukov was furious. 'If you think that your chief of staff can only talk rubbish,' he retorted, 'then demote me to a private soldier and let me defend my country with a rifle and a bayonet in my hand.'

Zhukov was arguably the most effective general of the Second World War, commanding northern, central and southern fronts. As soon as new or replacement equipment became available, either from Russian factories working flat out, or from the Western Allies, he turned the Blitzkrieg on to the Germans. Moreover, Russian soldiers were trained to live off the land, and were accustomed to the hideous winter conditions; the Germans were not.

5. As Fuller points out, Hitler's greatest mistake consisted in not winning over the populations of the Baltic states and the Ukraine, who initially welcomed the Germans as liberators from Stalinist tyranny, sending their women and children to present flowers to the invaders. Both the stupidity and the cruelty of Nazism are underlined by the Führer's insistence upon the brutalization and enslavement of peoples who might have been his willing allies.

6. The German invasion enabled Stalin to make a great appeal to the peoples of the Soviet Union, and to harness propaganda to his needs in a cry for unity of purpose based not upon communism, but upon 'Mother Russia' and Russian nationalism. holding aloft in defiance the Red Flag, under which all peoples of the USSR could unite. The Winter Campaign under Zhukov pushed the Germans back from Moscow. Their ordeal, had they known it, was in fact only just beginning.

On Sunday, 7 December 1941, Japan, allied to Germany, bombed without warning the US Pacific Fleet in the anchorage of Pearl Harbor, Hawaii, the intention being to cripple United States naval power and enforce a peace, so allowing Japan to take the economic prizes of South-East Asia: Malaya, Singapore, Burma, the Dutch East Indies, the Philippines, Hong Kong and a substantial chunk of China (which Japan had invaded in 1937). From December 1941 Japan attacked and conquered all save the last, and also occupied French Indo-China (now Cambodia, Laos and Vietnam). Admiral Isoruku Yamamoto achieved a brilliant tactical success at Pearl Harbor. Within two hours his carrier-launched aircraft had sunk or crippled 5 battleships and 14 smaller vessels, destroyed 120 aircraft, and killed some 2,000 US servicemen and 400 other people, for a loss of 29 aircraft from the 353 deployed. Strategically, however, the attack would prove to be a disaster for Japan. The Japanese naval task force failed to sink three American aircraft carriers, which were at sea at the time (and

three of the damaged battleships would be repaired and take part
in operations), and an outraged United States of America entered
the war, initially in the Pacific theatre. 'I fear we have only
awakened a sleeping giant and his reaction will be terrible,' said
Yamamoto.

Churchill promptly declared war on Japan, hoping to draw
America into the European theatre of operations. His task was
made easier by Hitler's casual declaration of war (in which Italy
joined) upon the United States on 10 December 1941. This was an
act of supreme folly, since the USSR, the USA and the British
Empire possessed between them 75 per cent of the globe's natural
resources. Hitler would lose the war he had come so close to
winning through an inability to understand that if he could not
win the initial campaign, as he had in Poland, Denmark, the Low
Countries and France from 1939 to 1940, then the odds against
him would in time become insuperable.

The Blitz, the Luftwaffe's bombing campaign against British
cities, principally by night, which lasted from 7 September 1940
until 10 May 1941, failed to shake British resolve. The U-boat war
in the Atlantic, supported by German surface raiders like the
battle-cruiser *Scharnhorst* and the 'pocket battleship' *Bismarck*,
was intended to destroy Allied merchant shipping and thus, as in
the days of Ludendorff, starve Great Britain into submission. The
British had the sense to continue with the convoy system, and
gradually came to support it with air power as longer-range
aircraft and better anti-submarine weapons, including radar, were
developed or became available. Even so, the Battle of the Atlantic
did not start well for the British. The U-boat fleet under Admiral
Karl Dönitz, who had played an important part in the building up
of Germany's submarine fleet from 1936 to 1939, managed to sink
496 Allied merchant ships with a gross registered tonnage of 2.42
million in 1941. In 1942 the U-boats and the German Navy sank
in the Atlantic 1,006 shops at 5.47 million GRT. British response
and retaliation, based upon the use of air power, lowered the
losses to 463 ships at 2.59 million GRT in 1943 and 132 at 0.77
million GRT in 1944. The German losses in submarines became
increasingly severe. For instance, though 98 German U-boats had
been commissioned between May and August 1943, 123 were
lost. Although the Allies lost shipping displacing 12 million GRT,

it can be argued that the Battle of the Atlantic, fought for vital supplies and equipment, was the most crucial victory of the Second World War.

In North Africa, Hitler had hoped that Mussolini's Italian forces (Italy had entered the war in 1940 when France was collapsing and a Nazi victory seemed certain) would put to rout the relatively small British force based in neutral Egypt to protect the Suez Canal, the key to Great Britain's hold on the Middle Eastern oilfields and the supply routes to South Africa, India and the Far East. The Italians met with disaster in Libya, and Hitler therefore sent reinforcements, the Afrika Korps under the brilliant General Erwin Rommel, whom the British called 'the Desert Fox'. Rommel proceeded to fight a superb campaign, all the while appealing to Hitler for fresh troops and supplies, knowing that if only he could take Suez, Germany would achieve a choke-hold on oil and other supplies to the British Empire's war effort which would ultimately force peace upon a still-defiant Britain.

Given the Royal Navy's dominance – not wholly uncontested, admittedly – in the Mediterranean, Hitler endeavoured to reinforce Rommel by drawing neutral Spain into the war. To that end, on 23 October 1940 he had met Generalissimo Francisco Franco, the fascist dictator of Spain, in a railway carriage at Hendaye, on the French border with Spain. If Franco had entered the war, his troops, hardened by the rigours of the Spanish Civil War (1936–39), would have ensured victory for the Axis forces in North Africa and, ultimately, a British withdrawal from the war. Franco, however, had chosen to practise *Sitzfleisch*, a German word meaning to sit on one's seat hour after hour, making moves that are sound but utterly uninspiring until one's opponent blunders through boredom. His country had been sundered and all but destroyed by the Civil War, and he was hoping for American economic aid, and above all money, in return for maintaining Spanish neutrality. This he later received. Hitler reminded Franco of the German military aid sent to assist his Nationalist forces during the Spanish Civil War – notably the air component known as the Kondor Legion which, among other raids, had bombed and destroyed Guernica in 1937. Franco had merely nodded. Afterwards, Hitler remarked that he would rather have a tooth pulled than deal with the Generalissimo again. Not for the first time, or the last, Hitler had neglected the power of American money.

By late 1941, Hitler was so preoccupied with the Eastern Front that he failed to send Rommel the troops and supplies the latter required, preferring to husband his resources for the war in Russia. The British base at Malta, though repeatedly bombarded from the air, contributed to the sinking of 75 per cent of Axis shipping in the Mediterranean. On 25 June 1942 General Sir Claude Auchinleck won a victory at the First Battle of El Alamein, halting the Axis advance into Egypt and saving the Middle East from German control. Churchill failed to appreciate the import of this success and replaced Auchinleck as C-in-C, Middle East, with General Sir Harold Alexander, with General Sir Bernard Montgomery as field commander of the Eighth Army (which Auchinleck, having sacked the army commander, had himself commanded at El Alamein). Montgomery proved himself to be a patient, meticulous and inspiring defensive commander, with a genius for raising his troops' morale, and careful of their lives. In August he defeated Rommel at Alam Halfa; then, having waited for reinforcements, he finally struck a decisive blow at the Second Battle of El Alamein, which began, after typically meticulous preparation, on 23 October 1942. Numerical superiority and sound generalship gave the Eighth Army a stunning victory and in four months Montgomery chased the Afrika Korps and its Italian allies westwards into Tunisia. In this he was aided by the Anglo–American landings in French North Africa, under the American General Dwight D. Eisenhower, in which Free French units also took part, as they had in the Western Desert campaigns. The Vichy-French forces in Algeria, under Admiral Jean Louis Darlan, were ordered not to fire on the Allies, with the result that the rest of France was occupied by the Nazis. On 12 May 1943 all Axis forces in North Africa surrendered; by then, Rommel had returned to Germany.

Hitler appears to have dismissed this matter from his mind as a minor sideshow, for he was concentrating all his attention upon the USSR. 'As for the cold, *I* will see to that,' he told General Guderian, 'Attack!' But whatever Hitler thought, whatever he desired, his armies simply could not hold their lines against the Russians during the savage winter of 1941–2, and suffered before

Moscow their first defeat of the war. By the spring of 1942, the campaign had cost 1,168,000 German casualties, excluding the sick.

Hitler's reliance upon his intuition, and his failure to take account of Russian reserves and resilience, must therefore take the blame for the losses suffered by the hitherto invincible armies of the Third Reich. On the other hand, he could also take the credit for ensuring that this defeat did not turn into a catastrophic rout. Guided once more by his sense of inevitable destiny, the Führer overruled his High Command and flew in the face of all established principles of military science by refusing to allow any tactical withdrawals. He insisted that his soldiers fight where they stood without yielding an inch of ground. Costly though this strategy was, it prevented the melting away of his armies in the frozen Russian wastes, the doleful fate of Napoleon's Grand Army. Unfortunately for his troops, however, Hitler would continue to insist upon repeating this strategy for the rest of the war; and so what had originally prevented disaster, ultimately brought about total defeat.

But for the present, in 1942 defeat on the Eastern Front had been averted, and Hitler was still convinced that victory would yet be his. It was during this period, however, that he developed to the full those traits of character which would finally negate any possibility of a German victory. Alan Bullock, in his *Hitler: A Study in Tyranny* (1960), puts forward the unarguable theory that Hitler came to believe completely in his own infallibility. Until 1942, the Führer's decisions, though prompted by his intuition, had been based upon calculation, and had to some extent taken account of military advice from his senior commanders; now, however, he adopted the view that whatever he did was right, simply because he did it, and only a handful of commanders, among them Guderian, dared check, criticize or even question his insistence upon his own omniscience. Previously he had based his decisions or theories upon facts, albeit in an extraordinary way; now he simply refused to accept the existence of facts that displeased him. So strong did his personal magnetism remain, however, that commanders who entered his headquarters with an iron determination to apprise him of the true facts of a military situation, left with the conviction that, somehow, their Führer knew better. All doubts vanished, moreover, in the spring of 1942, when the German offensive against Russia was renewed with startling success.

A series of spectacular victories brought Army Group C to the southern reaches of the River Volga, where it stood poised to take the oilfields of Batum and Baku, and to gain control of the Caspian Sea. As a result, there followed the great Battle of Stalingrad, arguably the most crucial encounter on land of the Second World War.

The Battle of Stalingrad, which lasted from September 1942 to February 1943, was initially just a battle of attrition. The turning point probably came when Zhukov took command of the Russian defence. He realized soon enough that although the crack troops of General Friedrich von Paulus's Sixth Army were pushing their way inexorably towards the centre of the city, their flanks were protected only by poorly armed Romanian conscripts. Unlike the dark days of 1941, supplies were now reaching the Soviet forces from the factories which Stalin had established behind the Ural Mountains, and from the convoys that brought American and British food and *matériel* into Russia. As a result, in the third week of November Zhukov was able to launch a series of devastating counter-strokes, principally against the weak German flanks. Besiegers now became besieged, and despite heroic German resistance, only a retreat in good order could have saved the situation, as Paulus realized. Hitler, however, refused to countenance even a reasoned discussion of such a possibility. Consequently, on 2 February 1943 the German Sixth Army surrendered. Of its 300,000 men, a lucky 35,000 had been evacuated by air; 175,000 had perished; and 90,000 had been captured, of which only 5,000 ever returned to Germany.

The Russians quickly tried to capitalize on the German disaster, but the German front was stabilized by a superb defensive mechanized counter-attack under General Erich von Manstein at Kharkov. This delayed, but did not cripple, the planned Russian advance. In July 1943, the Germans launched an onslaught upon that seemingly vulnerable Russian salient at Kursk. Two Panzer armies with 2,000 tanks sought to pulverize the Soviet defenders by trapping them with a pincer movement. Zhukov responded with a solid defence of 6,000 tanks, 6,000 anti-tank guns and minefields sown at a density of 5,000 mines to the mile. This defensive barrage separated the Germany infantry from its armour. Zhukov now launched his counter-attack, sending a heavy concentration of forces against the gaps he could discern in the enemy's positions, destroying 900 German tanks and, on 23 August, retaking Kharkov. The Red Army had finally seized the initiative from the Wehrmacht, which was henceforth condemned to fighting a long, bitter and bloody series of battles against the advancing Russians, battles which pushed it further and further back towards Germany.

In the Pacific, the Battle of Midway on 4 June 1942, in a fierce action decided by superior use of aircraft carriers, the US Navy defeated the Japanese navy to re-establish naval supremacy. Henceforth the Japanese would be fighting an increasingly bloody and desperate series of defensive actions and doomed counter-strokes.

In the west between 1943 and 1944, the Allies carried out three audacious amphibious operations. Sicily was taken in July 1943, and provided the springboard for the invasion of Italy in September. This brought about the fall of Mussolini, though he was later restored as a puppet dictator of the north by Hitler. Under Field Marshal Albert Kesselring, the Germans in Italy fought a clever and stubborn series of defensive battles which seriously delayed, and for a time halted, the Allied advance. The third and most vital operation was D-Day on 6 June 1944, the main landings designed to open a 'Second Front', relieve the pressure on Russia by drawing German forces away from the Eastern Front, and, in the end, liberate Europe. German-held Normandy was invaded by a total of 39 divisions (14 British, 20 US, 3 Canadian, 1 Free French and 1 Polish), carried by 6,000 vessels and supported by 11,000 aircraft, the Allies by now having achieved complete supremacy in the air. The ground phase of the invasion was initially commanded by General Montgomery under the Supreme Commander, Allied Expeditionary Force, General Eisenhower, with US General Omar N. Bradley commanding the American forces under Montgomery's overall command. The Allied plans dated from early in 1943, and had been constantly revised and refined by Eisenhower, Montgomery, and their staffs; without doubt, they had planned well. The troops were landed successfully on five beaches, despite fierce fighting, stubborn German resistence and, in some landings, notably at Omaha Beach, heavy Allied casualties.

Although Montgomery, commanding the British, Canadian, French and Polish forces in the eastern sector, found himself held for a time at Caen by a stiff German defence, to the west the US Third Army under General George S. Patton advanced swiftly southwards before turning east, trapping the Germans against the anvil of Montgomery's armies. Paris fell to the Allies on 25 August. For the Wehrmacht and SS troops, streaming headlong to the east, through Belgium and on into Holland, or through north-eastern France, Eisenhower's Operation Overlord had been a catastrophe. Out of fifty divisions committed to the defence of Normandy, only ten remained as effective fighting units. Within three months, the German Army had suffered twice the number of casualties that it had sustained at Stalingrad. It looked as though the Western Allies would be occupying Berlin in time for Christmas.

A part in the taking of Berlin was essential to Britain if she were to remain in the front rank of the Great Powers; only thus could she win a main place at the negotiating table when the future of Europe, post-war, came to be discussed. An astute summary of the failure to defeat Germany in 1944 was written by Alan Clark in a *Daily Telegraph* review of *A Genius for War: A Life of General George S. Patton* by Carlo D'Este (1996):

Of the army group commanders, Bradley wanted a 'short hook' to Falaise [in Normandy]; Montgomery, a long sweep behind the Seine – then changed his mind in favour of the tactically crazy scheme to vault the Rhine at Arnhem. Eisenhower favoured a political formula; no risks, keep up appearances, no one must get too much limelight. Most important of all, the Chief Logistician, US General Lee, was wholly unsympathetic to Patton and thwarted him all day long. Had Lee been overruled, had every gallon, every round, been diverted to the Third Army in early August, it is my belief that Patton would have driven the whole way. There was nothing in front of him except the obsolete, undermanned bunkers of the old Siegfried Line. And even with what he was allowed, he nearly made it.

Clark's judgement of Patton is balanced: 'What a perfectly dreadful human being! The man must have been pathological.... But Patton was the one man who could have won the war in an afternoon. Or, at least, over the last ten days of August in 1944.'

Whatever one may think of Patton, who was arrogant, abrasive, heedless of armies other than his own, daring, and sometimes reckless, one cannot doubt that General Lee ranks among the worst commanders of all time. Whilst Patton, Montgomery and Bradley were crying out for supplies so as to capitalize upon and consolidate the success of their lightning advance through France, Lee neglected to dispatch them and instead devoted his attention to what he considered to be far more important matters, such as writing memoranda which deplored the sloppy saluting practices and poor dress of the Allied troops in Paris. The essential notion of swift supply of fighting *matériel* to the troops at the front was replaced by a gross and undignified obsession with saluting, boot polish, Brasso and blanco, which last term might be said to describe, in military terms, the state of Lee's mind.

On 17 September 1944, Montgomery essayed his gamble at Arnhem. Why did he do this? Before Operation Market Garden, Montgomery had been characterized as a cautious general who attacked only when in possession of advantageous terrain and a greater weight of men, artillery, armour, air support and munitions. One reason is egotism. Vaulting ambition and jealousy of US generals Bradley and Patton had led him to believe that all resources should go to his 21st Army Group, which alone should drive for Berlin; and that he should thereby replace Eisenhower as Supreme Commander. The second reason was political pressure. Montgomery discerned that Great Britain, with its straining and near exhausted resources, could only remain a major power were the war to be won by the end of 1944.

The necessity of winning the war swiftly for the British Empire, a series of personal rivalries with Bradley and Patton, and his personal obsession in being the first to Berlin, caused Montgomery to attempt a series of airborne landings to lay a paratroop 'carpet' for the purpose of seizing, in turn from the south to the north, the key bridges in northern Holland over the River Maab, Waal, and at Arnhem, the lower Rhine. This would open the way for an armoured thrust across the Rhine and into the Ruhr. A daring operation, it was misconceived in the first place and then hastily planned without sufficient notice being paid to intelligence reports, and turned out to be a disastrous failure that destroyed the British 1st Airborne Division and dissipated the SHAEF Strategic Reserve, since the plans fell into German hands.

This was Montgomery's most hideous catastrophe. His defeat here was further occasioned by bad luck due to adverse weather conditions; by delays in the advance of the XXX Corps moving up a single road to link with the American and British airborne divisions, the lynch pin of the operation; catastrophic lack of information concerning the formidable defensive disposition of the German troops plus the presence of Panzer divisions; and over-cautious planning which led to the British 1st Airborne Division, dropped at Arnhem to secure the northernmost bridges, those over the Lower Rhine, being landed too far from their objectives. All objectives were achieved initially nevertheless and with incredible bravery but there was a fierce German counter-attack and after an heroic defence, the British 1st Airborne was forced to retire, having suffered savage casualties.

Despite this disastrous defeat, Montgomery continued to claim that Market Garden had been '90 per cent successful,' for reasons best known to himself, even though his delay in the capture of Antwerp was criticized by the Americans: he had by-passed that city, so allowing the German army there to escape, from which elements then regrouped at Arnhem in time to help defeat 1st Airborne's assault.

Insight into Montgomery's character can be gained from the anecdote of an occasion when Montgomery dined at Buckingham Palace with the Prime Minister, Winston Churchill, and King George VI. Montgomery dominated the conversation, delivering a lecture on the way in which Great Britain should be governed in peacetime and then excused himself, temporarily, as he left the room.

'I think he's after my job,' Churchill rumbled.

'Oh, th-thank heavens,' the King replied, 'I th-th-thought he was after mine.'

Nevertheless, it is true that Montgomery's subsequent generalship was sound, and that he was attentive to the needs of his troops, as it is also true of Patton. The latter made a swift and breathtaking advance to the River Meuse which was halted only because the abominable General Lee did not send the fuel required for its continuation. The Germans were thereby enabled to launch a counter-offensive in the Ardennes in December 1944, driving a deep wedge into Bradley's US Twelfth Army Group, in what came to be called the 'Battle of the Bulge'. In the crisis, Montgomery was given command north of the 'bulge', and Bradley himself to the south, both generals contributing to the steadying of the battered American units, before beginning to launch counter-attacks. To relieve the pressure on Bradley's troops, Patton moved with breathtaking speed, accomplishing in hours manoeuvres estimated as requiring days, wheeling his army, which had faced eastwards, north to counter-attack the Germans and halt their advance. 'No poor goddamn bastard ever won a war by dying for his country,' Patton declared; 'he won a war by making the *other* poor goddamn bastard die for *his* country.' His men called him: 'Old Blood and Guts', though they added cynically, 'our blood, his guts'. In common with General Sherman in the American Civil War, Patton destroyed utterly any village or town which offered his army the slightest resistance. It is probable that he could have taken Berlin before the Russians, but Eisenhower reined him in, as the result of the agreement between the US President Franklin Roosevelt, Stalin and Churchill at the Yalta Conference in February, which effectively resolved the post-war division of Europe. The Germans fought stubbornly to hold on to the west bank of the Rhine, and so keep the Allies out of the Fatherland. For a time they held; then, early in February, the Americans captured intact the bridge over the Rhine at Remagen, and poured men and equipment over the river. In March, at Wesel to the north, Montgomery commanded a combined amphibious and airborne crossing of the Rhine, and his Twenty-First Army Group, too, began to stream across into the German heartland. Still desperately fighting, hurling boys and old men and cripples into the action, the German forces fell back to the east.

On the Eastern Front, Marshal Zhukov had smashed Army Group B in June 1944, and the Russian advance towards Germany became relentless. The cutting of German supply lines by Russian partisans contributed to his victories, as did the surge of Russian nationalism that Stalin had inspired, but Zhukov also had a gift for selecting the best subordinate commanders and for winning the love and respect of his own men. No man in the Second World War was able to direct effectively such huge formations of troops upon so vast a field of battle. The siege of Leningrad, begun in August 1941, was finally relieved in January 1944 after which the Baltic states of Estonia, Latvia and Lithuania were taken, despite fierce resistance. Zhukov then directed two Red Army 'fronts' (army groups) and advanced through Poland to take Berlin by 2 May, having sent some of his forces racing westwards to the Elbe to ensure that the Western Allies would subsequently be in a weak bargaining position, with more than half Germany in Soviet hands. On 25 April 1945, troops from Bradley's Twelfth Army group linked up with the Russians at the Elbe.

On 30 April 1945, Hitler committed suicide. On 7 May 1945, his successor as Führer, Admiral Dönitz, ordered the unconditional surrender of all German forces still fighting.

In the Far East, the Japanese were slowly pushed back for their gains. The victory of Admiral William Halsey at Leyte Gulf on 17–20 October 1944 consolidated US naval supremacy, and finally proved that air power had rendered the battleship obsolete. Henceforth naval warfare would be predicated on the use of aircraft carriers, destroyers, missile cruisers, submarines and frigates. The Americans then proceeded to recapture the Philippines by July 1945, and to retake one Pacific island after another by daring amphibious operations, meanwhile using both submarines and aircraft to strangle the economic life of Japan, including the strategic bombing of Japanese cities. American losses were high, however, for Japanese resistance was stiff. On 25 July 1945, after one of the hardest, bloodiest, and least sung campaigns of the entire war, the British and Indian Army units of General Sir William Slim's Fourteenth Army, aided by Burmese guerrillas and American and Chinese forces, completed the reconquest of Burma, a two-and-a-half-year campaign which had taken them from the Indian border to Rangoon. Finally the decision was taken to end the war by dropping atomic bombs on Hiroshima and Nagasaki, on 6 and 9 August 1945 respectively. On the 14th, Japan surrendered unconditionally.

The Second World War cost the world roughly 50 million lives, of which an estimated 13 million – some 5.7 million of them

Jewish – died in concentration camps. It cost, too, more money than all previous wars combined. If this were not enough, it also brought the new superpowers into conflict, as Hitler had prophesied on 2 April 1945:

> With the defeat of the Reich ... there will remain in the world only two great powers capable of confronting each other – the United States and the Soviet Union. The laws of both history and geography will compel these two powers to a trial of strength.... These same laws make it inevitable that both powers should become enemies of Europe.

Ironically enough, and typically so, Hitler refused to accept any responsibility for the catastrophe he had brought about.

'Hitler did not destroy Germany alone,' writes Joachim C. Fest in his *The Face of the Third Reich* (1972),

> but put an end to the old Europe with its sterile rivalries, its narrow-mindedness, its selfish patriotism and its deceitful imperatives. He put an end too to its splendour, its grandeur and the magic of its *douceur de vivre*. The hour of that Europe is past and we shall never see it again. By the hand of the man whom it brought to power, the lights were really and finally put out over Europe.

22

The American War on North Vietnam (1965–1975)

In 1919, at the Paris Peace Conference in Versailles, a young man pleaded for the principle of national self-determination as enunciated by the US President, Woodrow Wilson, and was ignored by the victorious Western Allies. The young man's name was Ho Chi-Minh, and he wanted self-determination for his country, subsequently called Vietnam, which was then part of French Indo-China (the other dependencies forming Indo-China, then, being Annam, Cambodia, Cochin-China, Laos and Tonking). During the Second World War Ho organized resistance to the Japanese, who invaded in 1941, and in 1945 he declared a Republic of Vietnam, a country formed by the union of Annam, Cochin-China and Tonking. The French returned in 1945, however, and Ho Chi-Minh proceeded to stir up Vietnamese resistance to French colonialism. He appointed an excellent commander in General Vo Nguyen Giap, like him, a communist, and who had helped fight the Japanese. In March 1954, the French suffered a disastrous defeat when their principal fortress on the Laotian border, Dien Bien Phu, was overrun by the Viet-Minh (the Vietnamese liberation army), attacking with a force of 40,000 under Giap. The matter has been put well in *Battles of the Twentieth Century*, edited by Chris Bishop and Ian C. Drury (1989):

> Classic siege tactics were followed by Giap's men; trench lines were dug, forward saps ran ever closer to the next objective (on occasion underground to take mines), then one late evening a shattering bombardment would be followed by overwhelming infantry attack by waves of screaming and cheering riflemen.... The end came on 7 May. Giap had brought up some Soviet-made Katyusha rocket launchers and these added devastating weight to the bombardment which crashed down on the evening of 6 May, continued through the night and by morning had reduced the French position to a few hundred square metres around the southern end of the airstrip.

The French abandoned Indo-China and at the Geneva Congress in 1954 North and South Vietnam came into being, the former dominated by communism and the latter by capitalism, backed by the United States. Ho Chi-Minh, who was a ruthless communist ideologist, now employed the nationalist urge for a united Vietnam against the South, using both the regular North Vietnamese Army under Giap, and also the communist guerrillas, from North and South, known as the Vietcong, many of whom, in addition to seeking a unified country, resented the fact that the government of South Vietnam amounted to little more than plutocratic fascism backed by the imperial might of America. From 1961, the United States had provided aid to South Vietnam – increasingly in the form of military 'advisers' – as a means of strengthening that country as a bulwark against the encroachment of communism in South-East Asia. By mid-1964, it had become clear that this policy was not working, and in 1965 US forces began directly to intervene in Vietnam. Gradually America became drawn into the Vietnam War in order to protect her economic and political interests, though war was never officially declared by the US Congress and hence, in International Law, America had defaulted from the very position she had pledged herself to maintain at the Geneva Congress. By the beginning of 1969,

359,800 United States troops plus 144,100 supporting personnel had been committed to the anti-communist cause in Vietnam, a massive build-up from the very small beginnings of American involvement in 1959.

The Americans in Vietnam were misled by dogma and mistaken assumptions. The first of these was 'the Red Peril', the idea that communism in another very poor country could be a threat to the American way of life. The second was the 'domino theory', the idea that if South Vietnam fell to communism, then the whole of South-East Asia would follow, and that India would therefore become communist after that. The third was that American military might and technological superiority would bring about a quick victory.

Given the terrain of Vietnam, there was no fast way of winning this war by conventional military means. There was no front line, nor were there clearly defined positions to assault and capture. Moreover, the Americans failed utterly in their endeavour to capture 'the hearts and minds of the Vietnamese people'. They failed to capture the hearts and minds of their own people, too. The American attitude, which resulted in heavy losses, can best be demonstrated by a collage of quotes, starting with Lyndon B. Johnson, President of the United States from 1963 to 1969:

[If I had lost in Vietnam] there would be Robert Kennedy [US Attorney-General, brother of the assassinated John F. Kennedy whom Johnson had succeeded; assassinated himself in 1964] out in front leading the fight against me.... That I had let a democracy fall into the hands of the Communists. That I was a coward. An unmanly man. A man without a spine. Oh, I could see it coming all right. Every night when I fell asleep I would see myself tied to the ground in the middle of a long, open space. In the distance I could hear the voices of thousands of people. They were all shouting and running toward me: 'Coward! Traitor! Weakling!' (Quoted in Stanley Karnow, *Vietnam: A History, 1983*.)

It is difficult to believe that misguided machismo goes further, but it did so under the commander of US forces in Vietnam from 1964 to 1968, General William West-moreland, a man who did not object when American nuns instructed the children in their care to 'Kill a gook for God'. Westmoreland, an aggressive exponent of increased US involvement in Vietnam, was committed to a strategy of attrition, convinced that a massive deployment of helicopter squadrons, saturation bombing of targets in the North, and the use of munitions like napalm – one jellied drop of which can set a human being ablaze in a fire hot enough to melt the skull – would lead to the easy victories he kept announcing before he had won them. His strategy was in accordance with that expressed by US Air Force General Curtis Le May (who had commanded the squadrons which dropped the atomic bombs on Japan in August 1945): 'My solution to the problem would be to tell [the Vietcong] they've got to draw in their horns and stop their aggression or we're going to bomb them back into the Stone Age.'

Within the United States, however, there were dissenting voices.

'The Great Society has been shot down on the battlefield of Vietnam,' said Dr Martin Luther King, obliquely referring to the fact that the highest American casualties were among black soldiers. 'I ain't got no quarrel with them Viet Cong,' said the world heavyweight boxing champion, Muhammad Ali, who was unjustly stripped of his title in 1967 for refusing to be drafted into the US Army; 'no Viet Cong ever called me nigger.' 'To win in Vietnam, we will have to exterminate a nation,' Dr Benjamin Spock, the famous child-care expert, lamented. 'We are in the wrong place, fighting the wrong war,' pronounced Senator Mike Mansfield of the governing Democratic Party and Leader of the US Senate. Such objections, and thousands like them, left Westmoreland and his successors unmoved.

'General Westmoreland's strategy of attrition also had an important effect on our behaviour,' Philip Caputo wrote in *A Rumour of War* (1977):

Our mission was not to win terrain or seize positions, but simply to kill: to kill Communists and to kill as many of them as possible. Stack 'em like cordwood. Victory was a high body-count, defeat a low-kill ratio, war a matter of arithmetic. The pressure on unit commanders to produce enemy corpses was intense, and they in turn communicated it to their troops. This led to such practices as counting civilians as Viet Cong. 'If it's dead and Vietnamese, it's V.C.,' was a rule of thumb in the bush. It is not suprrising, therefore, that some men acquired a contempt for human life and a predilection for taking it.

Morale among American soldiers was appalling. Their senior commanders failed to solve the problem of defeating an enemy from an underdeveloped, technologically backward society which was fighting this war in a manner not yet experienced, a manner of 'Lurk! Withdraw! Upon them!' American troops had not been trained for this type of warfare and their brutal behaviour, in many cases, encouraged by the American propaganda designed to dehumanize the enemy, proved counter-productive and failed to win over the local population. In addition, there was fierce opposition to the war at home in the United States.

In common with many successful Asian generals, Giap appears to have studied *The Art of War* by the fourth-century Chinese writer Sun Tzu, and to have applied its lessons, most notably the following passage: 'Break the will of the enemy to fight and you accomplish the true objective of war. Cover the enemy's traditions with ridicule. Stir up the young against the old. The supreme excellence is to defeat the armies of your enemies without ever having to fight them.'

This is eminently relevant because the United States Army, supported by South Vietnamese forces amounting to no less than 1,000,000 men, was never formally defeated in the field. The US Marine base at Khe Sanh, near the Laotian border, which protected American supply lines, was successfully defended against savage onslaughts from January to April 1968, though the Marines were outnumbered by five to one. The Tet offensive by the North Vietnamese Army and the Vietcong in January and February of the same year, against Saigon, Hué, and ninety other towns and fifty villages, met with temporary success but was repulsed in the end with heavy communist losses. It did, however, have the effect of convincing the American public of the hopelessness of large-scale operations in Vietnam. It can be argued that the greatest ally of North Vietnam was the Western media.

Every day on their TV screens, the American people saw an apparently endless war which was cruelly dividing their nation. The fact that the lies of the commanders were exposed in the press did the war effort massive damage; as did the proven reports of American atrocities committed upon innocent civilians. In December 1972, President Richard Nixon adopted saturation bombing of the North as a means whereby to escalate the progress of peace talks. The bombing killed and maimed many Vietnamese, but accomplished little else in the way of strategic objectives. The Americans officially withdrew from Vietnam after the signing of a cease-fire agreement in January 1973, though they left behind a token presence. American endeavours had been crippled by military incompetence and by the dismal propaganda, between them resulting in at least half the nation demanding an end to this miserable and pointless war, which appeared to benefit no one other than financiers, the oil industry and armaments manufacturers.

The North Vietnamese took Saigon, capital of the South, in June 1975 after a devastating offensive which had commenced in March. Although the South Vietnamese Air Force was by now the fourth largest in the world, there was a complete collapse among all South Vietnam's armed forces. In common with most American soldiers, the South Vietnamese could not discern what they were fighting *for*; apart from a corrupt and cruel puppet government sustained by American multinational corporations for the purposes of exploiting cheap labour, and of marketing American products. As Ho Chi-Minh had desired at Versailles in 1919, Vietnam had finally been united; though hundreds of thousands had died to very little purpose, other than a communist takeover.

To twist the words of Winston Churchill: never in the field of human conflict has so much been loathed by so many on account of so few.

23

The Falklands War (1982)

The Falklands War between Britain and Argentina need not have occurred, and was fought by both sides largely for political rather than economic or strategical reasons. The origins of the conflict go back to 1833 when Britain seized the islands from Argentina; the British renamed them the Falkland Islands and introduced colonists from Britain. Argentina, although her troops had left voluntarily, continued to assert her territorial claim to sovereignty over these bleak, windswept islands in the South Atlantic, known in South America as the Malvinas (a corruption of the French name Les Malouines, after the sailors from St Malo who had first colonized them).

Diplomatic negotiations proceeded slothfully until 1965, when a United Nations Resolution called upon both sides to accelerate the talks in order to achieve an accord. Talks took place and nothing was agreed. In December 1981, Lieutenant-General Leopoldo Galtieri seized power in Argentina at the head of a military junta, and proceeded to arrest, maim, torture and kill all Argentinian citizens who opposed his regime or dissented from its policies. Within months, the junta had proved itself to be utterly incompetent, which led to catastrophic inflation and widespread shortages of essential goods. Galtieri therefore sought the classic

243

expedient of the failed and unpopular politician: he endeavoured to unite his country by sabre-rattling over a popular issue against another foe, and to that end occupied the Falkland Islands, and the neighbouring island of South Georgia in April 1982.

The Prime Minister of the United Kingdom, Margaret Thatcher, was at this time the most unpopular British leader since opinion polls had started recording such information in 1936. She too saw in the Falklands crisis an opportunity of uniting her country behind her, though it is difficult to ascertain the precise truth as to what followed. It seems scarcely possible that British Intelligence had no idea that Galtieri intended an invasion, or that Argentinian Intelligence had no appreciation of the 'Iron Lady's' resolve. Given Galtieri's notorious drinking habits, however, it is easier to believe that he was inept, and Thatcher astute.

Galtieri launched Operation Rosario at dawn on 2 April 1982. By 8.30 am, 1,400 Argentinian troops had been landed to march on a garrison of sixty-seven British Royal Marines. The British Governor, Rex Hunt, wisely ordered a surrender, though not before the Marines had fired on the invaders, killing one. On the following day, Argentinian forces occupied South Georgia, an island some 800 miles to the south, on which there was a whaling station. The response of Margaret Thatcher and the British Government was Operation Corporate, the dispatch, on 5 April, of a combined services and Merchant Marine Task Force to retake the islands. This carrier group was commanded by Rear Admiral John 'Sandy' Woodward, and included cruisers, destroyers, frigates, Fleet Auxiliary vessels, and merchant and passenger ships taken up from trade, as well as submarines operating in support, and carried Sea Harrier aircraft and Sea King and other helicopters. Eighteen Royal Navy ships, sailing from Gibraltar, linked up with this fleet at the British possession of Ascension Island, and were followed by troopships bearing the amphibious landing force, 3 Commando Brigade, under Brigadier Julian Thompson, Royal Marines. (They would later be joined by 5 Infantry Brigade with its support vessels, and also by the overall commander, under Woodward, of the land operations, Major-General Jeremy Moore, Royal Marines.) Many foreign observers felt this to be no more than a show of force. The United States, anxious over its image in South America, sought to preserve peace, as did the United Nations. On 12 April, Britain declared a 200-mile Total Exclusion Zone around the Falkland Islands: any enemy vessel or aircraft entering that zone would be attacked on sight.

On 25 April, after two abortive landings in atrocious weather conditions, the British recaptured South Georgia. America proposed that Argentina withdraw from the Falklands, that there be a joint Argentinian/British/US administration of the islands, and subsequent negotiation concerning the question of ultimate sovereignty. This was elaborated in a peace plan put forward by President Belaunde Terry of Peru. Both sides proved to be intransigent, with the British arguing, justifiably, that the Falkland islanders themselves had the right to national self-determination, and, truthfully, that they wished to remain under British, not Argentinian rule. On 30 April, the Americans finally sided with Britain, agreeing to assist with supplies whilst approving of an economic blockade of Argentina. The 'special relationship' Margaret Thatcher had constructed with the US President, Ronald Reagan, was a contributory factor in deciding American policy. The United Nations remained uncertain.

Given American approval – albeit qualified – and immense popular support in Britain, Thatcher ordered the commencement of hostilities on 1 May, when an RAF Vulcan dropped 21 1,000-pound bombs on the airfield at Port Stanley, though they did no permament damage. On the next day, the submarine HMS *Conqueror* sank the Argentinian cruiser *General Belgrano*, even though she was some thirty-five miles outside the Total Exclusion Zone and sailing towards Argentina. Three hundred and sixty-eight Argentinian lives were lost. Britain promptly offered to accept the reasonable Peruvian peace proposals. After the sinking of the *Belgrano*, Galtieri could not. The Argentinian occupation of the Falklands had made war probable; the British sinking of the *Belgrano* made war certain.

It was not certain, however, that the British would necessarily win. The Task Force had insufficient air cover, it was at risk from submarine attack as well as attack by aircraft and missiles, and it was operating at the end of very long lines of supply and communication. Argentina had Exocets, anti-ship missiles which can be launched from a ship or aircraft (or, as happened in the war, from land), and which skim the surface of the sea at very high speed so as to escape detection by their targets' radar. One of these sank HMS *Sheffield* on 4 May; HMS *Ardent* was sunk by bombs on 21 May; on 24 May HMS *Antelope* was sunk similarly; and 25 May saw the sinking by Exocet of the supply ship *Atlantic Conveyor*. It can be argued that just two more Exocet missiles would have ruined British strategy and led to a most ignominious defeat. British ships were sitting targets for attacks from the air, and *Glamorgan* was hit and damaged by a shore-launched Exocet.

It is fortunate the Galtieri was grossly negligent in his mining of the sheltered waters at San Carlos, in the Falklands Sound between East and West Falkland, which is where the 3 Commando Brigade landed on 20 May, with 5 Infantry Brigade joining them from 31 May. Moreover, had the Argentinian aircraft targeted the supply ships and transports in San Carlos Water, instead of bombing the defending frigates and destroyers, British casualties, in ships, men and *matériel*, would have been higher. The loss of supplies could well have caused the invasion to fail. This phase of the campaign was not won by Britain: it was lost by Argentina, for had Argentine pilots dropped their bombs from the correct height necessary for fusing, instead of allowing themselves to be driven down on to the deck by triple-A, then more of those bombs would have exploded, and more British ships would have been lost.

Most military experts estimated that once the highly trained and professional British troops had landed on East Falkland, they could destroy the Argentinian army of ill trained, poorly clad and badly supplied conscripts. Unfortunately not all were conscripts – there were, among others, some very effective Argentine Marines. Furthermore, they had (in the main) excellent US weapons and equipment, the Belgian FN rifle (fully auto version of the British semi-auto SLR). The Argentinians initially put up surprisingly stiff resistance. The initial brunt of the fighting was endured by the 2nd Battalion of the Parachute Regiment, which suffered casualties higher than anticipated in its attack on well dug-in forces at Darwin and Goose Green on 28 May but which, although heavily outnumbered, used superior tactics and fighting skills, based upon intelligent reconnaissance of the terrain, as well as artillery, air and naval gunfire support, to ensure a vital victory.

It had been intended that large twin-rotor Chinook helicopters would transport the troops to their main objective of taking the capital, Port Stanley, on East Falkland, but three of the four sent to the Task Force went down with the *Atlantic Conveyor*, which meant that most of the soldiers and marines had to march through bitter weather conditions and harsh terrain, carrying enormous loads, whilst continuously threatened by the Argentinian Air Force. However, in a series of classic infantry assaults, British forces, well supplied on this occasion by intelligence reports of weaknesses in the Argentinian defences, stormed Mount Longdon, Two Sisters and Mount Harriet, some ten miles west of Stanley, to occupy the hills above the port by dawn on 12 June. A night attack on 12 June and subsequent assaults the next day gained Wireless Ridge and the appropriately named defences at Mount Tumbledown by dawn on the 14th. Naval gunfire, 105-mm guns and light tanks supported the pressure on Port Stanley, which surrendered at 16.00 on 14 June. Galtieri resigned on 17 June; court-martialled in 1983, he was acquitted of violations of human rights, but sentenced to twelve years in prison for 'negligence' in starting and losing the Falklands War. When in October 1983, Argentina finally reverted to a democratic regime under President Raúl Alfonsín, the British could boast that they had been responsible for deposing a fascist, militarist dictatorship. Galtieri was released from prison and pensioned in October 1989.

The Falklands War had demonstrated quite a number of interesting points. Firstly, the Royal Navy had not altogether realized that such Armada-style operations are not possible without massive air cover unless the enemy is grossly inept, which in some respects the Argentinians were: British naval ineptitude would have led to catastrophe without that flaw in Argentina's high command. Secondly, there was a rapid need for improvement in military hardware, ranging from soldiers' boots to shipboard fire-fighting equipment to electronic warfare systems: at times, the campaign came very close to being lost. Thirdly, an invading infantry force of trained professionals can defeat a defending army of conscripts given sufficient intelligence data, good logistics, adequate firepower, and good air cover and air defence. Fourthly, skilful diplomacy in international relations is vital to the winning of a war. Prime Minister Thatcher managed to convince President Reagan that the fall of Galtieri would serve American interests; the instant that America gave limited consent, Britain commenced the war.

Finally, there was the matter of the media. Thatcher had learned from American mistakes in Vietnam, and sought to initiate and orchestrate a propaganda campaign which would arouse the full support of British nationalist feeling, as well as contributing to her initially unlikely posssibility of re-election. Myths of Boudicea, Drake and Churchill were paraded before the public. A conflict arose between the three issues of government propaganda, the obvious necessity for secrecy concerning crucial military operations, and the public right to information about the doings of its government.

'You must have been told you couldn't report bad news ...' a Ministry of Defence official informed the twenty-nine reporters, technicians and cameramen who had finally been allowed to sail with the Task Force, over the objections of the Royal Navy. He continued: 'You were expected to do a 1940 propaganda job.' 'It is the BBC's deep concern,' that corporation protested, 'that the Ministry of Defence has come very close to the "management" or "manipulation" of news, an idea that is alien to the concept of communication within a free society.' 'There are traitors in our midst,' the *Sun* newspaper responded, referring to the BBC, having distinguished itself during the war with such charming headlines as 'STICK IT UP YOUR JUNTA' and, when the *Belgrano* was sunk, 'GOTCHA!' The *Daily Mirror* commented: 'The *Sun* today is to journalism what Dr Josef Goebbels was to truth.'

Nevertheless, Margaret Thatcher won the war and temporarily united the bulk of the British people behind her, skilfully deploying that most crucial of weapons, propaganda. The campaign cost 1,000 lives on both sides, and the British taxpayers £2.6 billion. At the end of the war, matters were returned to the point at which they had been before the Argentine invasion; in 1996, Anglo–Argentinian negotiations over the fate of the Falkland Islands, or the Malvinas, once more proceed sluggishly.

In June 1983, a triumphant Margaret Thatcher was re-elected Prime Minister for her second successive term.

24

The Gulf War
(January–February 1991)

The Gulf War was made for the American media. There has never been a war which a superpower, the United States of America, looked more likely to win, unless one counts the skirmishes when the USA invaded Grenada in 1983 and Panama in 1989. President George Bush had learned vital lessons from the Vietnam War and from Margaret Thatcher's success in the Falklands: If you want your country united behind you and you are trailing in the opinion polls, go to war against an unpopular foreign enemy, plan the campaign meticulously, and establish as far as possible a choke-hold on the media.

Bush, whose policies all seemed to have the primary, indeed the sole, purpose of securing his re-election, was lucky in that his predecessor, Ronald Reagan, had pursued policies which had contributed, in the late 1980s, to the break-up of the formerly impregnable USSR and the collapse of Communism as an international force.

As has been said, a statesman thinks in terms of the next generation; a politician in terms of the next election. Even so, and although re-election was always the first aim of Ronald Reagan, here was a US President who was for once astute in statecraft, and never more so than when he used the superior economic resources of the USA to outspend the USSR in an arms race which left the latter virtually bankrupt; after which he concluded a series of peaceful agreements with President Mikhail Gorbachev of the Soviet Union. That country collapsed into an uneasy grouping of squabbling states, bereft of sound government and without adequate economic foundations, and the USA now became the one and only superpower as the Berlin Wall fell and the countries of Eastern Europe broke away from Soviet rule to embrace capitalism, with varying results. What was left of the Soviet Union, which urgently required US economic aid, would be unable to play a substantial part – on whichever side – in the Gulf War that followed.

During the long war between Iran and Iraq, from 1980 to 1988, the attrition of which reminded many of the First World War, the policies of both America and Western Europe towards the combatants was somewhat cynical: arms were supplied to both sides, sometimes secretly and in defiance of government guidelines, or even laws. When this atrocious war finally came to an end on 20 August 1988, at the cost of roughly a million casualties on either side without any significant gains, Saddam Hussein, the brutal dictator of Iraq, and leader of the ruling Baath Party there, found that his country was in debt to the tune of £70 billion, half of it owed to the Gulf States, with Kuwait the most prominent creditor. The latter, a major producer of oil, was now accused by Iraq of stealing Iraqi oil to the value of £1.3 million from the neutral zone that lay between the two countries. On 24 July 1990, Iraq moved 30,000 troops to the Kuwait border. At this point, the matter becomes diplomatically puzzling. America encouraged Kuwait to 'hang tough' in all negotiations. Simultaneously, the Iraqis were led to believe that the United States would not intervene. The US Ambassador to Iraq, April Glaspie, informed Saddam Hussein that Washington had 'no opinion of Arab–Arab conflicts, like your border disagreement with Kuwait'. Ms Glaspie left Baghdad two days before Saddam invaded Kuwait, and the Soviet Ambassador left on the same day. The British Ambassador was on holiday, and the chief of Israeli Intelligence was in Tel Aviv.

On 2 August 1990, Iraq invaded and overran Kuwait, positioning troops for a threatened strike into Saudi Arabia which never materialized. According to Jean Edward Smith in *George Bush's War* (1992), President Bush met with the Chief of the US General Staff, General Colin Powell, leading advisers such as Snowcroft and Richard Cheney; the White House Chief of Staff, John Sununu; Judge William Webster of the CIA; and other members of the National Security Council. The prevailing attitude among this grouping was apparently: 'Hey, too bad about Kuwait, but it's just a gas station and who cares whether the sign says Sinclair or Exxon?'

Curiously enough, US Central Command, which previously had never made plans for an Iraqi threat, had suddenly begun to plan for that eventuality just months before it happened. The USA secured the co-operation of the United Nations and Saudi Arabia, formed a twenty-eight-member Coalition with, among others, Britain, France, Egypt, Syria, and, on 16 January 1991, after the UN deadline for the withdrawal of Iraqi forces from Kuwait had expired, launched its military might and that of its allies against Iraq, in the form of massive air strikes. It would be hard to find in history an operation by America and her allies more meticulously planned and executed, other than Eisenhower's Operation Overlord, the invasion of Normandy on D-Day, 6 June 1944.

Operation Desert Storm was distinguished by three fine commanders. Colin Luther Powell, Chairman of the Joint Chiefs of Staff and principal liaison between President Bush and the US troops in the field, proved to be cool, calm and collected. The incidental fact that he was black was very useful for American propaganda purposes domestically. General 'Stormin'' Norman Schwarzkopf, the overall commander of United Nations forces in the Middle East, was considered to be an expert on desert warfare. Here he had learned from the brilliant Israeli commander, General Moshe Dayan, who in the Arab–Israeli Six-Day War of 1967, although vastly outnumbered, had defeated the forces of Egypt, Syria and Jordan with a series of pre-emptive air strikes, destroying 200 Egyptian planes for the loss of 19 Israeli aircraft, and then routed the opposing land forces by the swift deployment of tanks supported by mechanized artillery and infantry. Schwarzkopf, who of course was not outnumbered, instantly established air superiority. On the ground, Schwarzkopf was supported most ably by Lieutenant-General Sir Peter de la Billière, one of the British Army's most decorated serving officers, who had spent much of his career developing the SAS, which had originated in the deserts of North Africa during the Second World War. De la Billière was in command of the British forces, Britain having provided the largest number of troops after the USA.

This trio constituted a perfect piece of casting – quite aside from their considerable individual capabilities – as far as the American media was concerned. The United States needed a successful war against an unpopular enemy in order to erase the humiliation of national pride which Vietnam had brought about, and this time the US Government 'managed' the news with considerable skill. For the American public, the Gulf War was both a morally righteous cause and a sensationally dramatic occurrence on their TV screens each night. General de la Billière rightly predicted, before the ground war started, that the campaign would be over quickly, with only a few Allied casualties. The Americans could rejoice in defending both a small and allegedly oppressed nation, Kuwait; fighting an evil tyrant, Saddam Hussein, whom President Bush, once the Iraqi leader's ally, now compared to Hitler; and taking back oil wells, without which the price of gasoline would soar.

The Americans thrilled by the use of United States military hypertechnology, whereby an F-117A Stealth bomber could allegedly pinpoint a target so accurately that a bomb could be dropped down the chimney of Saddam Hussein's house. Or so it was said, and widely believed. Peculiarly enough, Interfax, the Soviet news agency, reported that out of 10,000 sorties made by the Allies, 90 per cent of bombs dropped missed their targets. Why Interfax should be thought any more accurate in its claims than the US Government – both being hardened exaggerators, if not liars – mystifies one. The truth is that both US and Soviet claims were 'inaccurate'. The USA blamed bad weather, although the sun kept shining on the theatre of operations.

The Allies appear to have been aided and abetted, though perhaps unwittingly, by the actions of Saddam Hussein, who had never had the benefits of military training. In studying this war one has to conclude that one of three possibilities defines Saddam:

first, that he might be insane; second, that he is the most stupid military leader ever to have lived; or third, that there was a hidden agenda in the American–Iraqi campaign.

It is hard to see why, when US forces arrived in the Gulf and were at their most vulnerable, Saddam waited, without attacking them. Nor is it clear why he gave every impression of having dug in, yet sent his elite Republican Guard to safety well behind the lines of battle, and the bulk of his air force – 100 aircraft – to neutral Iran. It is noticeable, too, that the Iraqi front-line troops consisted largely of soldiers from groups within Iraq opposed to the dominant, mainly Sunni, Baathists: 70 per cent were Shiites and 20 per cent were Kurds.

American technology was of course vastly superior to anything Iraq had to offer. When he unleashed his ground forces on 24 February, 'Stormin' ' Norman Schwarzkopf emulated Hannibal at Cannae in 216 BC, encircling the entire front-line Iraqi army in the field to win a brisk and brilliant victory. Here he was assisted by the fact that he had 683,000 troops – his own claim, contradicted by the Pentagon claim of 540,000 – to the 300,000 of Iraq. Saddam's threats to unleash terrorists upon Western civilian targets and biological and chemical weapons upon Coalition troops, proved to be empty. His televised appearances were extraordinary: they won him the sympathy, and even respect, of a good deal of the Arab world; and at the same time supplied Western sensibilities with a suitable ogre. His unsuccessful Scud attacks on Israel further demonized him. America made tremendous political capital by heralding the advance of her apparently unassailable Tomahawk cruise missiles and Patriot air-defence missiles, yet their military impact was negligible. After very few Allied casualties, Kuwait was liberated from Iraqi control and on 28 february 1991, Iraq accepted informally the peace proposals of the United Nations.

President Bush immediately called a halt to the Allied advance, which had originally been heralded as a thrust on Baghdad in order to drive a Middle Eastern Hitler out of the comity of nations. Nevertheless, the US Government encouraged a rebellion of Shiites in the south and Kurds in the north against Saddam, giving them to believe that they would receive American aid. This proved not to be the case, as the rebels found to their cost.

Norman Schwarzkopf gave Saddam permission to use helicopters, allowing him precisely enough force to suppress both Shiite and Kurdish rebellions. It would be interesting to learn the reason.

Operation Desert Storm gave the media many a field day. It certainly made for dramatic television, with news and other programmes continuously running stories of Iraqi atrocities, Allied weaponry, the evil of Saddam Hussein, the excellence of Allied fighting troops, the splendour of Allied commanders, and the glory of winning in a just cause – a victory which would, incidentally, prevent the prices at petrol pumps from rocketing. There were remarkably few Allied casualties, while very few people in the West cared about the 100,000 claimed Iraqi casualties; though subsequent estimates have put this figure at 8,000.

And the results? Kuwait had been recovered and was now more in debt to the United States than ever before. Despite his defeat, Saddam Hussein was a hero in the eyes of many in the Arab world, and had a tighter grip upon Iraq than ever before. The United States had demonstrated that in military terms, it was the one and only superpower, capable now, through its technology, of defeating any other nation anywhere on the globe: President Bush proudly proclaimed the advent of 'the New Order'. Certainly, and for the first time ever in its history, the United States persuaded its Allies to pay for military costs. Within America, national attention was undoubtedly diverted from severe, and severely neglected, domestic problems. The detached observer cannot help but remark that this was a war made for TV. As Stephen R. Graubard has it in his *Mr Bush's War: Adventures in the Politics of Illusion*: 'The war began with serial photographs of the bombing of Baghdad; it ended with a black American soldier reassuring an Iraqi prisoner of war that he was safe; all was well. *The war was a tale manufactured from beginning to end.*'

There is a certain horror in contemplating the serious possibility that a war might have been staged as a media event so as to re-elect the President. If this was so, then it would vindicate the view of Karl Marx that history repeats itself – the first time as tragedy and the second time as farce.

There were in fact some benefits for the West in consequence of the Gulf War. Kuwait was recovered from Saddam Hussein and returned to a regime less bad than his. Western technology capped the oil-well fires. The embryo nuclear industry of Iraq was temporarily dismantled. The United Nations Organization demonstrated its ability here to put together Christian and Muslim Arab forces in alliance against another Muslim force. Saddam Hussein, though he was taught never to essay such an adventure again without American further sanction, nevertheless remains more firmly entrenched in power over Iraq than ever before and is still mopping up all the dissidents.

This was the first instance of war being presented as a media event with all news manipulated for the excitement of TV couch potatoes. However, there is a sting in this tail and a twist to that tale. The Republican George Bush was not re-elected President of the USA in the 1994 election, since the voters opted for the Democrat, Bill Clinton. Perhaps Bush should have pondered upon the words of his rather more illustrious predecessor, Abraham Lincoln:

'You can fool all of the people some of the time, and some of the people all of the time; but you cannot fool all of the people all of the time.'

Epilogue

At the present stage of human evolution and whether one likes it or not, war is bound to play a substantial part in human affairs, whether impelled by a desire for political prestige, as in the Gulf, or as the consequence of embittered nationalist, tribal, racial or religious hostilities, as in Bosnia. An Internet survey gives the following summary of wars in progress:

> Afghanistan Resistance War
> Angola Guerrilla – Civil War
> Bangladesh Guerrilla War
> Bolivian Drug War
> Burma – Guerrilla War
> Central America
> War in Chad
> Conflict in Chile
> Colombia – Guerrilla War
> East Timor Resistance War
> Ecuador
> El Salvador Civil War
> Ethiopia–Eritrea War
> Guatemala, Guerrilla War in
> Holy War – Jihad
> India–Pakistan War
> India: Sikh–Hindu War

Iran–Iraq War
Kampuchea – Vietnam's War Against Guerrillas
Kurdish War of Independence
Lebanon
Liberia – Civil War
Morocco–Polisario War
Mozambique Guerrilla War
Nicaragua-Contra War
Northern Ireland Terrorist War
Peru's 'Shining Path'
Philippines 'Communist War'
Sudan – Civil War
Sri Lanka – Civil War
Togo
Zulu–ANC War

To this one can add the pan-Arab terrorism in Israel and the Israeli shelling of refugee camps in the Lebanon; the extreme right-wing anti-government terrorism in the USA; the 'drug/mafia' wars in Italy; the Graeco–Turkish conflict in Cyprus and the Kurds' fight for an autonomous state conducted against Turkey. Russia is fighting a number of wars, both overt and covert, to subdue various nationalistic minorities.

The majority of these wars are stupid and pointless but they will continue precisely on account of the fanatical territorial nationalism of egotistical, pig-headed dictators.

'War is hell,' as General Sherman declared: and yet some wars, the Second World War being the most notable, have actually advanced the state of human evolution. The finest commanders have always known that the whole point of warfare is to gain a strong position from which to negotiate a peace for the benefit of the future.

The worst commanders have always been fascinated solely by the notions of power and prestige and slaughter. A bad general cannot think of anything else.

A good general employs his or her tactics within a strategic context, using the weapons of politics, economics, diplomacy, technology and propaganda. Although political, economic and social forces determine the strengths of either side in war, it is often the genius of the individual general that determines the outcome of a battle. Such a battle may affect the course of history, though it will be won by the application of tactics based upon knowledge of terrain, of resources and of troops and their morale, inspired strategically by Will and Idea.

The Will is to win. The Idea is knowing how to do it.